THE ECONOMICS OF JOHN HICKS

The Economics
of
John Hicks

SELECTED AND WITH AN INTRODUCTION
BY DIETER HELM

Basil Blackwell

© Sir John Hicks 1984

First published 1984
Basil Blackwell Publisher Limited
108 Cowley Road, Oxford OX4 1JF, England

Basil Blackwell Inc.
432 Park Avenue South, Suite 1505
New York, NY 10016, USA

British Library Cataloguing in Publication Data

Hicks, John
    The Economics of John Hicks
    1. Economics
    I. Title   II. Helm, Dieter
    330   HB171
    ISBN 0-631-13616-9

Typesetting by Unicus Graphics Ltd, Horsham.
Printed in Great Britain by Bell and Bain Ltd, Glasgow.

Contents

Contents

Acknowledgements

I would like to thank Sir John Hicks for his help in making this selection, and for comments on my Introduction.

We are grateful to Oxford University Press for permission to reproduce material from chapter 1 of *A Theory of Economic History* (1969) and from chapter 14 of *Value and Capital* (1939).

Abbreviations used throughout this volume are listed at the beginning of the Bibliography 'The Published Works of John Hicks', p. 293.

Introduction

The essays that are included in this book are a selection from those that have been written by John Hicks over the last half-century. His economics has been predominantly, but not entirely, theoretical. His theories have nevertheless been constructed with an eye to application; he has continually been asking himself, What is this piece of theory for? He has accordingly been willing to work in many departments of theory, and on each of them he has made his mark. They include demand theory, the formulation of modern welfare economics, general equilibrium, monetary theory, growth theory and the theory of the cycle. His reformulation of the core of Keynes' *General Theory* is a familiar element in economic teaching.

Nevertheless, despite the breadth of his contribution, there is no Hicksian theory in the same way as one can speak of a Ricardian or Marxian theory. He has always moved on, never satisfied with his theory, always conscious of improvements and of different angles with which a problem could be viewed, and always conscious of changing institutions with the passage of time. What, however, is common to his work is the Hicksian method. It is not obviously a constant, yet the careful reader may detect it. And for the modern economist it is a method which is in danger of being lost, at least temporarily. In essence it is in the shaping of tools to be specific to the problem at hand.

There has not as yet been a spate of articles on Hicksian economics. Comments are mainly to be found in reviews of his work, and in specific theoretical developments. Furthermore, many such comments on Hicks' overall contribution, rather than individual responses to books, have been, to a certain degree, misguided to the extent that they have looked for and searched out disunity in the implications of the various Hicksian theories, rather than focusing on the method. The earlier work culminating in *Value and Capital* and divided off by the Second World War has been compared and contrasted with the work of his later post-war years, and writers have frequently been concerned to defend one or the other, but not both.

In the process rather gross simplifications and aggregations have been made, without due attention being directed towards the complex changes and alterations. Alternatively, reviewers have concentrated on those areas which suit their own opinions, and ignored other areas of Hicks' work more hostile to themselves.

Perhaps it is too early to place Hicks within the framework of the history of economic thought; perhaps the controversies should be allowed to settle. Yet one has the feeling that it will never be so, that his ideas have been and remain so central to economic theory that the disputes will go on indefinitely. But the one aspect which should be brought to more general attention is the diversity of Hicks' subject matter and the characteristic approach mentioned above. It is surprising that many students are aware only of his contribution to a specific area – to Keynesian economics, or welfare, or demand theory as examples – but not to others. Few students are now aware for example of the pioneering papers on real-income measurements. Many welfare economists know little of the Hicksian theory (or rather theories) of the demand for money. In part this reflects the direction towards specialisation within the subject.

This selection represents an attempt to bring that diversity of interest together within a single volume. In this introduction, some of the breadth of the contribution is presented, in chronological fashion, as well as a flavour of the methodological considerations.

Hicks' first work pre-dated his consumer theory by several years. In the tradition of the late 1920s when economic theory had not really gained the prominence that it has today, he began by looking at an industrial case study, which was published as 'Wage Fixing in the Building Industry' in 1928. It formed the non-theoretical background material for his first book, *A Theory of Wages* (1932). It was under the influence of Lionel Robbins at the LSE that he turned to theory, and in the theoretical discussion of wages he presented the production function and associated marginal productivity theory, a traditional view about which he was later to have severe doubts. The book represented a curious mixture of early influences; first Pigou, then Walras and finally Hayek. The results in the book were modified in his 'Wages and Interest' paper, which appeared just prior to Keynes' *General Theory* in 1935. This paper addressed a non-Keynesian question: it considered what would happen if real wages, rather than money wages, changed. The relation between the book and the article is not straightforwardly obvious, and this relation represented a difficulty to which Hicks returned much later, armed with various growth models and his 'Methods of Dynamic Analysis', in the 1963 commentary to the second edition of the *Theory of*

Wages, and in his *Crisis in Keynesian Economics*. The issue turns on whether a change in real wages leads to a positive or negative change in the interest rate (real); the book being concerned with the long-run effects and the article with the short-period effects.

If the theory of wages was one major component of his work prior to the publication of Keynes' *General Theory*, the general problem of the theory of value was perhaps the most important. It is the theoretical issue that still confronts all who come to economics: why do people attach the value to the things that they do? The Classical political economists had sought for an explanation in terms of costs and supply; their successors in terms of demand, and of preferences. Thus the focus had shifted towards exchange, and away from the Classics' concern with production and distribution. Indeed without the labour theory of value, it is quite difficult to consider value exclusively based on production. The cost approach to value, as opposed to technical efficiency, is unworkable. The insight which Hicks brought to value theory was comprehensive, and consisted of three stages – the 'Theory of Value' papers written with Roy Allen in 1934, *Value and Capital* in 1939, and *A Revision of Demand Theory* in 1956. In the first and most important of these contributions (essay one), there were in particular two advances: (a) the demonstration that the elasticity of substitution used in production theory by Joan Robinson had a parallel in consumer theory, and (2) the distinction of the income and substitution effects and the presentation of the fundamental formula clear of any reference to cardinal utility.

That Pareto had already managed to dispense with cardinality, and that Slutsky had already (though unknown to Hicks) derived results similar to Hicks and Allen does not detract from the importance of their papers. It is perhaps sometimes difficult for the modern student to see just how important the removal of cardinality was. Producing a similar result with one less assumption may be rather abstract; yet without that advance modern demand theory would have been much more objectionable. As Hicks put it in *Value and Capital*: 'Thus we can translate the marginal utility theory into terms of indifference curves; but, having done that, we have accomplished something more remarkable than a mere translation' (p. 17). Substitution and income effects could be identified without recourse to measurable utility. Indifference curves could be used to represent preferences, and the marginal method retained by the use of a ratio of marginal utilities, rather than an abstract cardinal marginal utility. The question, What would have to be true of preferences in order that stable downward sloping demand curves could be derived from them?, is the central issue of the theory of demand, and to demonstrate formally that an assumption deemed to be both necessary and at the same time so informationally demanding as to be unrealistic, was in fact redundant to the derivation of that result, was of unique importance. Interpersonal comparisons, rejected by Robbins,[1] were naturally untenable to an ordinalist.

The method of the margin had been in use for a long time – since Jevons, Walras and Menger independently set in motion the so-called marginal resolution of the 1870s. What Hicks achieved was a demonstration of just how powerful that method was. For although Hicks takes Marshall's consumer theory, employs Pareto's ordinal assumption, and then rigorously works out the implications, it is important to note that his development and orientation was not Marshallian, as Keynes' was, though he was careful to point out the relation between his own theory and that of Marshall. For Hicks, the line ran from Pareto to Walras and Edgeworth, a very different tradition, but one associated with the Robbins Circle[2] at LSE in the late 1920s and early 1930s. This group, the only one of which Hicks was ever a member, developed with the appointment of Lionel Robbins as Head of Department in 1929, and, besides Hicks, included amongst its members Allen, Sayers, Kaldor, Lerner, Shackle as well as Marian Bowley and his future wife, Ursula Webb. Hayek arrived somewhat later, though his impact on the group was, next to Robbins, the most profound. It was while a member of the Robbins Circle in the 1930s that Hicks produced most of his micro-theoretic work. He realised the power of his method, and its scope. One year after his famous 'Theory of Value' papers with Allen, he saw that the theory of money was amenable to the same method. To modern eyes, the two are somewhat apart – the one an issue in micro-economics, the other of macro. Yet it should be remembered that to value theorists of the eighteenth, nineteenth and early twentieth centuries, to explain the 'value' of something was intimately linked to explaining the *money* value at which it exchanged. A theory of money was naturally related to the more fundamental theory of value. Indeed as early as Adam Smith, in the first book of the *Wealth of Nations*, we find just this combination.

The background to this first paper on money, 'A Suggestion for Simplifying the Theory of Money' (essay 7 below), is, however, not

---

[1] Robbins gives his reasons explicitly in 'Interpersonal Comparisons of Utility', *EJ* (1938).

[2] See on the history of the group, as yet surprisingly little researched, Hicks himself 'The LSE group' in *Wealth and Welfare*, CEET I (1981), and Robbins *Autobiography of an Economist* (1971).

confined to the theory of value; Hicks had already written on the theory of risk, and on the theory of cycles. The paper suggests how one might use the same methodology as in value theory, but for both macro and micro behaviour. Hicks had never been keen on the divide, and to that extent the modern debate of the 1960s and 1970s on 'microfoundations' was out of tune with his work. To the extent that there was a reconciliation to be effected, Hicks was already addressing it in the 1930s, though from an individual point of view. Indeed what the 'Simplifying' paper does is to take the central concepts of his utility theory and apply them, with careful modifications, to the theory of money.

When combined with 'Wages and Interest' it can be seen that Hicks had, by 1935, and prior to Keynes' *General Theory*, reached his theoretical position with respect to the issue which was to divide Keynes from Robertson; the loanable funds and demand for money determination of the interest rate, and the relation between these two approaches. Indeed by 1935 Hicks already had three key components of his monetary theory: (1) the balance-sheet method, (2) that the choice of assets is one between probability distributions, and (3) that transactions costs are significant. Hicks' liquidity motive was not the same as that of Keynes' (even in his *Treatise on Money* formulation), because while the latter approach depended primarily on uncertainty, for Hicks transactions costs and their marginal impact on choice are also included. It was not well worked out in the 'Simplifying' paper; but it was there, and its presence is important to an understanding of his reaction to the *General Theory*. It was not until the 'Two Triads' that the theory was fully articulated, of which more below.

He had this work behind him when the *General Theory* appeared. His reaction to it has become part of the received tradition, and was accepted by Keynes and many, but by no means all, of his followers.[3] He was uniquely placed to interpret Keynes. He was not of the classical tradition which Keynes portrayed in such an uncompromising and crude formulation in the opening chapter of the *General Theory*. He understood value theory, he had worked on the labour market and the behaviour of wages, he had written with much originality on money, interest, risk and cycles, and he had already read and reviewed Myrdal's *Monetary Equilibrium* (1934). Most of all he faced what was and remains an undoubtedly difficult, confused and 'impressionistic' book with a clear analytical mind.

[3] For example, in Harrod's *Life of Keynes* (1951), Hicks receives one obscure footnote only. Since Hicks' interpretation has already become a standard one, this is odd in the extreme!

In his first published comment, 'The General Theory: A First Impression', he states at the outset the differing temptations (into which many subsequently fell) in approaching the book, and chose a typically Hicksian approach. He wrote:

The reviewer of this book is beset by two contrary temptations. On the one hand, he can accept directly Mr Keynes' elaborate disquisition about his own theory, and its place in the development of economics; praising or blaming the alleged more than Jevonian revolution. Or, on the other hand, he can concentrate upon investigating these disquisitions, and tracing (perhaps) a pleasing degree of continuity and tradition, surviving the revolution from the *ancien régime*. But it seems better to avoid such questions, and try to consider the new theory on its merits.

What did Hicks make of the new theory in his first attempts at reviewing it? Analytically he broke down its components in a fashion that would enable the Keynesian theory to be compared and contrasted with the position that it purported to attack, the Classical view. That is the origin of the famous, or perhaps infamous, *IS–LM* diagram of the second review, 'Mr Keynes and the Classics' (essay 8 below). The *IS–LM* framework was the tool of such a comparison; it is an expository device. It did not and does not represent Hicks' view; in this regard the 'Simplifying' paper is much more his.

From the first, Hicks did not accept the generality which Keynes claimed for his theory. Indeed if we were to do so, the *IS–LM* framework would not capture the analytical differences between Keynes and the Classics. Again in the 'First Impression' he writes:

The new theory is a theory of employment, in so far as the problem of employment and unemployment is the most urgent practical problem to which this sort of theoretical improvement is relevant. It is a theory of output in general *vis-à-vis* Marshall, who took into account many of the sorts of complications which concern Mr. Keynes, but took them into account only with reference to a single industry. It is a theory of shifting equilibrium *vis-à-vis* the static or stationary theories of general equilibrium, such as those of Ricardo, Bohm-Bawerk or Pareto. It is a theory of money, in so far as it includes monetary theory, bringing money out of its isolated position as a separate subject into an integral relation with general economics.

It is interesting to contrast this method of approaching the new book with those of others. Note three approaches in particular. One, led by Pigou, attempted to show how the old could in fact be preserved and buttressed against Keynes' attack. It tried to show that there was in fact nothing general about the 'general' theory, that it remained an interesting special case with inflexible or 'sticky' wages. While Hicks was prepared to accept that the 'general theory' was not general, equally he was not prepared to accept that the Classical position was either, and attempted, with the *IS–LM* framework, to provide a means of capturing both. The Pigouvians, however, wanted to reduce Keynes to a special case of their own theory. A second reaction took one aspect, namely the uncertainty surrounding the formation of expectations, as *the* theory, and neglected the rest. These so-called 'chapter 12 Keynesians' chose this chapter ('The State of Long Term Expectation'), which was inconsistent with the rest of the book, and developed it. In doing so they developed what at least some have seen as a nihilistic theory, whereas Hicks argued that since future events were unpredictable, one should employ the expectations formed about these variables as given data. In this he anticipated recent interpretations of Keynes,[4] that expectations are assumed to be exogenous.[5] The uncertainty theorists failed to perceive the inconsistency of the 'general theory'. The third approach has been relatively neglected. In the 1930s much debate centered not so much on the Classics' response, but on the relative merits of Hayek's theory as against that of Keynes. In his lectures on *Prices and Production* Hayek had considered an Austrian model in perfect foresight equilibrium except for the money market, which was allowed to deviate from its equilibrium levels. Policy could, however, be directed towards restoring equilibrium in that one deviant market, thereby rendering money neutral.

Hicks' approach took the essential component theories, and attempted to see what would happen if they were put together into a general framework. In order to do so, the Hicksian 'week' is introduced, which is not quite the same as the Keynesian short period, in that it is more restrictive. The Hicksian week assumes an equilibrium, a temporary equilibrium. A particular type of market separability is also assumed, and the diagram which has become so universal arises out of a mathematically convenient exposition. But as Hicks later realised, that temptation has not had uniquely good consequences. He returned later in a series of stages to say some fairly critical things about his own construction. Indeed he was to regard it as his own

---

[4] See for example Begg, D. *Rational Expectations, Wage Rigidity, Involuntary Unemployment, OEP* (1982), developing rational expectations models of Keynes' theory. Hicks, for other reasons, would not endorse the rational expectations approach.

[5] Keynes theory of probability admitted many kinds of uncertainty and hence both numerical and non-numerical probabilities. Hicks cut through all this by assuming the simplest case – exogeneity.

albatross.[6] His mind moved on, while the profession remained surprisingly static. The *IS–LM* framework was, as we pointed out above, a tool of exposition, not Hicks' theory. Alan Coddington expressed Hicks' position as two fold:[7]

We see Hicks as both one of the most severe critics of Keynes' own analysis *and* as one of the most rigorous and persistent of those who have tried to refine and strengthen the basic ideas that emerged from the controversy instigated by Keynes.

The continual revisiting of the *General Theory* occupied much of Hicks' post-war work. In particular he returned to a restatement of the Classics' position in his paper 'The Classics Again', in *Critical Essays in Monetary Theory*, and attempted to gain a more continuous view of theoretical development and change in his reflective article on 'Monetary Theory and History' in *EP*. He argued at this later stage that it is the short-run classical view, rather than the longer-run general equilibrium model, to which the *General Theory* should be compared. The revisiting also reflected his renewed concern with the alternative theories of Wicksell and Hayek.

With the *General Theory* behind him, what may be regarded as his greatest work, *Value and Capital*, was completed and published in 1939. It was perhaps an odd time to produce a book like that, but the contents represented 'unfinished business'.[8] In a manner which the *General Theory* of Keynes had failed to achieve, Hicks tried in this book to bring the strands of this thought together. It was more successful intellectually – it laid the foundations for general equilibrium theory and its mathematical exposition in the post-war period by Samuelson, Arrow, McKenzie and Debreu – and it made his name; in the sense that it stands as one of the central books of twentieth-century economics. As Harrod wrote in 1939:[9]

Professor Hicks, his place in the first rank of economic theorists long since secure, establishes by this volume his claim to admission to a narrow circle – the economists with a distinctive and distinguished style of writing. Take up any page of Pigou, Macgregor, Keynes, Robertson; you do not need to be told the author. And, henceforth, I think that Hicks' manner will be unmistakable.

---

[6] See '*IS–LM*: an explanation', essay 10 below.

[7] Coddington, A. 'Hicks and Keynesian Economics', *JEL* (1979).

[8] Hicks wrote in the Preface to First edition: 'The ideas on which this book is based were conceived at the London School of Economics during the years 1930–5.'

[9] *EJ*, p. 294, Review.

It is a rigorous book, taking the maximising principle through its paces. The first part of the book, on consumer behaviour and general equilibrium, is essentially static, and works out in the tradition of Walras and Pareto the ordinal theory of demand and the static general equilibrium model. The second part derives more from the tradition of Myrdal and Lindahl and represents Hicks' first full attempt at the theory of dynamics. However, in so far as the assumption of instantaneous adjustment is restrictive, in an important sense this first attempt fails to be fully 'in time' and was to be later more fully dynamised.

Value and Capital is sometimes misrepresented as an attempt to bridge the gap between micro and macro propositions, in a comparison between it and the *General Theory*. However, a much more reasonable interpretation would be as an attempt to bridge the gap between statics and dynamics, and in particular to extend static methods to dynamic cases. Just as consumer theory had been unrealistic in employing cardinality assumptions, so economic theory was in general unrealistic in being 'out of time'. *Value and Capital* should be perceived more as an attempt to drop the latter assumption. Dynamics[10] is defined here as economic theory under which 'every quantity must be dated' (p. 115, 1st edn). For Hicks, consumer theory in particular (but also production and monetary theory) is always a micro theory[11] in as much as it is given an optimising foundation based ultimately on individualistic explanation. Methodological objections to the practice of econometrics, best expressed for consumer theory in his *A Revision of Demand Theory* (1956), imply that the standard of judgement as to the realism of a theory must reduce to some kind of intuition, reminiscent of Hayek's view as expressed in 'Economics and Knowledge'.[12] Maximising behaviour is a characteristic for Hicks of the making of choices; in that sense it is *a priori* true, but its truth is also argued to derive

---

[10] Harrod offers a different definition in 'An essay in dynamic theory' as an economic theory of the constant and varying rate of change, (*EJ*, 1939). Hicks was later to combine the two versions in *A Contribution to The Theory of the Trade Cycle* drawing on Harrod's relationship between the accelerator and the multiplier. The problem with the Harrod approach, but not with Hicks', is that on Harrod's definition there is no room for short- and long-run periods; yet these represent very real problems for decision-makers. Harrod then has, on this definition, no period, and avoids precisely the problem of linking the periods together.

[11] Hicks has no macro consumption function as Friedman has, though of course he spawned it. See essay 2 below.

[12] *Economica* (1937), pp. 33–54; reprinted in his *Individualism and Economic Order* (1948).

from intuitive appeal. There can be no micro/macro distinction for Hicks; macro propositions cannot be allowed to float without foundation. He is never to be found picking out observations, in the manner of Keynes, such as 'a man's habitual habits having first claim on his income' or, in the long run, 'as a rule, a greater proportion of income (will be) saved as real income increases', without first deriving the result from simple principles. These have to be explained within the framework of rational behaviour. *Value and Capital* is completed by a mathematical appendix in which the amenability of the arguments in the book to this type of reasoning is demonstrated. But it is more than that; mathematical argument is used to prove the generality of the propositions to n commodities. It is the appendix where Hicks demonstrates the general equilibrium method to its full potential.

But *Value and Capital* should not be read as an uncritical exercise in the foundation of general equilibrium. Hicks was well aware of its limitations, and well aware of the cost of imposing the required assumptions. In discussing the fundamental problem of increasing returns to scale, he recognises that: 'it seems to be agreed that this situation has to be met by sacrificing the assumption of perfect competition' (p. 83), since the introduction of monopoly elements raises price above marginal cost. But he goes on to point out that:

it has to be recognised that a general abandonment of the assumption of perfect competition, must have very destructive consequences for economic theory. Under monopoly the stability conditions become indeterminate; and the basis on which economic laws can be constructed is therefore shorn away. (pp. 83-4)

It is worth quoting at length the arguments which Hicks uses to defend the continuing use of his assumption:

It is, I believe, only possible to save anything from this wreck – and it must be remembered that the threatened wreckage is that of the greater part of general equilibrium theory – if we can assume that the markets confronting most of the firms with which we shall be dealing do not differ very greatly from perfectly competitive markets. If we can suppose that the percentages by which prices exceed marginal costs are neither very large nor very variable, and if we can suppose (what is largely a consequence of the first assumption) that *marginal* costs do generally increase with output at the point of equilibrium (diminishing marginal costs being rare), then the laws of an economic system working under perfect competition will not be appreciably varied in a system which contains widespread elements of monopoly. At least, this get away seems well worth trying. We must be aware, however, that we are taking a dangerous step, and probably limiting to a serious extent the problems with which our subsequent analysis will be fitted to deal. Personally, however, I doubt if most of the problems we shall have to exclude for this reason are capable of much useful analysis by the methods of economic theory.

With hindsight, I suspect the conclusion would be revised. But it is important to realise the context: the alternative was the theory of imperfect competition which debateably did not get the economist very far. Modern theories of oligopoly were not then available, and it should not be forgotten that many of these turned out to be indeterminate. Hicks' requirement then, but perhaps not now, was determinateness of theory.

Much of the subsequent criticism of the neglect of increasing returns not only ignored the defence Hicks used for his perfect competition assumption, but also his attempts at that time to tackle it. For in 1939 his 'Foundations of Welfare Economics' appeared (essay 5 below), explicitly dealing with this issue, and his work on measuring real social income – his Valuation papers (essays 3 and 4 below) – explicitly face this issue by splitting the approach into cost and utility classifications.

Welfare economics had emerged with the marginal or Jevonian 'revolution' as the central concern of applied economics. But the aspects of public policy which it considered were concerned with partial adjustments in the system rather than with aggregate policy. To that extent, not only did Keynes attempt to dispute received theory, but he also tried to change the issues which it had sought to address. Keynes never wrote or concerned himself with the problems of welfare theory in the manner of Pigou. In contrast Hicks (along with Kaldor) did so, and with characteristic brilliance perceived first that the difficulties of Pigou's definitions could be replaced by the employment of the concept of Paretian optimality. Pigou was concerned not with welfare in general, but with a more restricted 'economic welfare' concerned with that which could be included under 'the measuring rod of money'. Hicks, following Pareto, was less restrictive; ordinal theory was built on a set of preferences which obeyed some minimal consistency criteria. It did not matter as it did to Pigou what sort of preferences were included. Later, in 'Preference and Welfare' and 'A Manifesto' (combined as essay 6 below) he was to call the Pigouvian tradition 'welfarist'.[13]

---

[13] The term welfarist, and its implications for the Paretian tradition, has subsequently been taken up in Amartya Sen's work. See in particular 'Personal Utilities and Public Judgements', *EJ* (1979), and 'Utilitarianism and Welfarism', *Journal of Philosophy* (1979).

Further to the defining of optimality conditions, Hicks also corrected, or rather extended, the Paretian framework to deal with cases where not only 'at least one person was made better off, and nobody worse off' but also where redistribution was involved; where there were both gainers and losers. It was here, in the case of gains from increasing returns to scale that Hicks tackled one of the criticisms of his *Value and Capital* discussed above. In this respect Kaldor and Hicks arrived at virtually the same solution simultaneously. The New Welfare Economics was an ingenious invention, which preserved with it, via the compensation tests, a modified form of the traditional theory. It was itself not complete without the exclusion by assumption of the Scitovsky case or paradox,[14] in which an agent can satisfy the Hicks–Kaldor criterion in both directions. But the road for future welfare economics was set and laid.

The concern with welfare economics and general equilibrium gained Hicks the Nobel Prize much later. But what passes for the subject today is somewhat different from what Hicks thought the subject should concern itself with. Quite recently, in 'The Scope and Status of Welfare Economics' (1975) (essay 10, *CEET* II) he was to point to the essentially Pigouvian tradition of the measurement of the social product, and its place in the Classical (Ricardo–Mill) thought. The difference between himself and Pigou was with what should and what should not be included in the idea of income. Hicks is quite general, Pigou quite specific. Hicks' methods, as with consumer theory, was to search for new foundations with minimal abstraction. And far from deserting theory to pursue issues of policy, the economists' economist tried to reformulate existing theory as he found it.

Until quite recently, in the dominant years of monetary theory and large-scale models, the interest in the status of welfare propositions has been rather a specialised activity. The Keynesian concerns of unemployment and the monetarist concerns with inflation tend to direct attention away from the more theoretical issues. Often it can seem somewhat bewildering to those new to the subject to have to work through welfare theory, rather than going straight to the 'answer'. Defining welfare changes, and defining real income, may seem curiously academic. Yet it cannot be stressed too strongly that many of the propositions about taxation, about allocation, about redistribution and equality, rest precisely on these abstract considerations; fundamentally on the concepts of income and welfare. Hicks never avoids this theoretical primacy; when the problems of cycles and their stabilisation became of practical concern, he re-

---

[14] For Hicks' comments on Scitovsky see *CEET* III, essay 11.

formulated the theory of cycles; when growth became a central concern he reformulated the theory; when it was inflation he turned (or rather returned) to the theory of money. It is in this context that the modern reader should understand the seemingly most abstract of his work, on consumer surplus and the measurement of real income. While others imagined (and to some extent did) that they were directing the management of the war economy and constructed somewhat utopian blueprints for the post-war period from Whitehall desks, Hicks continued at Manchester investigating the sources of welfare, and trying to maintain the remnants of that university in the war years. During the war years he was not, however, inactive or inattentive to the problems of the economic management of the war, nor to its aftermath. In an exchange with Keynes on the first war budget of Sir John Simon, he discussed the problems of imposing real-income losses, adamantly opposing the solution of allowing prices to rise on the grounds that wages would follow, making a real loss somewhat difficult to achieve. He was also clear in pointing to the dangers of proposed post-war policy and an excess of effective demand released the moment the war ended.[15]

Consumer surplus and changes in its level represented one way of comparing welfare. Hicks discovered four different measures and, eventually, that they could be placed in a general framework. Policies could be compared by reference to consumer surplus. But the central question of welfare economics as we noted above was the classical concern with the general problem: the measurement of real income.[16] Hicks perceived in his 1940 paper that there were two approaches to this problem – the utility approach and the cost or production possibility approach. These approaches were in fact quite differently and independently motivated to address different questions. Working on both the problems of social accounting and welfare theory, the realisation that the question of welfare was separate from the question of productivity was an important achievement which prevented some, but not all subsequent controversy. The Kuznets controversy reflected the slow absorption of the dichotomy in the late 1940s. This dichotomy is in fact profound, in as much as it captures the differing classical concern with production and the labour theory of value on the one hand, and the more modern concern with preferences and demand on the other.

[15] Quoted in a letter to Keynes (4 October 1939) in Keynes, C. W., vol. XXII, pp. 33–4. See also the important articles which appeared on post-war recovery, in particular essays 13 and 14 in *CEET* II.

[16] For a recent survey of real-income measurements, and comments on Hicks' role in the developments, see Sen 'The Welfare Basis of Real Income Comparisons', *JEL* (1979).

The motivation of this study is interesting, and the method of approach one from which much can be fruitfully learned. Dealing with 'the facts' of economic life requires both their meaurement and their organisation. In order to get the project going, to measure income, it is a necessary prerequisite to know what it is that you wish to observe. Facts are not so clear cut as in the natural sciences (if they are indeed so there); they are very often wrong. To get them 'right' for the purpose at hand, *and* the time period, the economist needs his theory. Theory helps to focus one's attention, it helps one know where to look. It has a classificatory role. But that means that 'facts' do not in the ordinary sense act as a check or test on the theory. Consistency of concepts is a necessary prior condition. The methodology is not that of econometrics, but rather of an older craft – making sure that the facts are what the economists think they are. If it is money that you wish to measure, first decide what money is. If it is income, work out what that income is. Modern econometricians frequently employ statistical methods of really great complexity; but their own material is only as adequate as the selection and filtering to which it has been subjected. In the nature of things, and because time passes, there will never be a perfect set of 'facts'. Hicks' articles on the valuation of social income, and his most popular book, *The Social Framework* (1942) represent exercises in the definition of the more important economic 'facts'.

Careful concern over the facts and their measurement was at least as important in Hicks' study of money. The 'Two Triads' is perhaps the best example of careful reflection on the idea and concept of money with the traditional textbook triad of functions which money is deemed to perform. Indeed Hicks introduces a selection of his own work on money, published as *Critical Essays in Monetary Theory*, with a statement which may act as a summary of the Hicksian method. He writes that his conception of monetary theory at that time had been reached over a long period. He says:

All the while I have been learning; as time has gone on, first one thing has become clear, then another. I have realised that truth is many sided. Any uniform presentation could only be a photograph from one angle; by changing my approach I hope that I have achieved something more stereoscopic.

It is important to realise that Hicks' monetary theory reflects developments from three influences: (1) Keynes' 'Treatise on Money', (2) Hicks' own development of the theory of consumer behaviour, and (3) the challenge presented by Hayek's notion of 'neutral money' as explored in the first essay of his *Prices and Production*. These influences form the background against which Hicks' thought out his theory of liquidity, left incomplete by Keynes. For although Hicks claims to come to money from risk, it may perhaps be a better representation to say that he came via risk to liquidity, and hence to money. The balance sheet approach in the early 'Simplifying' paper represented a continuum or spectrum of assets each referring to different degrees of risk, return and liquidity. It is not the simplistic theory of money and bonds within which Keynes operated; Hicks was to extend this analysis to include a breakdown of the different types of assets, including financial and industrial securities, as well as real assets. In this respect it is perhaps fairer to point back to Wicksell rather than Keynes, or even to suggest that Hicks gave a Wicksellian interpretation to Keynes. Hicks repeatedly points out that the controversies which divide monetary theorists are not new, but rather of quite old pedigree. He has tried to see continuity in thought, whereas others have seen revolutions. The history of economic thought is the route by which we come to a problem. Without understanding how we arrived at a problem, it is hard to imagine how it might be solved. In monetary theory, to modern students the controversy between the Currency and the Credit schools is economic history; to Hicks the issues of that debate form the dividing lines of the more recent fields of conflict.

In the post-war work on liquidity, the concept is presented as a problem of temporal co-ordination, reflecting a movement away from the more static portfolio approach of the 'Simplifying' paper and its value theory approach. Liquidity is the connection between the past and the future, so it is to be represented by sequential choices. The portfolio approach is not sufficiently in time to reflect speculative demand for money. The liquidity problem is the area where Robertson's thought had most impact on Hicks, especially with regard to the conflict between Keynes' liquidity preference theory and the Classics' loanable funds theory. Transactions demand does not have the voluntaristic character it does for Keynes; and as such cannot, at least in Hicks' later work, be analysed by choice models.

This is not the place to provide a review or critique of Hicksian monetary theory, or rather theories. In this selection, two samples of that plurality of views are represented; the early 'Simplifying' paper, and the much later one on 'The Credit Economy'. The early paper, as has already been indicated, is the value-theory approach; the later paper is the more mature Hicks, and perhaps the closest to his more recent views.

Keeping monetary matters firmly in mind, Hicks had always been dissatisfied with the static framework within which much marginalist thinking had been conducted. It may have been a necessary first step in economic analysis, but it was hardly sufficient for an explanation of economic behaviour. Indeed after the Second World War, having been isolated from the American economists for most of its duration, he was somewhat surprised by the extent to which they had concentrated on the static general equilibrium sections of *Value and Capital*, while somewhat neglecting the dynamic sections to which half the book had in fact been devoted. The dynamic extensions which were made, by Samuelson in particular, Hicks felt were too mechanical, and although useful for possible economic application, lacked tangency with the real economy and treated expectations too roughly. As Hicks put it in the appendix to the second edition of *Value and Capital*: 'for the understanding of the economic system we need something more, something which does refer back, in the last resort, to the behaviour of people and the motives of their conduct' (p. 337). With the problem of dynamics in mind, Hicks had turned his attention to trade cycle, to methods of dynamic analysis, and most importantly back to money and monetary theory. The Walrasians, with Walras' Law at hand, could happily ignore these matters by assuming such problems away. Hicks, ever mindful of the real economy, could not be so complacent. Indeed his general avoidance of the rather specialised 'general' equilibrium debate, and especially the 'existence' part of that debate, in the post-war years reflects his disinclination towards the pursuit of theory for its own sake, and a pre-occupation with the pursuits of questions relevant to the real economy. What theories should include, and what they should leave out, is related, as Hicks had continued to stress, to the problem at hand. Money is necessarily an imperfect institution, since risk and uncertainty reflect an imperfection of knowledge. The Walrasians were not concerned with such an imperfect world; rather they were concerned with the exposition of perfection. Money is not an equilibrium phenomena, and in this Hicks follows Hayek's lead. Disequilibrium occurs where expectations are disappointed. The American economists of that period included in varying degrees three strands within their thought, none of which appealed strongly to Hicks. These were the idealisation of the free market, the pursuit of theory for its own sake, and a reliance on econometrics to make contact with reality.

It is not an easy task to introduce Hicks' Methods of Dynamic Analysis, since they introduce necessarily added complexities. Yet an understanding of these methods is essential if one is to grasp his theories on money, the trade cycle and growth. The major contribution in this area is not his most Keynesian book on the trade cycle, nor indeed the book on growth, but rather a paper which appeared in the Lindahl Festschrift with that name. Its appearance there was not accidental; the paper attempts to spell out theoretically the relation between the ex-ante/ex-post method of the Swedes and the methods of Keynes. To put the paper in perspective, we can identify four stages in the development of Hicksian dynamics. These are: the *IS–LM* model, the *Value and Capital* position, the reaction to Harrod, and the fix-price/flex-price models. The idea of dynamic models is a relation between capital and time, of analysing processes rather than static outcomes. The set of possible models were for Hicks classified into a two by two matrix, where the division in one direction is, (1) *ex ante/ex post*, and (2) stock-flow models. To be set against these to form the four possible types, Hicks has (1) *p* models (flex-price) and (2) *q* models (fix-price).

Essentially these are the models which Hicks works out in the 'Methods of Dynamic Analysis' paper. This, and the addendum which is attached to the paper in *CEET* II, are reproduced below as essay 9; for it is of crucial importance to realise, as the addendum points out, that what Hicks has in mind in the fix-price, flex-price distinction is not the economists' exogenous and endogenous. The assumption represents models of dynamic adjustment, ways in which markets respond with the passage of time to particular changes else-where in the system. Exogeneity assumptions, related as they are in a special way to the notion of 'cause' may say something more about this dynamic process, but they are no part of its classification. A flex-price market is where equilibrium is established by the equating of supply and demand with the aid of a merchant. Fix-price markets are organised and administered; and as time passes they may tend to dominate flex-price markets.

Now the idea of flex-price methods is what Hicks has called a 'temporary equilibrium method', whereas fix-price is a disequilibrium method. For Hicks, however, the way to examine disequilibrium is by reference to equilibrium; it needs a benchmark or reference point. Furthermore, whereas we can allow flex-price to remain unconcerned with stocks, we cannot do so for fix-price. Indeed stock behaviour is a natural way for disequilibrium to manifest itself, and with this in mind perhaps the most interesting box in the above scheme is the *ex ante/ex post*, *q* model, reflecting disequilibrium stocks where there may be incomplete information and perhaps, therefore, risk aversion. In this domain, Hicks in the *Crisis in Keynesian Economics* (1974) explains the multiplier behaviour. Equilibrium concepts are clearly fundamental to this analysis, and in particular their relation to the adjustment of markets to the passage of time. With regard to the idea of temporary equilibrium, Hicks had in mind what he calls a 'week'. In this week, all flex-price markets could clear, but the fix-price markets could not. Stocks and expectations remain constant, and a temporary equilibrium is established where this partial clearance condition is met for a vector of prices.

There remains to this introduction three areas of discussion: capital and growth theory extensions of the dynamic models, the theory of economic history, and causality. The first relates to the application of dynamic models discussed above, while the issue of causality relates to the problem of dynamic sequences, and with the relation to the problem of expectations.

Capital and growth theory naturally grows out of Hicks' concern with dynamics; indeed, it is hard to see what a static theory would amount to here. But the relation is peculiarly defined for Hicks: growth theory is in fact for him 'one of the *methods* of Economic Dynamics'. In *Capital and Growth* (1965) the first nine chapters are devoted to an elucidation of the appropriate methods, and in particular to the methodological construction of macroeconomic theory. One of the building blocks of a growth theory is capital; and the continuum of Hicks' concern with capital can be seen through his three books on the topic: *Value and Capital, Capital and Growth*, and *Capital and Time*. These may be regarded as different angles on the same theme. The third of the books received perhaps the most mixed reception since it was seen as a departure from his earlier positions. But it should be stressed that the Austrian approach had always held a particular attraction to Hicks, because of its treatment of time. From his early days at the LSE, it was the influence of Hayek which had a strong attraction. The presentation of the views of *Prices and Production* was one of the strands of thought of the inter-war Robbins group. But the reason behind Hayek's impact can be traced back to Menger, whom Hicks has always regarded in the highest of lights. For it was the Austrians who, while embracing the marginalism of the late nineteenth century, kept their gaze firmly fixed on the importance of time in economics, and the effects of its passage. *Capital and Time*, far from being an episode in Hicks' work, was in fact a long-overdue statement of an important strand of his thinking. In it the steady state model of *Capital and Growth* is presented in Austrian style. For a more explicit treatment of time, readers are referred to his article 'Time in Economics', reprinted below as essay 14.

Economists with a theoretical inclination have neglected Hicks' *A Theory of Economic History* (1969). Historians have not, and for good reason. The logical extension of a concern for the passage of time in economic theory is to apply one's theory to economic history (see essay 13 below). In particular the distinction of fix- and flex-price markets needs a supporting story of the evolution and dominance of the fix-price over the flex-price. The flex-price world is an unorganised world requiring an intermediary, and this intermediary is the merchant. *A Theory of Economic History* is in part a theory of the evolution of the merchant, as an institution to facilitate the clearing of markets. He is a merchant who actually trades, rather than a Walrasian auctioneer who just registers prices. As time runs on more organised and administered markets appear; and these tend towards the fix-price variant. *A Theory of Economic History*, however, stops at the industrial revolution, for it is concerned more with the simplicity of the market than with the more difficult task of explaining the great upheaval of the late eighteenth and nineteenth centuries. The latter problem Hicks grapples with in his essay 'Industrialism' in *EP*, which may be regarded as a continuation of *A Theory of Economic History*. In this he introduces the concept of an impulse, a shock which can be traced through a sequence of consequences flowing from the potential of a major new invention. It is the same impulse which *Capital and Time* attempts to model.

The final area from the point of view of this selection of Hicks' contribution is his short book on *Causality in Economics* (1979), and his more recent methodological writings, about which there have been strongly divergent opinions. It was a brave book to write; it strays on to others' territory, and it contains a particular view as to the nature of economics as distinct from science, history, and other areas of social concern, yet requiring all three types of consideration. But its importance for the student of Hicks' work lies with the critique which it provides of the possibility of economic theory. In particular it provides careful reasons as to why prediction is not a strong possibility, and thus it explains Hicks' dislike of econometric practice. The book provides careful categorisation of different kinds of 'cause' from two dimensions; first with regard to time in terms of contemporaneous, sequential and static causality, and second in terms of strength of influence. This latter division is between 'strong' and 'weak' causality, where to claim that A strongly causes B is to say that A is the only cause of B. If A is a weak cause, then it is one of potentially many, and in explanation must be protected by a series of *ceteris paribus* clauses. Now it is only in cases of strong causality that prediction is possible, and it is unlikely, Hicks points out, that there are any cases of strong causality in economics. Economists are doomed to deal with weak causality, and are thus limited in their ability to predict. Falsification, at least in its naive form, is inapplicable, as the *ceteris paribus* clauses cannot be tested for. And the evolution of economic theory is not to be perceived as the rationalistic programme encapsulated by the philosophers of science such as Lakatos and Popper.

In his paper on the history of economic thought, ' "Revolutions" in Economics' (essay 12 below), Hicks is at pains to point to the essential continuity of theory, as a focusing of thought, rather than to a continual series of advances towards scientific knowledge. And since institutions change with the passage of time, theory depends for its relevance on the time period it addresses. In this regard the Hicksian theory of economic thought is far more tolerant than that of Schumpeter (1954); economics does not possess scientific status, nor can this be attained. There does not exist a standard such as that employed by Schumpeter to judge theories against; economics is for Hicks 'a discipline, not a science', and it might be added, a pluralistic one.[17] It is the discipline of which Hicks has become a master.

---

[17] See essay 32, *CEET* III.

Part I
Value

Hicks has contributed to value theory in four main areas, three of which are represented in this selection. The first contribution is the exposition of the ordinal theory of demand, replacing the assumption of measurability of utility by the ranking of preferences. 'A Reconsideration of the Theory of Value', essay 1 below, was written with the aid of Roy Allen and was first published in *Economica* (1934). The reader is referred to Hicks' 'A Revision of Demand Theory' (1956) for further developments and comments.

The second contribution is a series of essays on the measurement of income. The first of these, essay 2 below, is taken from *Value and Capital* and considers definitions of individual income which maintain spending power intact over time. There are shown to be a variety of ways of constructing this concept, which is a precursor of permanent income measures. Next Hicks considered the measurement of social income, and develops an important distinction. He points out that measurement depends on the *rationale* of the valuation of National Income. The correct method of adjusting market values, themselves distorted by elements of monopoly, taxation, and so on, depends on the purpose the economist has in mind. These purposes include the desire for an index of economic welfare (following Pigou), which derives a measure of want satisfaction or utility, and the need for a measure of productivity, deriving a cost measurement. Only under optimal conditions do the two measures coincide. Social income and social product are, under all other economic arrangements, different in quantity. These points were made in his 1940 paper, 'The Valuation of Social Income' published in *Economica*, and reprinted in *CEET* I. Two subsequent papers, reproduced below as essays 3 and 4, extended the analysis, and largely superseded the 1940 paper. The first, taking the utility approach, appeared in 1958 as 'The Measurement of Real Income', in *Oxford Economic Papers*. The second, 'Valuation of Social Income: the Cost Approach', although promised in the 1958 paper, did not appear until 1981 in *CEET* I.

The third area of value theory to which Hicks has contributed is the foundations of welfare economics, discussed in Part II. Finally mention should be made of his consumer surplus papers, and the four measurements which he isolated. These are presented and discussed in *CEET* I (essays 4 and 5).

1

A Reconsideration of the Theory of Value

This essay was published jointly with Roy Allen in *Economica*, February (1934). A second part appeared in May of that year, and is reprinted in *CEET* I.

The pure theory of exchange value, after a period of intensive study by economists of the generation of Jevons and Marshall, has received comparatively little attention from their successors in the twentieth century. Apart from some very interesting enquiries into what may be called the dynamics of the subject, due to contemporary writers of the school of Vienna,[1] there has been only one major achievement in this field since 1900. That achievement was the work of Pareto, whose *Manuel* (and particularly its mathematical appendix) contains the most complete static theory of value which economic science has hitherto been able to produce.

Of all Pareto's contributions there is probably none that exceeds in importance his demonstration of the immeasurability of utility. To most earlier writers, to Marshall, to Walras, to Edgeworth, utility had been a quantity theoretically measurable; that is to say, a quantity which would be measurable if we had enough facts. Pareto definitely abandoned this, and replaced the concept of utility by the concept of a scale of preferences. It is not always observed that this change in concepts was not merely a change of view, a pure matter of methodology; it rested on a positive demonstration that the facts of observable conduct make a scale of preferences capable of theoretical construction (in the same sense as above) but they do not enable us to proceed from the scale of preference to a particular utility function.

[1] Schönfeld, *Grenznutzen und Wirtschaftsrechnung*; Hans Mayer, *Der Erkenntniswert der funktionellen Preistheorien (Wirtschaftstheorie der Gegenwart II)*; Rosenstein-Rodan, 'La Complementarità' (*Riforma Sociale*, May 1933).

The first signs of a breakdown of the old conception of utility had already made their appearance in Irving Fisher's *Mathematical Investigations into the Theory of Prices*. Fisher had pointed out (1) that the whole theory of equilibrium in a market depends on the assumption of directions of indifference, and does not involve anything more; (2) that with three or more commodities the directions of indifference may not be integrable, so that it is impossible to deduce any utility function from a knowledge of these directions.[2] This latter point also makes its appearance in Pareto; it led him to his celebrated but mysterious theory of 'open cycles'; however, it is *not* with that point that we are at present concerned. It is with Pareto's more general and economically more significant contention, that even if it is possible to deduce a utility function from the directions of indifference, that utility function is to a very large extent indeterminate.

Though Pareto states this conclusion in the text of the *Manuel*,[3] he does not prove it there, and this has no doubt been responsible for the failure of many readers to see its significance. But a proof is given in the mathematical appendix;[4] it is not a difficult proof, and its sense can be set out in words quite easily.

Suppose, for the moment, that we have a utility function given; that is to say, we know, for the individual in question, how much utility he would derive from any given set of quantities of the goods on the market. Then we can deduce from this function (assuming always that he will prefer a higher to a lower utility) a scale of preferences; we can say, of any two sets, whether he will prefer one to the other, or whether they will be indifferent to him. If there are only two sorts of goods, this scale of preferences can be represented by a diagram of indifference curves.

It is thus possible to proceed from a utility function to a scale of preferences; but is it possible to proceed in the reverse direction? The answer is no; for the function with which we started is not the only function which will determine the scale in question. It is not only that there may be an indeterminate constant (this would not matter very much); but we can take as an 'index' of utility any variable which has the same value all along an indifference curve, and which increases as we proceed from one indifference curve to a higher one. Thus we might take the function with which we started; or we might take double that function (but this would only mean

---

[2] *Mathematical Investigations*, p. 88.
[3] *Manuel*, p. 159.
[4] *Ibid.*, pp. 540-2.

a change in units); however, we might also take its square, or any variable having a more complex relation with the first, so long as the essential condition of increasing in preferred positions is preserved.

To take an arithmetical illustration: Successive positions might be numbered 1, 2, 3, 4, 5; or 1, 4, 9, 16, 25; or 1, 2, 4, 5, 7; or any increasing series we like to take. So far as the actual behaviour of any individual can possibly show, any such series would do absolutely as well as any other.

The methodological implications of this 'ordinal' conception of utility have been discussed elsewhere;[5] they are very far-reaching indeed. By transforming the subjective theory of value into a general logic of choice, they extend its applicability over wide fields of human conduct. Two opportunities for the exercise of this new freedom seem of particular importance for the future of economics. One is the economic theory of the state, where the shackles of utilitarianism have always galled; the other is the theory of risk, where the application of the same logic seems fundamental to any progress in economic dynamics.

The present paper, however, is not concerned with these wide questions. Its task is the more pedestrian one of examining what adjustments in the statement of the marginal theory of value are made necessary by Pareto's discovery. As it happens, this task was not by any means completely carried through by Pareto himself. Much of his theory had already been constructed before he realised the immeasurability of utility, and he never really undertook the labour of reconstruction which his discovery had made necessary.

There are, however, two later writers whose work goes some way towards supplying this deficiency; they are W. E. Johnson and R. G. D. Allen. Johnson's work[6] does not appear to spring directly from Pareto; it is based rather upon Edgeworth; but it is much less dependent upon a 'cardinal' conception of utility than any of theirs.

---

[5] Cf. Zawadski, *Les Mathématiques appliquées à l'économie politique*, ch. III; Schönfeld, *Grenznutzen und Wirtschaftsrechnung*, Part I; Wicksteed, *Common Sense of Political Economy*, ch. V; Robbins, *Nature and Significance of Economic Science*, ch. VI.

Reference should also be made to Edgeworth's interesting remarks on Pareto's doctrine (*Papers*, vol. II, pp. 472–6). It has become increasingly hard to accept Edgeworth's contention that the existence of theories of Public Finance and Industrial Conciliation depending on the measurability of utility ought to be regarded as an argument in favour of maintaining that assumption. For its abandonment need not imply the abandonment of these undoubtedly valuable doctrines; it serves instead as a stimulus to the construction of new theories of wider validity, into which the traditional teaching can subsequently be fitted as a special case, depending on the introduction of a particular ethical postulate.

[6] 'The pure theory of utility curves', *EJ*, 1913.

It was further developed by Mr Allen in a pair of articles written before our collaboration began;[7] the present paper is the result, first, of my own reflections about Mr Allen's work, and secondly, of our collaboration in working out the details of a theory which shall be free of the inconsistencies detected in Pareto.[8]

What has now to be done is to take in turn a number of the main concepts which have been evolved by the subjective theory; to examine which of them are affected by the immeasurability of utility; and of those which have to be abandoned, to enquire what, if anything, can be put in their place. It is hoped in this way to assist in the construction of a theory of value in which all concepts that pretend to quantitative exactitude, can be rigidly and exactly defined.

I

1. *Marginal utility.* If total utility is not quantitatively definable, neither is marginal utility. But the theory of value does not need any precise definition of marginal utility. What it does need is only this; that when an individual's system of wants is given, and he possesses any given set of goods, $X, Y, Z, \ldots$ we should know his *marginal rate of substitution* between any two goods. The marginal rate of substitution of any good Y for any other good X is defined as the quantity of good Y which would just compensate him for the loss of a marginal unit of X. If he got less than this quantity of Y, he would be worse off than before the substitution took place; if he got more he would be better off; there must be some quantity which would leave him exactly as well off as before.

It will be evident to the reader that this *marginal rate of substitution* is nothing else than what we have been in the habit of calling the ratio of the marginal utility of X to that of Y; we might have called it the 'relative marginal utility'. My reasons for suggesting what is certain to be a rather tiresome change in terminology are these.

[7] 'Nachfragefunktionen für Güter mit korreliertem Nutzen' (*Zeitschrift für National-ökonomie*, Mar. 1934); 'A Comparison between different definitions of complementary and competitive goods' (*Econometrica*, 1934, p. 168).

[8] Our co-operation has been so close that it has been completely inpossible to separate out his results from mine in any orderly presentation. It has therefore seemed best that I should present our whole theory in a non-mathematical form, while Mr Allen follows it with a mathematical version. But this division does not of course correspond in any way to the actual process by which the theory was constructed. Mathematics and economics went hand in hand; nor would the reader find it easy to identify our respective shares by a consideration of the technique necessary to reach particular points.

If once we introduce marginal utilities, then, with the best will in the world, it is extraordinarily difficult to keep these two marginal utilities together; they have an almost irresistible tendency to wander apart. It would be possible to work out the whole of the following theory, using as our basic concept the ratio of the marginal utility of X to that of Y, the quantities possessed (or consumed) of all commodities being given; but we should have to keep a strong hold on ourselves, or we should soon be finding some indirect way of talking about one marginal utility by itself – or, what is equally indefensible, talking about the ratio of the marginal utility of X (when one set of quantities is possessed) to the marginal utility of Y (when the quantity possessed is in some way different).

A second reason may perhaps become clear in what follows. There does seem to be some advantage to be gained from concentrating our attention at this early stage on the essentially substitutional character of the concept.

If an individual is to be in equilibrium with respect to a system of market prices, his marginal rate of substitution between any two goods must equal the ratio of their prices. Otherwise he would clearly find an advantage in substituting some quantity of one for an equal value (at the market rate) of the other. This is the form in which we now have to write the law of proportionality between marginal utilities and prices.

When quantities of X and Y are represented on an indifference-diagram (quantities of all other goods possessed being therefore supposed given), the marginal rate of substitution between X and Y is measured by the slope of the indifference-curve which passes through the point at which the individual is situated. This depends simply upon the system of indifference-curves; given the indifference-map, we can read off directly the slope at any point; given the slopes at all points within a region, we can reconstruct the indifference-map for that region.[9]

---

[9] For more than two commodities the corresponding proposition is not necessarily true. For n goods, we have $n-1$ independent marginal rates of substitution (those of X and Y, X and Z, X and W, etc.; the rest can be deduced from these). But from these $n-1$ marginal rates of substitution it is only possible to construct an indifference-diagram (or what corresponds to an indifference-diagram in n-dimensional space) if some further conditions are satisfied (the integrability conditions). This proposition, which exercises a great fascination over the minds of mathematical economists, remains of doubtful economic significance. Some conclusions which are only valid if the integrability conditions are satisfied, will be given below.

2. *Diminishing marginal utility.* The principle of diminishing marginal utility must similarly give place to *increasing marginal rate of substitution.* Starting with given quantities of all the goods X, Y, Z, . . . ; if we first replace a marginal unit of X by that quantity of Y which just makes up for it; and then replace a second marginal unit of X by that quantity of Y which just makes up for this second unit: the second quantity of Y must be greater than the first. In other words, the more we substitute Y for X, the greater will be the marginal rate of substitution of Y for X.

This condition is expressed on the indifference diagram by drawing the indifference-curves convex towards the axes. (The curves must of course always slope downwards if the goods are both positively desired.)

The replacement of *diminishing marginal utility* by this principle of *increasing marginal rate of substitution* is something more than a mere change in terminology. When we seek to translate the principle of *diminishing marginal utility* into definable terms, it does not appear at first sight evident that this is the condition we must use. And it is an interesting historical fact that when Pareto found himself confronted with this question, he first of all gave the condition that the indifference-curves must be convex to the origin, and then went on to add a further condition: that the marginal rate of substitution will increase, not only when Y is substituted for X, but also when the supply of Y is increased without any reduction in the supply of X. This condition looks as good a translation of *diminishing marginal utility* as the other, but (as Pareto ultimately realised[10]) it stands on an altogether different footing. Cases which do not satisfy this latter principle undoubtedly exist in plenty, and there is no particular difficulty in fitting them into a general theory.[11] Exceptions to the true principle of increasing marginal rate of substitution would be much more serious.

For it is certain that for a position to be one of stable equilibrium at given prices, the marginal rate of substitution *at that point* must be increasing. If it is not, then, even if the marginal rate of substitution equals the price ratio, so that the sale of one marginal unit of X would not give any appreciable advantage, nevertheless the sale of a larger quantity would be advantageous. Equilibrium would be unstable – the individual would be at a point of minimum, not maximum, satisfaction.

[10] *Manuel* (French edition), pp. 573-4; cf. the earlier Italian edition, pp. 502-3 (of the 1919 reprint).
[11] See below, sec. II, 1, of this paper.

The assumption that the principle of increasing marginal rate of substitution is universally true, thus means simply that any point, throughout the region we are considering, might be a point of equilibrium with appropriate prices. There must be some points at which it is true, or we could get no equilibrium at all. To assume it true universally is a serious assumption, but one which seems justifiable until significant facts are adduced which make it necessary for us to pay careful attention to exceptions.[12]

3. *Elasticity of substitution.* The replacement of *diminishing marginal utility* by *increasing marginal rate of substitution* has this further advantage: it becomes significant and useful to ask: 'Increasing how rapidly?' Economists whose theory was based on diminishing marginal utility have rarely had the courage to ask a corresponding question; and when they have done so they have not derived much advantage from it. But our conception is strictly quantitative; and the rate of increase of the marginal rate of substitution may be expected to play an important part in the development of theory.

It is obvious that the two main conditions under which indifference lines are drawn – (1) downward slope, since an increase in either commodity leads to a preferred position; (2) convexity to the origin, from the principle of *increasing marginal rate of substitution* – leave open a wide variety of different shapes which may be taken by the curves. They may vary from the one extreme of straight lines at an oblique angle to the axes (the case of perfect substitutes) to the other of pairs of perpendicular straight lines parallel to the axes (the case of goods which must be used in fixed proportions). Between these extremes any degree of curvature is possible.

The curvature of the indifference-curve describes the same property as the 'rate of increase of the marginal rate of substitution'. But to take either as our measure without correction for units would be impossible – the result would have as little significance as the uncorrected *slope* of a demand curve. A measure free from this objection fortunately now lies ready to our hand. It is the *elasticity of substi-*

---

[12] Exceptions would presumably take the form of 'blind spots' on the indifference diagram – regions within which no stable equilibrium would be possible. These would also involve the possibility of cases of 'Buridan's ass'; the consumer with given income, confronted with given prices, would still be unable to decide between a number of different distributions of expenditure.

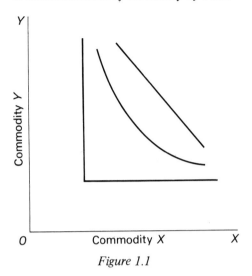

Figure 1.1

tution, when defined in a way analogous to that used by Mrs Robinson and Mr Lerner.[13] Applied to this problem it becomes

$$\frac{\text{relative increase in the proportion possessed of the two commodities } (Y/X)}{\text{relative increase in the marginal rate of substitution of } Y \text{ for } X}$$

when a small amount of Y is substituted for X, in such a way as to compensate the consumer for his loss. (That is to say, it is taken along the indifference-curve.)

One of the advantages of this particular measure is that it is symmetrical; if we write X for Y, and Y for X, in the above, the result is unchanged. It is therefore a general measure of substitutibility; when the commodities are perfect substitutes (so that the rate of increase of the marginal rate of substitution is zero), the elasticity of substitution becomes infinite; when they have to be used in fixed proportions (the other extreme) the elasticity of substitution is zero. Negative elasticities of substitution are, of course, ruled out by the principle of increasing marginal rate of substitution.

---

[13] Robinson, *Economics of Imperfect Competition*, p. 256; Lerner, 'Elasticity of Substitution' (*RES*, Oct. 1933, pp. 68–70). The definition given in my *Theory of Wages*, though appropriate, under certain assumptions, to the theory of production, is not valid here.

4. *Complementarity.* If (as appears from the above) any two goods are to be regarded as more or less substitutes, what becomes of the traditional doctrine that two goods may be either competitive or complementary? It will not be possible to give a full answer to this question until much later in this paper, but it is already possible to indicate why the traditional conception entirely fails to accommodate itself to our present construction. The definition of complementary (and competitive) goods given by Pareto and Edgeworth[14] (these seem to be the only major economists who have given an exact definition in terms of the general theory of wants) is completely dependent on the notion of utility as a determinate function. On their view, complementary goods are such that an increase in the supply of one will increase the marginal utility of the other; competitive goods are such that the marginal utility of the other will be lowered. This test cannot be translated into terms of marginal rates of substitution; it becomes definitely ambiguous when account is taken of the immeasurability of utility. In the vast majority of cases, the goods will be complementary or competitive, *on this definition*, according to the particular arbitrary measure of utility we choose to take.[15]

For the moment, then, let us put complementarity aside.

II

1. *The expenditure curve.* We have in the elasticity of substitution one of the fundamental concepts on which our further enquiries will be based; but it is not by itself an adequate foundation for a theory of value. For the elasticity of substitution refers only to one possible kind of change: that which takes place if one commodity is substituted for another, if, that is to say, the individual moves from one position to another on the same indifference-curve. But this kind of movement is not the only one of which we have to take account.

---

[14] Pareto, *Manuel*, p. 268; Edgeworth, *Papers*, vol. I, p. 117.

[15] If the utility function could be uniquely defined as $\phi(x, y)$, then the Paretian test would be given by the sign of ϕ_{xy}. But if we adopt his own doctrine that any other function of ϕ, $F(\phi)$, could equally well be taken as the utility function, this test breaks down. For

$$\frac{\partial^2}{\partial x\, \partial y} F(\phi) = F'(\phi).\phi_{xy} + F''(\phi).\phi_x \phi_y$$

and in general there is no reason why this should have the same sign as ϕ_{xy}, even though $F'(\phi)$ should be taken as positive.

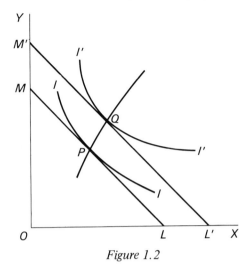

Figure 1.2

When the conditions of the market change, the individual does not usually move along the same indifference-curve; he is usually made better off or worse off by the change, so that he moves from one indifference-line to another. We, therefore, need information, not only about the shapes of particular curves, but about the mutual relations of the curves.

Take any point P on a given indifference-map, and draw the tangent at P to the indifference-curve that passes through P. Now draw a series of straight lines parallel to that first tangent, and mark off on each line the point where it touches a curve of the system. (By the principle of increasing marginal rate of substitution there can for each line be only one such point.) Now join these points. The curve so formed I shall call an *expenditure-curve*. It follows from the same principle of increasing marginal rate of substitution, that this expenditure-curve can cut any indifference-curve in one point only, and that there can be only one expenditure-curve through any point. But through any point an expenditure-curve can be drawn.[16]

The significance of this construction should be clear. The point P is a position of equilibrium (income being spent wholly upon commodities X and Y), when the relative prices of X and Y are as

---

[16] The reason why these further elaborations are not necessary in the theory of production – at least in its elementary stages – is that the assumption of a homogeneous production function implies that all 'expenditure-curves' are straight lines through the origin.

OM/OL, and when the income of the individual is OL (measured in terms of X) or OM (measured in terms of Y). The point Q is a position of equilibrium when the relative prices are the same (since the tangents are parallel) but income has increased (from OL to OL', or OM to OM'). The expenditure-curve thus describes the way in which the consumption of the two commodities varies, when prices remain unchanged, but there is a change in total expenditure.

What is the relation between the expenditure-curve through P (or rather its slope at P) and the elasticity of substitution at P? Strictly, they describe different things, for while the latter is a characteristic of a single indifference-curve, the former describes the relationship of one indifference-curve to others. Expenditure-curves of all sorts of slopes are compatible with elasticities of substitution of all sorts of magnitudes.

There is, however, one limitation on this. Since no expenditure-curve can cut an indifference-curve more than once, the variety of possible slopes the expenditure-curve can show is a little more restricted when the elasticity of substitution is low than when it is high. For finite changes, at any rate, an expenditure-curve through P which slopes very much to the left, or very much downwards, becomes distinctly more probable the flatter the expenditure-curve at P is, though this probability is reduced if there are stretches of greater curvature (or lower elasticity of substitution) in the neighbourhood of P.[17] In the case of fixed proportions (elasticity of substitution zero) the expenditure-curve must of course slope to the right and upwards.

Now if the expenditure-curve is positively inclined, this means that an increase in income will increase the consumption of both commodities (X and Y). If the expenditure-curve is downward-sloping, an increase in income will increase the consumption of X but diminish that of Y; if it is backward-sloping, X will be diminished and Y increased. These latter cases may arise whether or not the goods are easily capable of substitution, but they are distinctly less likely when the elasticity of substitution is low.

It is these cases which are ruled out by Pareto's condition, which we quoted above as a possible interpretation of *diminishing marginal utility* – the interpretation which we discarded. If, for example, the expenditure-curve is backward-sloping, this means that the point Q (where the higher indifference-curve has the same slope as the lower

---

[17] Very abnormal expenditure-curves (downward or backward sloping) are undoubtedly most likely at the extremities of the indifference-curves; for most indifference-curves become fairly flat as they approach the axes.

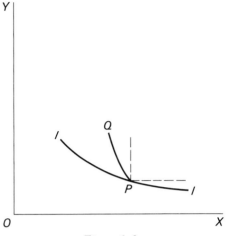

Figure 1. 3

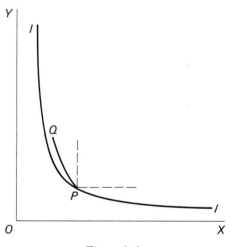

Figure 1. 4

curve at *P*) lies to the left of *P*, and since (by *our* principle of increasing marginal rate of substitution) the slope of any indifference-curve must increase from right to left, or diminish from left to right, the higher indifference-curve must have a smaller slope at the point vertically above *P* than the lower indifference-curve has at *P*. The marginal rate of substitution therefore diminishes when *Y* is increased and *X* is left unchanged.

Pareto's condition would thus limit us to positively-inclined expenditure-curves; but there is no particular reason why we should limit ourselves to cases which satisfy this condition.[18] Negatively-inclined expenditure-curves do occur; they are found whenever one of the commodities is an 'inferior' good, which is most largely consumed at relatively low levels of income, being replaced (or partially replaced) by goods of higher quality when income increases.

The most convenient measure for that property expressed by the expenditure-curve is simply the elasticity of demand for X (or Y) *in terms of income*. (The two are interdependent.) We shall find it convenient in this paper to use the conception of elasticity of demand in several senses additional to that given it by Marshall. Strictly speaking, the individual's demand for any commodity depends, not only on the price of that commodity, but also on the prices of all other commodities purchased, *and on his income*. A change in any one of these variables may affect the demand for X; and we can measure the dependence of demand on any of these variables by an elasticity. (Of course, many of these elasticities will usually be negligible.)[19]

The income-elasticity of demand for X therefore

$$= \frac{\text{relative increase in demand for } X}{\text{relative increase in income}}$$

when income is increased by a small amount, but the prices of all goods remain the same.

If there are only two goods purchased (the case to which our expenditure-curve directly refers), then a negative income-elasticity of demand for X means that the expenditure-curve is backward-sloping. A zero elasticity gives a vertical expenditure-curve. An elasticity of unity indicates that the consumption of each good increases in the same proportion as income, so that the slope of the expenditure-curve becomes the same as that of the line OP. If the expenditure-curve is downward-sloping, the income-elasticity of Y must be negative, and consequently the income-elasticity of X must

---

[18] A theory limited by this condition (and by this alone), would not be appreciably simpler than a more general theory; and it would certainly fail to cover all the facts.

[19] Cf. Lange, 'Die allgemeine Interdependenz der Wirtschaftsgrössen und die Isolierungsmethode' (*Zeitschrift für Nationalökonomie* 1932).

be greater than $1/k_x$, where k_x is the proportion of income initially spent on X.[20]

The conception of income-elasticity of demand is obviously applicable, however many are the goods on which income is spent.

2. *Constant marginal utility.*   A simple application of the preceding argument is the translation of Marshall's 'constant marginal utility' into exactly definable terms. If the marginal utility of commodity Y is constant, the marginal rate of substitution between X and Y must depend on X only. If the quantity of X is given, the marginal rate of substitution (or the slope of the indifference-curve) is given, too; the tangents to the indifference-curves at all points with the same abscissa must be parallel.

Since the expenditure-curve is drawn through points of parallel tangency, the expenditure-curve must be vertical, and the income-elasticity of demand for X must be zero. This property is again capable of extension to any number of goods. If the marginal utility of any one commodity out of many is constant, the income-elasticities of all the rest will be zero.[21]

III

1. *The demand-curve.*   The two indices we have now developed, the elasticity of substitution and the income-elasticity of demand, describe the two most important characteristics of the individual's scale of preferences in the immediate neighbourhood of the position where he happens to find himself. They are the analytical tools which we may now proceed to apply; and the first object of analysis must inevitably be the ordinary demand-curve.

[20] This latter proposition follows at once from the condition that $k_x \times$ income-elasticity of demand for $X + k_y \times$ income-elasticity of demand for $Y = 1$; for the small increase in income is supposed to be spent wholly upon X and Y. A similar proposition holds for any number of commodities.

[21] When restated in accordance with this, the argument of Marshall V.2. (that notable incursion into the dynamic theory of value) remains of course perfectly valid. If the article on which interest is concentrated is only one among many, only a small part of the increase in income due to an early favourable bargain is likely to be spent on that particular article; so that the demand curve for further units is unlikely to be much affected by such market aberrations. That is essentially all Marshall's argument comes to.

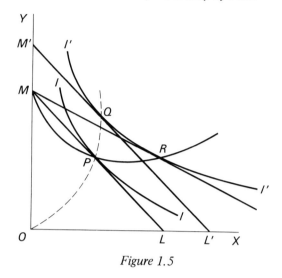

Figure 1.5

Here we may conveniently begin with a geometrical treatment, concentrating in consequence on the case where income is spent on two goods only – the case most amenable to the geometrical method.

Income is now to be taken as fixed, and the price of Y as fixed: but the price of X is variable. The possibilities of expenditure open to him are thus given by straight lines joining M (OM = income measured in terms of Y) to points on OX which vary as the price changes. Each price of X will determine a line LM (OL increasing as the price falls); and the point of equilibrium corresponding to each price will be given by the point where the line LM touches an indifference-curve. Joining these points, we get a demand-curve.[22]

Now it is obvious (again from the convexity of the indifference-curves) that any single indifference-curve must be touched by a line through M at a point to the right of that where it is touched by a line parallel to LM and above it. Therefore, as we move on to higher indifference curves, the demand-curve through P must lie to the right of the expenditure-curve through P; that is to say, the slope of the demand-curve must be less than the slope of the expenditure-curve.

Further, it is fairly evident from the diagram that the difference between these slopes – the extent to which R will be pushed to the right of Q – will depend upon the curvature of the indifference-

[22] Strictly speaking, demand-and-supply curve reversed. Supposing the individual to start with a given amount OM of Y, we might subtract each ordinate of the above curve from OM, and get a demand-and-supply (or offer) curve of the ordinary type.

curves, that is to say, upon the elasticity of substitution. The greater the elasticity of substitution – the flatter, therefore, the indifference-curves – the greater will be the divergence between the expenditure-curve and the demand-curve.

The increase in demand for a commodity X, which results from a fall in its price, depends therefore partly upon the income-elasticity of demand for X, and partly upon the elasticity of substitution between X and Y. We can in fact look upon the increase in demand as consisting of two parts, one of which is due to the increase in real income which a fall in the price of X entails, the other to the opportunity of substituting X for other goods which results from the fall in the *relative* price of X.

The relative importance of these two components depends fairly obviously upon the proportion of income initially spent on X. The larger that proportion, the greater will be the increase in real income resulting from a given fall in the price of X; and this will increase the importance of the income-elasticity relatively to the elasticity of substitution.

These geometrical and verbal reasonings hardly enable us to proceed to a formula for the elasticity of demand for X (in the ordinary sense, elasticity with respect to the price of X). But they are exactly corroborated by the algebraic analysis which will be given by Mr Allen.[23] It is there rigorously proved that with two commodities:

Price-elasticity of demand for X

$= k_x \times$ income-elasticity of demand for X
$\quad + (1 - k_x) \times$ elasticity of substitution between X and Y

(where k_x is the proportion of income spent upon X).

The price-elasticity of demand is thus not an independent index; it is reducible to the two primary characteristics which we described above.

2. *Extension to more than two goods.* Our formula has this further convenience, that it is capable of extension, with the slightest possible amendment, to the much more important case where more than two goods are consumed. We have only to write, instead of 'elasticity of substitution between X and Y', 'elasticity of substitution between X and all the other goods taken together'. For the rest, the formula remains unchanged.[24]

[23] See Part II of this article in *CEET* I, sect. I, 3(*b*).
[24] See Part II, sect. II, 4(*b*).

The sense of this extension can be interpreted as follows: Since it is only the price of X which varies, while the prices of $Y, Z, \ldots$ remain unchanged, these latter goods remain freely substitutible for each other at fixed ratios given by their relative prices. They behave, therefore, just like perfect substitutes, and a collection of perfect substitutes can be regarded as a single commodity. But the single composite 'commodity', which is thus formed by $Y, Z, \ldots$ taken together must be regarded as similar to a commodity with a wide variety of *uses*; the substitution among themselves of $Y, Z, \ldots$ is of precisely the same character as the reshuffling of quantities of the second commodity among different uses which might very well take place, even if there were only two commodities altogether.

Now it is fairly clear that with two commodities only, the elasticity of substitution between X and Y is likely to be greater, other things being equal, if Y has a wide variety of uses than it will be if Y is very specialised – this is evidently one of the main influences affecting the elasticity of substitution. Applying this to the 'many commodities' case, it follows that the elasticity of substitution between X and the 'composite commodity' is likely to be greater the more various the components of the latter are, i.e. the smaller are their mutual elasticities of substitution.[25]

Consequently, the elasticity of demand for any commodity is likely to be greater the more various are the objects of consumption with which it is in competition.

3. *The 'rising' demand-curve.*   Our analysis has now provided us with an exact definition of the conditions on which the elasticity of an individual's demand for a particular commodity X must depend. Since, of the two terms of which our formula is composed, the second must be positive, but the first is not restricted in sign, a highly inelastic demand is possible either (1) if both terms are positive and very small, or (2) if the first term is negative. Now, as we have seen, when X is only one good among several, it is unlikely that the elasticity of substitution between X and the other goods together will be very small, so that a highly inelastic demand is less probable in case (1) than in case (2). In that second case, where X is an inferior good, the elasticity of demand will clearly be smaller, the higher the proportion of income spent on X.

When the income-elasticity is negative, there is no absolute reason why we should be limited to positive price-elasticities of demand,

---

[25] The elasticity of substitution between X and YZ thus varies inversely with the elasticity of substitution between Y and Z.

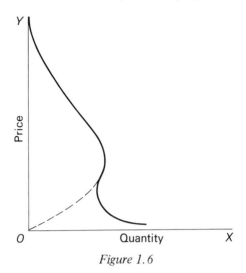

Figure 1.6

i.e. to downward-sloping demand-curves. If X is a good very decidedly 'inferior', so that its income-elasticity is negative and fairly large; if k_x is also large, so that a large proportion of income is spent on X; if, finally, the elasticity of substitution between X and other goods is moderately small; then the first (negative) term in our formula may outweigh the second (positive) one.

This possibility can easily be recognised as the celebrated Giffen case referred to by Marshall,[26] when the consumption of bread may actually be reduced by a fall in its price. Our analysis shows that it is perfectly consistent with the principle of *increasing marginal rate of substitution*; but it is only possible at low levels of income, when a large proportion of expenditure is devoted to this 'inferior' commodity, and when, among the small number of other objects consumed, there are none that are at all easily substitutible for the first. As the standard of living rises, and expenditure becomes increasingly diversified it is a situation which becomes increasingly improbable.[27]

[26] Marshall, *Principles*, 8th edition, p. 132.
[27] The demand curve on our diagram (Fig. 1.5) must first descend from M as the price of X falls (its elasticity >1). After a time it may rise again (become inelastic); and then – only then – it may curl back towards the Y-axis.

On a price-quantity diagram the resultant curve would look like Fig. 1.6. But it might conceivably continue to curve back to the price-axis (dotted line).

IV. Complementarity

1. It is perfectly consistent with the theory we have so far elaborated, to suppose that all goods are more or less related in consumption; yet we have made no use of the conception of *complementary and competitive goods*. We have not used it, because we had no need to use it; we had not yet come to the problem where it is relevant.

Substitution, indeed, comes into the theory of value from the start. Any two goods are substitutes – more or less. But complementarity, in the strict sense in which we shall define it, is not a possible property of two goods; it only has sense when the goods in question are at least three.

We have already examined the reaction of a fall in the price of one good on the quantity demanded of that good; and we have discovered that our analysis was applicable, however many other goods are simultaneously consumed. We have now to enquire how such a fall in price reacts on the demand for one particular good out of these other goods.

The same principle which we have previously applied will obviously hold here. The change in the demand for Y resulting from a fall in the price of X will again consist of two parts:

(1) There will be the change in demand for Y resulting from the increase in real income;
(2) there will be the change in demand resulting from the substitution of X for the rest, owing to the fall in its relative price.

Of these two components, the first will normally be positive, but will be negative if Y is an 'inferior' good. The second will depend on how far the substitution in favour of X takes place at the expense of Y rather than of the other goods (Z). If Y and Z are more or less on the same footing in the scale of wants, so that they are sacrificed fairly equally, then the second component will evidently be negative; and such negativeness we clearly ought to regard as the normal case. When the second component is negative, we shall say that Y *is competitive with X against Z*.

On the other hand, it is possible that the substitution in favour of X may not, as in this case, take place partly at the expense of Y, partly at the expense of Z. It may carry with it a simultaneous substitution of Y for Z; so that the whole effect of the substitution in favour of X is that the consumption of X *and* Y is increased, but that of Z is diminished – of course, more than in the preceding case. If this is so, we shall say that Y *is complementary with X against Z*;

and here the *second component* of the preceding paragraphs will be positive.

For three goods, we may thus distinguish three possible cases; either Y and Z are both competitive with X (against Z and Y respectively); or Y is complementary and Z competitive; or Z is complementary and Y competitive. It is impossible for both Y and Z to be complementary with X, since this would infringe the principle of increasing marginal rate of substitution.

For more than three goods, the possibilities are obviously extended; but it remains impossible for all of the other $n-1$ goods to be complementary with any one good. It is possible, however, for all the remaining $n-1$ goods to be competitive with the first.

2. The definition of complementarity just given, although it indicates the most important property of complementary (or competitive) goods, is, as a definition, not altogether satisfactory. For there is implied in it the assumption that when X is substituted for Y and Z, the ratio of the prices of Y and Z remains unchanged, and it is only the price of X relatively to these prices which varies. (Any change in the YZ price-ratio would of course affect the quantities substituted.) Since there is implicit in our definition this assumption about price-ratios, we have not succeeded in defining complementarity (as we ought to do) purely in terms of the individual's preference-scale; we are making a reference to the market which is better avoided.

Since there is an indefinite number of ways in which two goods Y and Z can be substituted for a marginal unit of X, it is best to concentrate our attention on that case which is the watershed between competitiveness and complementarity – the case when substitution in favour of X tends to leave the amount consumed of Y unchanged. Suppose then that X is substituted for Z, but Y remains unchanged. This simple substitution will affect not only the marginal rate of substitution between X and Z (in the way previously analysed), it will also affect the marginal rate of substitution between Y and Z. Since the quantity of Z is being diminished, the 'normal' effect will be to shift the marginal rate of substitution between Y and Z in favour of Z, or against Y;[28] Y is then competitive with X against Z. But if (as is possible) the marginal rate of substitution is shifted in the opposite direction (in favour of Y), then Y is complementary with X.

This second definition is really nothing more than a restatement of the first, and their equivalence is readily shown. If the marginal rate

---

[28] That is to say, it will increase the amount of Y needed to replace a marginal unit of Z.

of substitution is shifted against Y, then (if the price ratio between Y and Z remains unchanged), there will be a tendency to substitute Z for Y, i.e. some Y will be sacrificed. If the marginal rate of substitution is shifted in favour of Y, then not only is X substituted for Z (as we are already supposing to be the case), but Y increases at the expense of Z as well.[29]

3. The test of complementarity or competitiveness is thus established: the change in the marginal rate of substitution between Y and Z which follows on a marginal substitution of X for Z. Not only does the direction of this change indicate *whether* the goods are complementary or competitive, but also the degree of change (when properly adjusted) can be used as a *measure* of complementarity. But the definition of this 'elasticity of complementarity', and the detailed analysis which it makes possible, are so complex, that we must content ourselves here with a mere statement of results, whose proof must be left over to Mr Allen's mathematical version.[30]

It is there shown that:

(*a*)   the elasticity of demand for Y relatively to the price of $X = k_x$ × (Income-elasticity of demand for Y + Elasticity of complementarity of Y with X against Z).

(The elasticity of complementarity is, of course, positive or negative, according as the goods are complementary or competitive.)

(*b*)   If the integrability conditions are satisfied (and as a general rule we may probably take it that they are), so that *a* utility function could be formed, though not one utility function only; then it is true that the elasticity of complementarity of Y with X against Z *equals* the elasticity of complementarity of X with Y against Z. In general, therefore, it is quite correct to talk about X and Y being complementary (or competitive) with respect to Z, without having recourse to the more elaborate terminology we have hitherto employed.[31]

(*c*)   From this it can be shown in precisely what way complementarity will be reflected in demand relations. For the elasticity of demand for X relatively to the price of $Y = k_y$ × (Income-elasticity of demand for X + elasticity of complementarity of XY against Z).

---

[29] See Part II, sect. II, 4, 5, in *CEET* I.

[30] See Part II, sect. II and sect. III, 1, 2, in *CEET* I.

[31] Subject to the same condition, it follows that of three goods, X, Y, Z, only one pair at most can be complementary.

Whether or not this will have the same sign as the elasticity of demand for Y relatively to the price of X thus depends on the difference between the income-elasticities of the two commodities. If this difference is small, the two cross-elasticities of demand will generally have the same sign; but they may not if the difference between the income-elasticities is considerable. If, for example, one of the income-elasticities is positive and the other negative, then we may get reactions of price on demand which go in completely opposite directions – unless the goods are sufficiently complementary (or sufficiently competitive) for this variation to be swamped by the complementarity term.[32]

(d) Since the elasticity of complementarity of Y with X against Z measures the extent to which a substitution of X for YZ takes place at the expense of Y (when the relative prices of Y and Z are unchanged); and since the elasticity of complementarity of Z with X against Y measures the extent to which the same substitution takes place at the expense of Z; there must be a relation between these two elasticities and the elasticity of substitution of X with YZ taken together. In the general case, where there are six elasticities of complementarity and three elasticities of substitution (X for YZ, etc.) we get three equations connecting them, and could thus write the elasticities of substitution in terms of the elasticities of complementarity.

But when the integrability conditions are satisfied, and the six elasticities of complementarity therefore reduced to three, we can also use these three equations to give us the elasticities of complementarity in terms of the elasticities of substitution.[33] Hence we can derive the following propositions:

(1) XY are more likely to be complementary with regard to Z, the lower is the elasticity of substitution between X and Y, relatively to those between X and Z, and Y and Z.

(2) XY are more likely to be complementary with respect to Z, the larger is the proportion of total income spent upon Z, and therefore the smaller the proportion spent on X and Y together.

[32] The valuable investigation into this problem by Professor Henry Schultz ('Interrelations of demand', *Journal of Political Economy*, August 1933) is limited by the assumption of 'constant marginal utility of money' (i.e. of our third good Z). This comes to the same thing as neglecting the income-elasticities of demand, which the present analysis shows to be highly significant for the problem, as they may easily be of comparable magnitude with the (symmetrical) complementarity term.

[33] See Part II, sect. III, 2, in *CEET* I.

(3) If the elasticity of substitution between X and Y is zero, they must be complementary with respect to any third good less closely related; if the elasticity of substitution between them is infinite, they must be competitive.[34] If the elasticities are equal, they must be competitive.

V. Independence

1. According to the Edgeworth–Pareto definition of complementarity (based on the reaction of the marginal utility of one commodity to a change in the quantity of the other), it was natural to regard the case intermediate between complementarity and competitiveness (where the effect on the marginal utility is zero) as a case of 'independent goods'. This definition must be abandoned for the same reason as we have abandoned their definition of complementarity.[35]

Nor is it in any way appropriate to regard the watershed between complementarity and competitiveness (on our definition)[36] as a case of independence. For, if, as would happen at our watershed, the marginal rate of substitution between Y and Z is unaffected by compensating changes of X and Z, this does not mean that the goods are in any useful sense 'independent' – there subsists a very complex relation between them.

But there does exist another property to which the term *independence* can much more usefully be applied. If the marginal rate of substitution between Y and Z is unaffected by the quantity of X possessed, then we may say that YZ is *independent* of X.[37] If this condition holds, then it is clear that a substitution of X for Z can exert an influence on the marginal rate of substitution between Y and Z in only one way. The increase in X has no influence at all; it is only the decrease in Z which is effective. But that decrease in Z may still affect the marginal rate of substitution between Y and Z in either direction. For although the normal effect will undoubtedly be to move the marginal rate in favour of Z, nevertheless, if the

---

[34] In this sense, therefore, and in this sense alone, is it possible to say that competitive goods are easily substitutible; complementary goods not easily substitutible. This statement, so agreeable to common sense, turns out to be correct – so long as we speak in relative, not absolute, terms.

[35] It was a feeling of disquiet about this definition in the mind of Dr Rosenstein-Rodan which first led me to a consideration of the whole problem of this paper.

[36] When the elasticity of complementarity is zero.

[37] Similarly, for more than three goods, if the marginal rate of substitution between any pair depends on the quantities of these goods alone, it may be said to be 'independent'.

relationship between Y and Z is such that, were they to be consumed in isolation, Y would be an *inferior* good, then the marginal rate of substitution would be shifted in favour of Y.[38]

It is therefore possible for YZ to be independent of X, and at the same time XY may be either competitive or complementary against Z.

2. To say that YZ is independent of X, is a very different matter from saying that X, Y, Z, are independent goods. Can we give any meaning to the latter statement?

There is only this. If YZ is independent of X, and XZ is independent of Y, then XY may also be independent of Z.[39] If this is the case, then X, Y, Z are clearly independent in a wider sense, which approximates more closely to the older definition.[40] (This can be extended to any number of goods, which will be independent if the marginal rate of substitution between any pair of them depends on the amounts of those goods alone.)

Independent goods may be either complementary or competitive; but it follows from the preceding section that X and Y can only be complementary if Y is an *inferior* good. Further, since the integrability conditions must always be satisfied for independent goods, a substitution of Y for Z must also move the marginal rate of substitution between X and Z in favour of X, i.e. X must be an *inferior* good too. There are thus two possible cases of independent goods:

(1) where all pairs are competitive, and all the income-elasticities positive.
(2) where one pair is complementary, and two income-elasticities negative.

It will be shown in the mathematical analysis that this relation between complementarity and income-elasticity (in the case of independent goods) refers not only to sign, but to magnitude as well. If three goods are independent, then their income-elasticities depend on their complementarities.[41] It would not be difficult to demonstrate this on a three-dimensional indifference-diagram, where it would emerge in the following form: that in this case, given one

---

[38] See above, sect. II, 1.

[39] It will be if the integrability condition is satisfied.

[40] The marginal rate of substitution between any pair XY must then be of the form $f(x)/g(y)$, where x, y, are the quantities possessed. (This can be used as definition of independence in the case of two goods.) In cases of complementarity and inferiority, $f'(x)$ or $g'(y)$ may be positive, i.e. we must avoid being entrapped again in the law of diminishing marginal utility!

[41] See Part II, sect. III, 3, in *CEET* I.

indifference-surface, all the other indifference-surfaces of the system could be deduced.

This property, however, does not reproduce itself in the case of two commodities. The independence condition[42] is not then sufficient to enable us to deduce other indifference-curves from one curve alone. And so, in the two-commodity case, but only in this case, it is always possible, however the goods are in fact related, to find a pair of independent utility functions which will give us an indifference-map, closely approximating, over a small region, to the true map. This suggests a method of mathematical economic analysis which is much simpler than the quite general analysis followed in this paper, and which will, for small variations, give a close approximation to correct results.

Substantially, that method is the method of Marshall; it is one which has rendered great services to economics, even when *rationale* was not fully understood. But it is a method which is applicable, in strictness, only to the case of two commodities; for more than two commodities it loses its generality altogether.

---

[42] See note 41.

2

The Concept of Income

This is an extract from chapter 14 of *Value and Capital* (1939).

1.   The purpose of income calculations in practical affairs is to give people an indication of the amount which they can consume without impoverishing themselves. Following out this idea, it would seem that we ought to define a man's income as the maximum value which he can consume during a week, and still expect to be as well off at the end of the week as he was at the beginning. Thus, when a person saves, he plans to be better off in the future; when he lives beyond his income, he plans to be worse off. Remembering that the practical purpose of income is to serve as a guide for prudent conduct, I think it is fairly clear that this is what the central meaning must be.

However, business men and economists alike are usually content to employ one or other of a series of approximations to the central meaning. Let us consider some of these approximations in turn.

2.   The first approximation would make everything depend on the capitalised money value of the individual's prospective receipts. Suppose that the stream of receipts expected by an individual at the beginning of the week is the same as that which would be yielded by investing in securities a sum of £M. Then, if he spends nothing in the current week, reinvesting any receipts which he gets, and leaving to accumulate those that have not yet fallen due, he can expect that the stream which will be in prospect at the end of the week will be £M plus a week's interest on £M. But if he spends something, the expected value of his prospect at the end of the week will be less than this. There will be a certain particular amount of expenditure which will reduce the expected value of his prospect to exactly £M. On this interpretation, that amount is his income.

This definition is obviously sensible in the case when receipts are derived entirely from property – securities, land, buildings, and so on. Suppose that at the beginning of the week, our individual possesses property worth £10 000, and no other source of income.

Then if the rate of interest were 0.1 per cent per week, income would be £10 for the week. For if £10 were spent, £10 000 would be left to be reinvested; and in one week this would have accumulated to £10 010 – the original sum.

In the case of incomes from work, the definition is less obviously sensible, but it is still quite consistent with ordinary practice. Not having to do with a slave market, we are not in the habit of capitalising incomes from work; but in the sorts of cases which generally arise this makes no difference. Fluctuations in receipts from work are not usually easy to foresee in advance; and any one who expects a constant stream of receipts (and does not expect any change in interest rates) will reckon that constant amount as his income, on this definition. If fluctuations are foreseen, they are nearly always so near ahead that interest on the variations is negligible. With interest neglected, calculation by capitalising reduces to mere arithmetical division over time. £20 per month of four weeks can be taken as equivalent to £5 per week.

Income 1 is thus the maximum amount which can be spent during a period if there is to be an expectation of maintaining intact the capital value of prospective receipts (in money terms). This is probably the definition which most people do implicitly use in their private affairs, but it is far from being in all circumstances a good approximation to the central concept.

3.   For consider what happens, first, if interest rates are expected to change. If the rate of interest for a week's loan which is expected to rule in one future week is not the same as that which is expected to rule in another future week, then a definition based upon constancy of money capital becomes unsatisfactory. For (reverting to the numerical example we used above), suppose that the rate of interest per week for a loan of one week is 0.1 per cent; but that the corresponding rate expected to rule in the second week from now is 0.2 per cent, and that this higher rate is expected to continue indefinitely afterwards. Then the individual is bound to spend no more than £10 in the current week, if he is to expect to have £10 010 again at his disposal at the end of the week; but it he desires to have the same sum available at the end of the second week, he will be able to spend nearly £20 in the second week, not £10 only. The same sum (£10 010) available at the beginning of the first week makes possible a stream of expenditures

$$£10, £20, £20, £20, \ldots,$$

while if it is available at the beginning of the second week it makes possible a stream

$$£20, £20, £20, £20, \ldots.$$

It will ordinarily be reasonable to say that a person with the latter prospect is better off than one with the former.

This leads us to the definition of Income 2. We now define income as the maximum amount the individual can spend this week, and still expect to be able to spend the same amount in each ensuing week. So long as the rate of interest is not expected to change, this definition comes to the same thing as the first; but when the rate of interest is expected to change, they cease to be identical. Income 2 is then a closer approximation to the central concept than Income 1 is.

4. Now what happens if prices are expected to change? The correction which must be introduced suggests itself almost immediately. Income 3 must be defined as the maximum amount of money which the individual can spend this week, and still expect to be able to spend the same amount *in real terms* in each ensuing week. If prices are expected to rise, then an individual who plans to spend £10 in the present and each ensuing week must expect to be less well off at the end of the week than he is at the beginning. At each date he can look forward to the opportunity of spending £10 in each future week; but at the first date one of the £10s will be spent in a week when prices are relatively low. An opportunity of spending on favourable terms is present in the first case, but absent in the second.

Thus, if £10 is to be his income for this week, according to definition 3, he will have to expect to be able to spend in each future week, not £10, but a sum greater or less than £10 by the extent to which prices have risen or fallen in that week above or below their level in the first week.

Some correction of this sort is obviously desirable. But what do we mean by 'in real terms'? What is the appropriate index-number of prices to take? To this question there is, I believe, no completely satisfactory answer. Even when prices are expected to change, there is, indeed, still available a very laborious criterion which would enable us to say, for any given set of planned expenditures, whether it is such that the planner is living within his income or not.[1] If the

---

[1] If he is living within his income he must be able to plan for the second Monday the same stream of purchases as for the first, and still have something left over. Suppose he plans to purchase of commodity X quantities $X_0, X_1, X_2, \ldots$ in successive weeks; of commodity Y quantities $Y_0, Y_1, Y_2, \ldots$; and so on. The condition for him to live within his

application of this test were to show that the individual's expenditure equalled his income, then of course it would determine his income; but in all other cases it does not suffice to show by how much he is living within his income, that is to say, exactly how much his income is.

Income 3 is thus already subject to some indeterminateness; but that is not the end of the difficulty. For Income 3 is still only an approximation to the central meaning of the concept of income; it is not that central meaning itself. One point is still left out of consideration; by its failure to consider this even Income 3 falls short of being a perfect definition.

This is the matter of durable consumption goods. Strictly speaking, saving is not the difference between income and expenditure, it is the difference between income and consumption. Income is not the maximum amount the individual can *spend* while expecting to be as well off as before at the end of the week; it is the maximum amount he can *consume*. If some part of his expenditure goes on durable consumption goods, that will tend to make his expenditure exceed his consumption; if some part of his consumption is consumption of durable consumption goods, already bought in the past, that tends to make consumption exceed expenditure. It is only if these two things match, if the acquisition of new consumption goods just matches the using up of old ones, that we can equate consumption to spending, and proceed as before.

But what is to be done if these things do not match? And worse, how are we to tell if they do match? If there is a perfect secondhand market for the goods in question, so that a market value can be assessed for them with precision, corresponding to each particular degree of wear, then the value-loss due to consumption can be exactly measured; but if not there is nothing for it but to revert to the central concept itself. If the individual is using up his existing

---

income in the first week is that the stream of purchases actually planned for later weeks,

$$X_1 Y_1 Z_1 \ldots, \qquad X_2 Y_2 Z_2 \ldots, \qquad X_3 Y_3 Z_3 \ldots,$$

valued at the prices at which each is actually expected to be made (those of the second third, fourth etc. weeks respectively), should have a greater value than the original stream

$$X_0 Y_0 Z_0 \ldots, \qquad X_1 Y_1 Z_1 \ldots, \qquad X_2 Y_2 Z_2 \ldots,$$

valued, not at the first, but at the second, Monday, and valued at the same prices as that of the other stream (those of the second, third, fourth weeks etc.), that is to say, valued at prices expected to rule 1 week later in each case than the dates at which these purchases are expected to be made in fact.

stock of durable consumption goods, and not acquiring new ones, he will be worse off at the end of the week if he can then only plan the same stream of purchases as he could at the beginning. If he is to live within his income, he must in this case take steps to be able to plan a larger stream at the end of the week; but how much larger can be told from nothing else but the central criterion itself.

5.   We are thus forced back on the central criterion, that a person's income is what he can consume during the week and still expect to be as well off at the end of the week as he was at the beginning. By considering the approximations to this criterion, we have come to see how very complex it is, how unattractive it looks when subjected to detailed analysis. We may now allow a doubt to escape us whether it does, in the last resort, stand up to analysis at all, whether we have not been chasing a will-o'-the-wisp.

At the beginning of the week the individual possesses a stock of consumption goods, and expects a stream of receipts which will enable him to acquire in the future other consumption goods, perishabe or durable. Call this Prospect I. At the end of the week he knows that one week out of that prospect will have disappeared; the new prospect which he expects to emerge will have a new first week which is the old second week, a new second week which is the old third week, and so on. Call this Prospect II. Now if Prospect II were available on the first Monday, we may assume that the individual would know whether he preferred I to II at that date; similarly, if Prospect I were available on the second Monday, he would know if he preferred I to II then. But to inquire whether I on the first Monday is preferred to II on the second Monday is a nonsense question; the choice between them could never be actual at all; the terms of comparison are not *in pari materia*.

This point is of course exceedingly academic; yet it has the same sort of significance as the point we made at a much earlier stage of our investigations, about the immeasurability of utility.[2] In order to get clear-cut results in economic theory, we must work with concepts which are directly dependent on the individual's scale of preferences, not on any vaguer properties of his psychology. By eschewing *utility* we were able to sharpen the edge of our conclusions in economic statics; for the same reason, we shall be well advised to eschew *income* and *saving* in economic dynamics. They are bad tools, which break in our hands.

[2] See *VC*, p. 18.

6. These considerations are much fortified by another, which emerges when we pass from the consideration of individual income (with which we have been wholly concerned hitherto) to the consideration of social income. Even if we content ourselves with one of the approximations to the concept of individual income (say Income 1, which is good enough for most purposes), it remains true that income is a subjective concept, dependent on the particular expectations of the individual in question. Now, as we have seen, there is not reason why the expectations of different individuals should be consistent; one of the main causes of disequilibrium in the economic system is a lack of consistency in expectations and plans.[3] If *A*'s income in based on *A*'s expectations, and *B*'s income upon *B*'s expectations, and these expectations are inconsistent (because they expect different prices for the same commodity at particular future dates, or plan supplies and demands that will not match on the market), then an aggregate of their incomes has little meaning. It has no more to its credit that its obedience to the laws of arithmetic.

The conclusion seems unavoidable, but it is very upsetting, perhaps even more usetting than our doubts about the ultimate intelligibility of the concept of individual income itself. Social income plays so large a part in modern economics, not only in the dynamic and monetary theory with which we are here concerned, but also in the economics of welfare, that it is hard to imagine ourselves doing without it. It is hard to believe that the social income which economists discuss so much can be nothing else but a mere aggregate of possibly inconsistent expectations. But if it is not that, what is it?

In order to answer this question, we must begin by making a further distinction within the field ˙of individual income. All the definitions of income we have hitherto discussed are *ex ante* definitions[4] – they are concerned with what a person can consume during a week and still *expect* to be as well off as he was. Nothing is said about the realisation of this expectation. If it is not realised exactly, the value of his prospect at the end of the week will be greater or less than it was expected to be, so that he makes a 'windfall' profit or loss.[5] If we add this windfall gain to any of our preceding definitions of income (or subtract the loss), we get a new set of definitions, definitions of 'income including windfalls' or 'income *ex post*'. There is a definition of income *ex post* corresponding to each of our

---

[3] *VC*, p. 133.

[4] To use a term invented by Professor Myrdal, and exported by other Swedish economists.

[5] To use a term of Mr. Keynes's.

previous definitions of income *ex ante*; but for most purposes it is that corresponding to Income 1 which is the most important. Income 1 *ex post* equals the value of the individual's consumption *plus* the increment in the money value of his prospect which has accrued during the week; it equals Consumption *plus* Capital accumulation.

This last very special sort of 'income' has one supremely important property. So long as we confine our attention to income from property, and leave out of account any increment or decrement in the value of prospects due to changes in people's own earning power (accumulation or decumulation of 'Human Capital'), Income 1 *ex post* is not a subjective affair, like other kinds of income; it is almost completely objective. The capital value of the individual's property at the beginning of the week is an assessable figure; so is the capital value of his property at the end of the week; thus, if we assume that we can measure his consumption, his income *ex post* can be directly calculated. Since the income *ex post* of any individual is thus an objective magnitude, the incomes *ex post* of all individuals composing the community can be aggregated without difficulty; and the same rule, that Income 1 *ex post* equals Consumption *plus* Capital accumulation, will hold for the community as a whole.

This is a very convenient property, but unfortunately it does not justify an extensive use of the concept in economic theory. *Ex post* calculations of capital accumulation have their place in economic and statistical *history*; they are a useful measuring-rod for economic progress; but they are of no use to theoretical economists, who are trying to find out how the economic system works, because they have no significance for conduct. The income *ex post* of any particular week cannot be calculated until the end of the week, and then it involves a comparison between present values and values which belong wholly to the past. On the general principle of 'bygones are bygones', it can have no relevance to present decision. The income which is relevant to conduct must always exclude windfall gains; if they occur, they have to be thought of as raising income for future weeks (by the interest on them) rather than as entering into any effective sort of income for the current week. Theoretical confusion between income *ex post* and *ex ante* corresponds to practical confusion between income and capital.

7.   It seems to follow that any one who seeks to make a statistical calculation of social income is confronted with a dilemma. The income he can calculate is not the true income he seeks; the income he seeks cannot be calculated. From this dilemma there is only one way out; it is of course the way that has to be taken in practice. He

must take his objective magnitude, the Social Income *ex post*, and proceed to adjust it, in some way that seems plausible or reasonable, for those changes in capital values which look as if they have had the character of windfalls. This sort of estimation is normal statistical procedure, and on its own ground it is wholly justified. But it can only result in a statistical estimate; by its very nature, it is not the measurement of an economic quantity.[6]

For purposes of welfare economics it is generally the *real* social income which we desire to measure; this means that an estimate has to be made which will correspond to Income 3 in the same way as the above estimate corresponds to Income 1. Here we have the additional difficulty that it is impossible to get an objective measurement of Income 3, even *ex post*; since Income 3 always depends upon expectations of prices of consumption goods. But something with the same sort of correspondence can be constructed. Variations in prices can be excluded from the calculation of capital values, in one way or another; one of the best ways theoretically conceivable would be to take the actual capital goods existing at the end of the period, and to value them at the prices which any similar goods would have had at the beginning; any accumulation of capital which survives this test will be an accumulation in *real* terms. By adding the amount of consumption during the period, we get at least one sense of real income *ex post*; by then correcting the windfalls, we get a useful measure of real social income.[7] But it is just the same sort of estimate as the measure of social money income.

---

[6] Since the statistician must adopt this line, it is not surprising to find him turning for assistance to those other seekers after objective income – the Commissioners for Inland Revenue. The best thing he can do is to follow the practice of the Income Tax authorities. But it is the business of the theoretical economist to be able to criticise the practice of such authorities; he has no right to be found in their company himself!

[7] The process of correcting for windfalls will usually be less important in this case of real income, since all windfalls due to mere changes in money values have already been excluded; only such things as windfall losses due to natural catastrophes and wars are left to be allowed for.

3

Valuation of Social Income –
the Utility Approach

This essay was originally published under the title 'The Measurement of Real Income' in *OEP* (1958).

I. Utility and Cost Measures

1. The scope of the paper may be explained most conveniently if I present it as having the same relation to my much-controverted 1940 paper on Valuation as my 1956 book *A Revision of Demand Theory* (*RDT*) had to the corresponding sections of *Value and Capital* (*VC*).

There were two main contentions in the 1940 paper; (1) that measurement in real terms may mean valuation in respect of utility, or in respect of cost, and that these two meanings are in principle different; (2) that the utility measure is independent of the possibility of aggregating utilities. The first of these contentions appears to have stood up quite well to the fire of controversy; though there has been some criticism of the practical consequences which I drew from it,[1] the theoretical validity of the distinction itself remains unimpugned. But the second, as presented, has been shown to be fallacious. How much remains, when this error has been corrected, is a matter that has been much discussed by others; but I think that I have some right (or perhaps duty) to examine it myself.[2]

I propose in this paper to take for granted the distinction between cost and utility measures; and to concentrate attention on the utility measure – the valuation of the Social Income on the side of utility.

[1] See the controversy with Kuznets described in the addendum to essay 3, in *CEET* I.

[2] I have so much to do in the way of constructive work in this essay that I must beg to be excused from any survey of the extensive literature on 'New Welfare Economics', highly relevant as much of it is to what I shall be saying. Some reference must, however, be made to Samuelson's 'Evaluation of Real Income' (*OEP*, 1950); I have learned more from that article than from any other source, in relation to the particular matters which I shall be discussing. Much of what follows is no more than the imposition of a somewhat different 'slant' upon Samuelson's argument.

C

This is not because I am uninterested in the cost measure. I now think that in my 1940 article I claimed too little for the cost measure (perhaps because, as a result of the mistake in my argument, I was claiming too much for the other). After all it is the cost interpretation, in terms of resources applied, which is the interpretation which for most purposes we mainly want. Social Accounting proceeds for the most part in terms of Factor Cost; and I do not question that it is generally right to do so. The elucidation of the cost measure may therefore be a more important task than the elucidation of the utility measure. Nevertheless, it is the utility measure which has been the object of most of the theoretical controversy; and I have quite enough to say about it to occupy the present essay. Somewhat regretfully, therefore, I shall put the cost measure on one side.[3]

2. I have been speaking rather loosely about utility and cost 'measures'. I should, however, make clear at the beginning of our discussion that the basic distinction is not one between different measures, in the statistical sense; it is a distinction between different interpretations. The statistical measure of Real Income which we are examining is throughout a simple price-weighted index-number of Σpq type. Our problem is not one of the kind of measure to use, for we have no choice about that; it is a problem of the meaning which we can give the measures which we have to employ.

It is true that the question of meaning reacts back on the statistical problems of measurement. There are many components of the Social Income which do not have well-defined prices, so that we have to look to the purpose of the calculation in order to get guidance on what price to apply. (The celebrated case of indirect taxes may be taken as the leading example of this; but the issue arises in other connections also. There are goods which we may want to include though they do not have a price, such as food consumed on farms. There are goods with administered or controlled prices, where we may doubt whether the price given to us is the price we really want. Finally, there is the general problem of stock accumulation and fixed capital depreciation, items which may be utimately priced, but where the relevant prices do not fall within the period under consideration.) It is worth remembering these problems, because they serve to show that our inquiry has a practical bearing. But we cannot deal with them until after we have made up our minds on the theoretical issue. The first thing to be done is to determine the meanings that can be

---

[3] Though I shall come back to it at the end (see below, pp. 93–5). See also essay 4 below.

given to the concept of Real Income, and the relation between those meanings and the index-number measure, taken (for the present) in a simple and uncomplicated sense.

Nevertheless, when the matter is looked at in this way (with the results which have emerged from the controversies of these last years in our minds), there is one negative result which we can already foresee. We must not expect to find *any* general meaning which a price-weighted index-number (however skilfully constructed) can always, in all circumstances, be relied upon to express. Or, if there is any such meaning, it is something so empty and formal as to be scarcely interesting. We have been beaten back from the search for that Philosopher's Stone; but more modest objectives may still lie within reach. If we merely look for meanings which can often, or perhaps usually, be ascribed to our index-numbers, we are looking for something which may be more attainable.

But if we do limit ourselves in that way, there is a further duty, not previously noticed, which is laid upon us. We should be looking for criteria of reliability. We should be seeking for tests which would tell us when the verdict of the index-numbers is a good verdict and when it is open to suspicion. What we want is something which corresponds, on the theoretical plane, to the statisticians' 'standard error'. What we want is some better means of telling, in a practical instance, whether we are talking sense or not.

That is the general direction in which I want to turn my inquiry. But we shall only reach that point at the end of a fairly long discussion. It is necessary to begin much farther back.

II.   The 'Classical' Assumptions

3.   Since the real social income is made up out of flows of different sorts of goods and services (together with increments – and perhaps decrements – in the stocks of various sorts of capital goods), any method of measuring it implies a rule for establishing an equivalence between goods of different kinds. The simplest rule of equivalence is equivalence of market price; but though we are bound to rely on that equivalence very largely in practice, we cannot (for the reasons just explained) accept it as an ultimate criterion. We require some means of testing the suitability of the prices offered, and of penetrating into the penumbra where market prices cease to be available. Two alternatives then remain. Either we seek an equivalence in terms of cost – goods are equivalent if they are substitutable for one another, as alternatively producible from given resources; or

we may seek it in terms of utility – goods are equivalent if they are substitutable for one another, as alternatively usable in the attainment of given ends.

Some conception of substitutability in use is, I think, essential to any attempt to measure real income on the utility side; but there is quite a gap between this general notion (which, to me at least, appears quite unexceptionable) and the specialised forms which are needed to make it an instrument of analysis. To make it a convenient instrument, we need some special assumptions; and it must be freely admitted that the character of these assumptions is very questionable. It would be wrong to introduce them, if one proposed to leave them at the end wholly unmodified; but as a piece of scaffolding, by which one can mount up, so far as one is able, to a more general theory, they seem still to have a place.

The theory which is based on these assumptions needs a name; I have decided, after much hesitation, to call it the 'classical' utility theory. The theory which is to be associated with the classical economists, as that term is commonly used, is of course the theory of the cost measure; but we can surely recognise (in this mid-twentieth century) that utility has its classics as well as cost – neo-classics as some call them. It is not altogether wrong to mark some association between my classical theory and such 'classical' writings as those of Marshall and Pigou; but it would be wrong to label it with the name of any particular economist. For I am going to take the characteristic assumptions of the theory rather strictly; and when they are so taken it becomes obvious that they are too questionable to be accepted without reservation by any economist who has thought deeply about his subject. They can only be accepted, as I am here going to propose that they should be accepted, on a very provisional basis.

I shall accordingly set out the utility theory of the Social Income in two stages. First of all, I shall give the classical version (only, however, after explaining rather carefully why we are not to expect too much from it). I shall then go on to examine some ways in which we can relax the assumptions, so as to build up a utility theory which is not confined within quite such narrow bounds.

One special advantage which we shall derive from this procedure deserves mention at this point. Our decision to treat the classical theory as a provisional theory, due to be modified when the time comes, will enable us to make a fuller exploration of it, while we are concerned with it, than we should dare to do, if we proposed to make it our substantive theory, when we should be continually oppressed by its obvious weaknessses. This exploration will be very well worth while. For in the course of making it we shall discover techniques, which remain usable (at least to some extent) even when we modify the classical assumptions. One of the things which has been blocking a full development of the utility analysis has been a natural tendency to become preoccupied with its obvious weaknesses *too early on*.

4. The assumptions which are needed for the validity of the classical theory could be set out in a fairly long list; but it makes for convenience in handling if they are amalgamated into two. I shall call these the *Assumption of Integrated Wants* and the *Assumption of Revealed Wants* respectively.

(1) *Integrated wants*. If the wants which are to be satisfied by the set of real goods included in income are integrated, it is possible to arrange all relevant alternative sets in a single consistent ordering. This may be a weak ordering,[4] in which some possible alternatives come on the same level; but it must be a complete ordering, which obeys the axiom (or axioms) of transitivity. Granted this assumption, it is possible to construct a Utility Function (or, to adopt Bergson's famous phrase, a Social Welfare Function), in which Utility is shown as a Function of the quantities of the various commodities. Instead of considering the outflow from the productive process as an output of physical commodities (as common sense, followed in this respect by the more general utility theory, has to regard it) we can allow ourselves, once we grant this assumption, to follow the Welfare economists in regarding it as an outflow of Utility.

The Integration assumption is accordingly equivalent to assuming that the further ends (to which all utility theory must regard the real commodities as means) can be subsumed under a single end; so that the physical outputs can be treated like inputs that co-operate in the production of one single product. Now if all inputs did co-operate in the production of one single product, the measurement of the Real Social Product would be a simple matter; we should simply look at the quantity of the single product that was produced. It has accordingly been tempting (it was a characteristic mark of the 'Old Welfare Economics' that it succumbed to the temptation) to think of the measurement of Income as being ultimately a measurement of this one (subjective) product – that is, of Utility. The productive system produces Economic Welfare; it produces more, the more Economic Welfare it produces.

[4] *RDT*, chs. 3–5.

The arguments which have been advanced against this notion are familiar; it is unnecessary, at this time of day, to go into them in detail. In the form in which the question of measurable utility arises in this place,[5] it is completely disposed of by the classic demonstration of Pareto: that the ordering of the sets, which is all that is required by the Integration assumption, does not suffice to determine a single Utility function.[6] If $u(q_1, q_2, \ldots, q_n)$ is a utility function which expresses the given ordering, then $f(u)$, where f is *any* increasing function of u, will express the same ordering, so that it will serve as a measure of utility just as well as u. The single 'product', utility, is a mere construct; it is inadequately defined to be an object of measurement. The idea of measuring utility, or welfare, as such, is a blind alley.

It is, however, of much more importance, in this place, to look at the reverse side of this celebrated argument. Even if we do not seek to measure utility, we can still hold (if we choose) to the Assumption of Integrated Wants; and we can use it (by methods which will be explained in the next section) as a means of measuring, not Utility, but Real Income. If the cardinalists have gone too far in one direction, contending that it is possible to have an unambiguous measure of utility itself, ordinalists have often gone too far in the other, contending that we must limit ourselves to the mere comparison of a pair of positions, putting one above (or below) the other, without having any indication of the extent (or degree) of the difference. This is not so, as can be seen in general terms in the following way.

Let us suppose that our various sets of commodities are weakly ordered, so that the ordering can be represented by a set of indifference levels, or (sufficiently for the moment) by a set of two-dimensional indifference curves. Pareto's ordinal principle teaches us that the utility-indices which we can attach to these curves may be any set of numbers that rise as we go 'up' the curves. We may grant this, and still notice that there are various sets of numbers, which satisfy this condition, and which are in fact exhibited on the diagram. If the indifference curves intersect either axis, the intercepts along that axis will be one such set of numbers. Other sets can be found by drawing straight lines through the origin (or, indeed, any upward-sloping line – it need not even be a straight line), and

---

[5] For a discussion of the same question in other contexts, see *RDT*, ch. 2.

[6] It would of course have been more correct, historically, if I had taken the Integration assumption to include the specification of a determinate utility function. But I shall hope to convince the reader that this would have been a less fruitful way of arranging the argument.

noting the co-ordinates (either co-ordinate) of the points at which the line intersects the successive indifference curves. It has been a foundation of the ordinalist case that, of all the multitudinous measures that may be turned out by such a rule, no one is better than any other; there is a sense in which that is clearly correct. But it remains possible, even when that is granted, that there may be some of these measures which are more interesting and appropriate than others; I shall try to show that this is in fact the case. If we can grant the Integration assumption, we can find such measures; they will serve most of the purposes which the Old Welfare Economists sought to attain by the measurement of utility. But these measures (as is already apparent from what has just been said) are not reckoned in terms of utility; they are reckoned in terms of physical commodities, or combinations of commodities. They are not measures of Utility; they are measures of Real Income.

5.   If we can grant the Integration assumption, this is the kind of thing we can do; but can we grant it, even provisionally? The obvious objection against it lies in the multiplicity of consumers. The wants, which are satisfied out of the Social Income, do not form a single system; there are as many systems of ordering as there are consuming units. 'Integrated Wants' (it may be argued) is nothing else but the Addibility of Utilities in another guise.

   The connection must, of course, be admitted; I think, nevertheless, that it is worth while to exhibit the critical assumption in this less familiar form. The multiplicity of consumers is not the only reason why we may be unwilling to admit the assumption of Integration. To assume that the individual consumer has a fully integrated scale of preferences is quite a big assumption. It is an assumption that economists have allowed to pass because of its undoubted convenience; but the more one thinks about it, the more dubious it becomes. Taken literally, to mean that the consumer is capable, at any time, of ordering all the alternatives that may be presented to him, it is obvious nonsense. Many of them will be alternatives about which he has not begun to think. And though, when an actual choice is presented to him, he must make some decision, it is by no means necessary that his successive choices (they must, in practice, be *successive* choices) should fit together into an integrated system. It is true that if his choices fail to fit together, we can always get out of the difficulty by saying that his tastes have changed. But that makes it altogether arbitrary to say that the change is a change from one *system* of wants to another.

This is a difficulty for the econometric theory of demand, as well as for the 'welfare' theory. In the econometric theory, as I have else-where maintained,[7] it can be overcome by postulating an Ideal Consumer, whose tastes will only change for identifiable reasons; it is the Ideal Consumer, not the actual consumer, who is assumed to have a given (and fully-formed) scale of preference, so that to him the Assumption of Integrated Wants does apply. It is not necessary to assume that the actual consumer (you or I, or the person one meets in the street) does have an integrated scale; we can allow for a considerable degree of randomness in *actual* preferences. All that is necessary, in the econometric theory, is to assume that the random element really is random; so that a population of actual consumers, if it is a sufficiently large population, will behave in the aggregate very much as a population of ideal consumers would do. This is a more credible hypothesis, and for econometric work it is sufficient.

It is not inevitable that the same interpretation, which fits the econometric theory, should be suitable for the application with which we are here concerned. But it can hardly be doubted, when we face up to the issue, that some corresponding construction is required here also. The crude identification of the 'preference machines', whose working we analyse so finely in Demand theory, with real human beings, is just wrong; it has been the source of a large part of our difficulties. The 'individuals', whose want-structures we are here considering, are not actual consumers; they are ideal con-sumers, or (as it may be more appropriate to put it in the present application) *representative* consumers. To assume that the represen-tative consumer has an integrated want-structure is a tolerable assumption; to apply the same assumption to actual consumers is, when we think it out, not tolerable at all.

A major consequence of this reorientation is that the old trouble about Addibility loses a good deal of its force. The Classical Utility theory, which assumes Integrated Wants for the whole economy, emerges as the theory which is appropriate, so long as we are pre-pared to work with representative consumers, who stand for the whole body of consumers. Formally speaking, we then neglect both differences in wants and differences in incomes, and suppose that the whole supply of each commodity is divided among a large number of representative consumers, each of them being (for all that we take into account) identical with every other. The consumers are identical and they get equal shares. For purposes where distribution is not

[7] *RDT*, pp. 16 ff.

important, this is a perfectly sensible and useful construction. It is perfectly proper, in appropriate places, to define a rise in real income to mean that that representative consumer is better off.

Obviously, however, it will not do for all purposes. When we are not satisfied with it, we must go farther. But it is senseless to go to the other extreme, to a population in which every individual has his own idiosyncracies; that is an assumption which we are entirely unable to manage, and it is not necessary. All that is necessary is a half-way house. We may think of our whole population as divided into sub-groups, with a representative individual in each sub-group; this is an assumption that can be dealt with by a modest extension of the classical method, and it gives us all that we can seriously want. For whatever may seem to be the case from the course of our arguments, the important conclusions of economics are not concerned with individuals; they are concerned with society and with the classes of society. With these we can deal on the lines I have been describing.[8]

To break up the total population into sub-groups is the same thing as to abandon the assumption of Integrated Wants for the whole economy; instead of assuming that all the wants can be integrated into a single system, we have a number of separate systems. Now I think that I shall be able to show that this is also the important thing that happens when we abandon the Integration assumption for a single individual.[9] Thus the procedure we have set before ourselves, of beginning with the classical (integrated) theory, and then modifying it somewhat, is doubly justified. We can deal with distribution, and with some disintegration of wants, at one blow.

6. *Revealed wants.* The second assumption of classical theory I am calling the Assumption of Revealed Wants. There is, of course, in this title an acknowledgement to the Revealed Preference of Samuelson; but I am making a slight change in his wording, to mark a slight change in meaning. He was concerned with the deduction, from observed market behaviour, of the system of wants which is assumed to motivate it; my approach is less behaviouristic. I assume the existence of wants, independently of the market; whether these

---

[8] On this interpretation (it may be noticed) the question of population changes, which has worried some critics of my 1940 article (Kuznets, 'The Valuation of the Social Income', *Economica*, 1948; J. de V. Graaf, *Theoretical Welfare Economics* (1957), p. 160), is easily disposed of. There is no difficulty in changing population with constant tastes if the numbers in the various sub-groups change proportionately.

[9] This is one of the ideas which I owe to Professor M. Morishima's stay in Oxford. See his 'Stability of multiple exchange', *RES* (1957). The point is elaborated on pp. 89–90 below.

wants are 'revealed' on the market is not a question which (in general) I want to prejudge. Instead, I propose to mark off a portion of theory in which I do assume that wants are revealed on the market; but it is a provisional assumption, which we may seek to modify (at least in some respects) later on.

The precise significance of this second 'classical' assumption will become clearer if we examine some of the things which it obliges us to leave out of account. It is evident, in the first place, that wants cannot be revealed upon a market unless there is a market; a market-less economy, such as that of Robinson Crusoe or of a self-sufficient monastery, may have a Real Income, but it cannot be measured by the methods of classical theory. Even in more normal cases, there will be some commodities, which we shall want to include in the Social Income, but which have no market, so that the corresponding wants cannot be revealed in market demand in the way the assumption requires. Goods consumed by their own producer, without contact with the market, and public services provided by the State, are the main examples of this phenomenon; from the Real Income which is measured by classical theory they must be left out. We can only include them when we can find ways of stepping outside the classical model.

Even with respect to those goods that are sold upon a market, there are several ways in which we may doubt whether the market bids do properly reflect the wants which the goods are to serve. For one thing, the market may not be *free*; a rationed market, for instance, must be differently treated from a market that is free in the ordinary sense. Again, we should not be afraid to admit that there may be a failure of 'revelation' due to consumer irrationality, or lack of information; there is no reason why we should rule out the possibility that satisfactions may be improved by more instructed buying. It is, after all, the case that people do earn their living by providing such instruction; to treat the instruction itself as a commodity contributing to the social product in its own right, may be unavoidable, but is a clumsy way of proceeding. It does seem to be a better arrangement at this point to mark a distinction, which is to be deliberately neglected in the 'classical' theory, but which is left as one of the things which may be considered when we widen out. In any case it will serve as an introduction to the points which come next on my list.

When a consumer knows that he is ignorant, he may pay for instruction; but he may also pay to have decisions made for him. Doctors and lawyers and architects and stockbrokers may be paid to take certain sorts of economic decisions for their clients; these instances serve to remind us that the people who make choices are not necessarily the same as those whose wants are satisfied, to whatever extent, by the choices that are made. Even in the most perfectly individualistic economy, the distinction between the 'consumers' who choose, and the 'consumers' who enjoy, does not disappear altogether. In any economy that is not perfectly individualistic (that is, in any real economy) there are other forms of the distinction which are still more important. Every kind of voluntary association provides an example; and the two basic permanent associations, the family and the State, are of course the most important examples of all. In all these cases there is a question how far the wants that are 'revealed' by the choosers, do in fact coincide with the ultimate wants of the people for whom the choice is being made.

We need these distinctions for clarity of thinking; but we are still on ground that looks most intractable to economic analysis. In the end, we can hardly hope to do more than to find some polite way of evading these difficulties; yet, if they are indeed over the edge, they are nearly on the edge of the matters with which we do have to deal. And they lead up to an issue which we cannot shirk.

The investment goods, which we shall certainly want to include in some way or other as a part of the social income, are themselves (so far as they are acquired on the market) the prime example of commodities acquired *on behalf of* other people. They are the clearest and most important case where a distinction between choice-making and want-satisfaction is essential. It is indeed just because this is a case where the distinction forces itself upon us, so that we cannot avoid it, that the inclusion of investment goods in a utility-measured income has been felt to be paradoxical. Investment goods which are purchased by the ultimate consumer for his own satisfaction, whether the satisfaction be direct (as in the case of a gramophone) or indirect (as in the case of a spade to be used in the vegetable garden) do not cause trouble; we are content to treat them as if they were consumption goods. We do this in spite of the fact that some of the utilities they will yield are future utilities, running outside the period under consideration; we do it because we are content to regard the wants that are satisfied by such commodities as directly revealed. Where difficulty arises is where the saver entrusts his savings to someone else to make investment for him. The distinction between chooser and enjoyer is then so marked that we are unable to overlook it.

In classical theory, as I have insisted, we keep to the Assumption of Revealed Wants and therefore rule out *all* these complications. With an eye on the last point only, it may then be said that the thing we are measuring is Consumption, not Income. I would, however, prefer to say that we are measuring Income, but are measuring it under restrictive assumptions, so that the problem of saving and investment (along with other complications) does not, at the Classical stage, arise. For if we cut it out altogether, we should be pushing it off to be dealt with in some quite different way than by present methods. I would prefer to leave it with a place where it does belong in the present analysis; though the opportunity which we thereby leave open is one that we shall hardly be able to explore within the limits of this paper.

III.   The Classical Theory

7.   It is easy, once the Classical Assumptions are granted, to proceed to the familiar conditions under which an index-number comparison will tell us that one position of the consumer is better than another, or yields a higher real income than the other. These conditions[10] are implied in the theory which follows, but I shall refrain from setting them out in the conventional form, since I propose to be more ambitious. As explained above,[11] I am looking for a measure of gain, for something more than a test whether or not a gain exists. It is a consequence of ordinal utility that there is no single measure which will do for all purposes; we are not starting after a wild-goose chase after that single measure. It does, however, remain possible that we can find outstanding measures, which are more interesting than their possible rivals. Such measures I now believe can be found.

We are comparing two positions (of the representative consumer) which I shall call A and B. At A he is purchasing the set (q_1) of quantities of commodities at the set (p_1) of prices; at B (q_2) at (p_2). Quantities and prices being different, there is in general no way of making a direct comparison between the two positions. We can only make an indirect comparison, by setting up an 'intermediate' position α, that is comparable in one way with A and in another way with B. α is comparable with A if it is indifferent with A; but then (since transitivity is part of the Integration assumption) it cannot, in general, be indifferent with B. α may nevertheless be comparable

[10] See, for instance, essay 3, *CEET* I, pp. 82–3.
[11] See pp. 62–3.

with *B* in another manner. We may, as is well known, be content to find an α which is clearly higher (or lower) on the scale of preference; but this, though it is sufficient for a test of gain, does not suffice to give a numerical comparison. For that, α must be comparable with *B* numerically. There are two basic ways in which an α which is numerically comparable with *B* can be selected.

These correspond to the two basic cases in which we can treat a basket of goods if it were a single commodity. On the one hand, if the quantities of all the goods in the basket are changed in the same proportion, we can say that the basket as a whole has changed in that proportion. A basket whose 'product-mix' remains unchanged is directly measurable in some appropriate unit. On the other hand, if the prices of all the goods in the basket remain unchanged (or change in the same proportion) the composite basket can again be treated as if it were a single commodity. These are the two basic principles of measurement which we shall use in what follows.

The existence of these two principles of measurement (or methods of standardization) imposes upon the ensuing theory the same dualism as I have shown elsewhere to run through Demand Theory generally. There is, indeed, a close correspondence between the method of measurement which reduces to proportional quantities, and the demand theory which is based on quantities – what in my book[12] I called the Marginal Valuation theory, or *q*-theory. There is a similar correspondence between the other method of measurement and the demand theory that proceeds from prices to quantities (the *p*-theory). I shall accordingly take over the terms which I used in that other place, and shall call the two measures the *q*-measure and the *p*-measure respectively. I shall begin by setting out the two theories quite independently of one another, and (for reasons which will become clear as we go on) I shall in this case take the *q*-theory first.

8.   It is, I think, more or less inevitable, when we are analysing the wants of a representative consumer, that we should take the commodities consumed to be finely divisible. If, among 100 million consumers, there was one purchaser of a pet okapi, one hundred-millionth part of an okapi should enter into the representative consumer's budget. We shall seek to disembarrass ourselves of this inconvenience, to some extent, as we go on; for the present, however, divisibility must be assumed. Let us accordingly take one *m*th part of the quantity of each commodity that is consumed in

[12] *RDT*, chs. 9, 16.

position *A*, and combine them together to form a unit of a composite commodity (an *A*-bundle). The *A* consumption (q_1) can then be represented as *m A*-bundles. *B* consumption can be similarly reduced to *m B*-bundles. This makes it possible to proceed to an indifference diagram, essentially of the familiar type, in which *A*- and *B*-bundles appear as the two commodities.

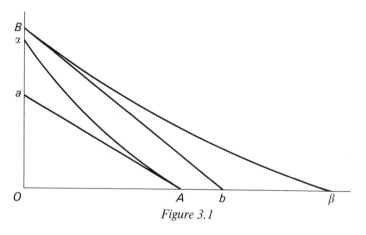

Figure 3.1

In Fig. 3.1, *A*-bundles and *B*-bundles are measured on two axes, and the *positions A* and *B* are represented by the points *A* and *B*. (There is some slight convenience in making the distances *OA* and *OB* geometrically equal; since the units in which *A*- and *B*-bundles are measured are entirely arbitrary, there is no reason why we should not do so.) As in the elementary application of the diagram, a point (*x*, *y*), not on the axes, represents the combination of *x A*-bundles with *y B*-bundles. Any collection of commodities which is capable of being expressed as a combination of *A*-bundles with *B*-bundles is accordingly representable on the diagram. These, of course, form no more than a small part of the set of collections from which a choice might be made; if we desired to represent a collection which was not expressible in this manner we should have to introduce a third dimension. It does, however, turn out that all collections which are relevant for *q*-measurement are capable of being represented on the two-dimensional diagram thus defined.[13]

[13] If there are no sorts of commodities in the *B*-bundle which are not in the *A*-bundle, and vice versa, there will be some collections of positive quantities of commodities which will be representable as *differences* between so many *A*-bundles and *B*-bundles. It may accordingly be proper to think of the indifference curves and price-lines as extending a little way beyond the *A*- and *B*-axes.

Let Oa be the number of B-bundles which has the same value, at A-prices, as OA A-bundles. Then, since the ratio OB/Oa is the ratio of two numbers of B-bundles, which will be the same at whatever set of prices commodities are valued, it can be expressed as the ratio between the value of B-quantities at A-prices and the value of Oa quantities at A-prices, which is the same as the value of A-quantities at A-prices. OB/Oa is accordingly equal to the Laspeyres quantity-index $(p_1 . q_2)/(p_1 . q_1)$. Further, since Oa is the number of B-bundles which the consumer could have acquired, if he had had his A-spending-power and could spend it at A-prices, the straight line Aa can be regarded as a price-line,[14] indicating those alternatives (representable on the diagram) which are open to the consumer when he is in his A-position. Out of these alternatives, and the many other alternatives (not shown) that are open to him, he chooses the point A; since (as assumed) he reveals his wants in this choice, there can be no point on the line Aa which is on a higher indifference level than the point A actually chosen. Thus the *indifference curve* between A- and B-bundles, which passes through A, cannot cross the line Aa; we will take it that they touch at A, just as any well-behaved indifference curve touches its price-line in ordinary Paretian theory.[15]

Let us call this indifference curve $A\alpha$, α being the point where it intersects the B-axis. As for its shape, I have drawn it convex to the origin, in the usual manner; this convexity can be demonstrated, in the usual way, if we are prepared to grant that each point along the curve represents a collection that could be chosen at some set of prices.[16] It is, however, worth observing that we are not obliged to make this additional assumption. The shape of the curve between A and α does not really matter for our present purposes; so we are not

[14] It is of course a section of the hyper-plane which represents the whole set of alternatives open in a space of n dimensions (n being the number of commodities). The whole of the present construction is based upon the observation that for purposes of comparing *two* positions we do not need the whole n-dimensional 'diagram', but merely the plane section of it which is determined by the origin and the two points A and B.

[15] If (see note 13) the indifference curve and the price-line can cross the axis to its negative side, positions on both sides of A are rejected in favour of A; then, granted that the indifference curve is a smooth curve, there must be tangency. Otherwise (and it is not difficult to spell out that this is correct) it is possible that the curve and the line may meet at A at an angle; but it remains true that the indifference curve lies wholly outside the price-line, and that (as we shall see) is all that matters.

[16] For this implies that at each point between A and α the curve lies outside its tangent, just as we have shown that it lies outside its tangent at the point A. (There is now no question that the curve must lie outside its tangent *on both sides*.) See also *RDT*, ch. 19.

obliged to assume that the other points on the curve could be chosen points, nor even that α itself could be a chosen point. Since the collections that are represented by these points must often be very odd collections, in which commodities are combined in very peculiar proportions, it is just as well that we can avoid doing this. What does matter is that a (that is, Oa B-bundles) is among the alternatives rejected at A; it is accordingly impossible that it should lie on a higher indifference curve than A. α, which represents a real set of quantities of goods[17] (which the consumer might be given, even if he would not buy it of his own volition), does lie on the same indifference curve as A, and must therefore tend to lie outside a. The important thing is that $O\alpha$ is greater than Oa (save in the special case where the two bundles of goods are perfect substitutes); this is independent of the shape of the indifference curve between A and α.

9.   We may now proceed to identify the position α, as just defined on our diagram, with the 'intermediate position' for which, at the beginning of this section, we decided to look. α is comparable with A, because it is indifferent with A; it is comparable with B, because it is a collection of commodities that is combined in B-proportions. A utility measure of the change in real income from A to B is accordingly that which is expressed on Fig. 3.1 by $OB/O\alpha$. Since $O\alpha > Oa$, we learn at once that this is *less* than the Laspeyres index which we have identified as OB/Oa.

Now, before going further, let us see what happens if A and B change places, so that instead of measuring from A towards B, we measure from B towards A. It is evident that the whole construction can be repeated on this basis (as indeed, I have shown it repeated on the diagram). Here we proceed to select an intermediate position β, which is indifferent with B, but comparable with A (because it is measured in terms of A-bundles). We can draw a price-line Bb, which (in the same sense) 'touches' the indifference curve $B\beta$. Ob is necessarily less than $O\beta$ (unless the bundles are perfect substitutes). The utility measure $O\beta/OA$ (writing it, for convenience of comparison, that way up) will now tend to be greater than the Paasche index (as it now becomes) Ob/Oa.

That there are two price-weighted indices, according as we work from A towards B, or from B towards A, is very familiar. What is

[17] It is, however, not to be excluded that the indifference curve through A might fail to intersect the B-axis, as would be the case if A contained an irreplaceable 'necessary' that was not included in the B-bundle. Even so, the rules which follow continue to hold, though α 'goes to infinity'.

less familiar, though it is made quite clear from our diagram, is that there are two utility measures also. The same change (from one indifference level to another) is measured by $OB/O\alpha$ if we work in terms of B-bundles, and by $O\beta/OA$ if we work in terms of A-bundles. There is no single measure of real income. Every measure is infected by relativity; every measure depends upon the point of view from which the measure is taken.

In spite of this, the utility measures (as defined) do have one great theoretical advantage over the price-indices, and indeed over any other measure of real income or real product which we might invent. So long, at least, as we can grant the classical assumptions, there is a necessary *coherence* between the utility measures. On the classical assumptions, the two indifference curves $A\alpha$ and $B\beta$ belong to the same want-system; and it is impossible that two indifference curves, which belong to the same (integrated) want-system, should intersect one another. Thus β must lie on the same side of A as B does of α; our two ratios are either both of them greater than 1 or both less than 1. In spite of the fact that we have two measures, so that the *size* of the change may look different according as we adopt the one measure or the other, each will show the same direction of change. If one says up, the other says up; if one down, the other down.

We cannot, of course, hope to estimate the utility measures directly; though the more precise formulation of the measures which has just been given may perhaps help in the search for indirect ways in which we might get some notion of their magnitudes. The obvious use of the analysis is to give us a means of evaluating the significance of the price-indices. Though the reformulation of the rules about the price-indices which it permits does not add much to what is known in other ways, we shall need it later on, and must therefore set it down.

Let L and P be the Laspeyres and Paasche price-indices; let p be the utility index $OB/O\alpha$ and l be the utility index $O\beta/OA$.[18] We then have $L \geqslant p$, $l \geqslant P$. If we could assume that $l = p$, it would follow that $L \geqslant P$. But we cannot assume that this equality is true in general. All that we know is that l and p lie on the same side of unity. Thus if $L < 1$, $p < 1$; therefore $l < 1$, and $P < 1$. Also if $P > 1$, $p > 1$; therefore $l > 1$, $L > 1$. We can argue each sequence its own way round, but not the other.

---

[18] This notation is of course a pure convention; we could have labelled them the other way. But it turns out to be handier to do it this way. As a mnemonic, let l's and p's suggest *large* and *petty*, as well as Laspeyres and Paasche.

There are therefore the following possible cases:

(1) If **L** and **P** are both greater than 1, it follows that l and **p** are greater than 1, so that there is a rise in real income.
(2) If **L** and **P** are both less than 1, l and **p** are both less than 1, and there is a fall in real income.
(3) If $L > 1$, $P < 1$, l and **p** may both be greater or both less than 1; nothing is shown whether there is a gain or a loss.
(4) This is, finally, the 'impossible' case – that $L < 1$, $P > 1$. There is, of course, no reason why this case should not occur, on occasion, in practice; but if it does, what is shown is that the classical assumptions will not do. Behaviour of this kind is incapable of being interpreted as the 'revealing' of an unchanged integrated want-system by a representative consumer.[19]

10. All that has been said, so far, belongs to the q-theory. It is complete in itself, and the results which it gives are in accordance with those which economists have long been willing to accept, in some form or other. There is only one reason why we may want to look further.

Consider the case (common enough in practice) where the two price-weighted indices (**L** and **P**) give quite harmonious results. Each of them (let us say) registers a rise of 5 per cent. We can then deduce from the above argument that the Laspeyres utility index (if we could find it) must register a rise of at least 5 per cent.; and that the Paasche utility index (which must move in the same direction) must rise by something between 0 and 5 per cent. If we were also prepared to admit that the two utility indices (though not necessarily equal) could not diverge from one another *very much*, it would be easy to conclude that the 5 per cent. rise, shown by the statistics, was 'pretty representative' of the real rise that had occurred. I suppose that it is by faith in this kind of proposition that economists do justify to themselves the use they make of index-numbers. If it checks up both ways, it must be right!

It must, however, be observed that the conclusion only follows if the indifference curves ($A\alpha$ and $B\beta$) are nearly linear; but it by no means follows from parallelism of the price-lines that the indifference curves are straight lines. There is, it is true, a limit to the extent to which they can curve; but they can curve quite enough to make nonsense of our measure. It is entirely possible, on the figures given,

---

[19] It will, of course, be recognised that these rules are nothing more than a restatement of the familiar rules of Revealed Preference theory.

that l might show a big rise (say 20 or 30 per cent.) while **p** showed scarcely any rise at all. If this were really the case, we could state that real income had risen, but we should be quite baffled on the amount of the rise; neither of the figures just quoted would have much significance.

Now there is some reason to suppose that the case just isolated is by no means a freak case; it may indeed be fairly general. It is by no means impossible that the proportions in which commodities are combined in the consumer's budget depend quite largely on the level of real income which he attains; they are more sensitive to changes in the level of real income than they are (excepting among groups of close substitutes) to changes in relative prices. If there is anything in this (and one's impression is that there is a good deal in it), the equi-proportional changes which we have been using as a standard of reference are a good long way away from the changes which the consumer, in ordinary market conditions, would spontaneously desire. If he is to be moved from an actual position on to a considerably higher indifference level by an equi-proportional expansion, it will have to be a big expansion; while an equi-proportional contraction (from an actual position) will cut his satisfactions very considerably, even if it is only a small cut.

The alternative method of measurement (the p-theory), to which I now turn, may be presented as a means of overcoming this difficulty. Instead of amalgamating a bundle of commodities into a single commodity by keeping quantities in fixed proportion, we amalgamate them by keeping them exchangeable for one another at fixed prices.

11. The p-theory can be put upon a diagram in the following way. (This diagram, the reader should be warned, is not – like the last – a mere adaptation of the ordinary indifference diagram; it is a kind of inversion of the indifference diagram. But there is a close correspondence between it and the indifference diagram which we have been using.)

We start, as before, with a position A, in which prices are (p_1), quantities consumed (q_1) and 'income' accordingly $(p_1 . q_1)$. If income were to increase, while prices remained unchanged, the consumption of each commodity would change in a particular manner, tracing out its own income-consumption curve (or Engel curve). The successive positions taken up could then be *defined* by the corresponding levels of income. If we measure income along a line (the A-axis in Fig. 3.2), and suppose that prices remain at (p_1)

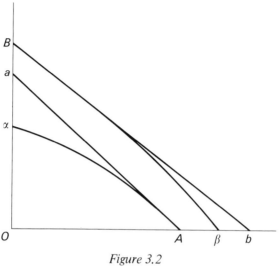

Figure 3.2

while income moves along that line, the situations of the consumer at successive points are completely defined, and the positions reached can be compared with one another by considering the change in income. We may mark a position A (as before) as the first of the positions we seek to compare; it is determined, once the prices (p_1) are given, by the income shown as OA. Other points on the A-axis are to represent the positions taken up at (p_1) prices with the incomes shown.

At B, prices are (p_2); so B cannot be placed on the A-axis. We draw a new B-axis for it, along which incomes, spent at prices (p_2) define a second set of positions in a similar manner.

Though it is not absolutely necessary for most of what follows, it will make for clarity if we give a meaning to positions which are not on either axis. These should be positions which are taken up when prices are in some sense intermediate between (p_1) and (p_2). The point $(x, 0)$ on the horizontal axis represents the collection of goods purchased when income is x and prices (p_1); the point $(0, y)$ that when income is y and prices (p_2). It would seem by analogy that (x, y) should represent the goods which would be purchased if the consumer had an income x, spendable at (p_1) prices, *and* an income y, spendable at (p_2) prices; this is nearly, but not quite what we want. For we want to compare conditions in which the consumer is spending his income at given, uniform, prices; and this means that the choice whether to pay for a particular purchase out of one 'purse' or the other is not a choice which should be left open. We can close it if we impose the additional condition that equal proportions of the various commodities purchased are to be paid for out of the two 'purses'. If the ratio is kept the same for all commodities, the quantities consumed will be the same as if income had been $x + y$, and the prices of the various commodities had been 'similarly intermediate' between their p_1 and p_2 prices – that is, they had divided the gap between p_1 and p_2 prices in the same ratio.

This being understood, we begin by looking for an expression for the price-weighted indices (as in the corresponding stage of the q-theory). Let Oa be the income, spent at (p_2) prices, which would just suffice to purchase the actual set of commodities purchased at A. Thus Oa is $(p_2.q_1)$; OB/Oa is $(p_2.q_2)/(p_2.q_1)$, which is the *Paasche* price-weighted index **P**. (It is important to notice the crisscrossing, which is a natural result of the change from working in terms of quantities to working in terms of prices; OB/Oa was the Laspeyres index in the other theory.) Now if the consumer were actually at a, with income Oa and prices (p_2), he would (in general) not purchase the A collection (q_1), though that collection is available to him for purchase; other alternatives are open to him which were not available to him at A, so that he can move to something else which he prefers. Thus a, which (it must be remembered) represents the actual set of goods which would be purchased if prices were (p_2) and income Oa, will (in general) be on a higher indifference level than A. If we define $O\alpha$ as the income, spendable at (p_2), which makes it possible to reach the same indifference level as was reached at A, α must tend to lie inside a, as drawn.

We may now (as in Fig. 3.1) draw a straight line joining A to a, and an 'indifference curve' joining A to α. What are the meanings of this line and this curve?

Since Oa is the cost of (q_1) quantities at (p_2) prices, the line Aa will exhibit that set of incomes which will enable (q_1) quantities to go on being purchasable, while prices change over, by steps, from (p_1) to (p_2). This is the same thing as saying that it exhibits the incomes which would be payable if income were adjusted, for each change of prices, by a cost-of-living index based on A. It must accordingly be insisted that Aa does not represent a set of simultaneously available alternatives, like the corresponding line in the other diagram. Instead of calling it a quantity-line (to match the price-line of the q-theory), it will help us to be clear about its character if we call it a *bonus line*.

Thus at each point on the bonus line, the A quantities (q_1) remain available. These quantities are chosen at A, but at the other points on the line they need not be chosen. The quantities actually chosen (which, I repeat, are those that are to be taken to be marked by the points on the diagram) cannot therefore, at any point on the bonus line, lie on a lower indifference level than the point A. The indifference curve, $A\alpha$, if we take it to join those incomes which permit of the attainment of the same level of satisfactions as was reached at A, will therefore tend, except at A, to lie below the bonus line. On substantially the same grounds as in the q-theory, it may therefore be taken to touch the bonus line at A.[20]

It then follows that the shape of the indifference curve must be as I have drawn it in Fig. 3.2. It is indeed possible that the indifference curve may coincide with the bonus line over a stretch, as will happen when the change in prices (with income bonus) leaves consumption unaffected. Tangency must be interpreted to include this possibility. Nevertheless, apart from the possibility of such linear stretches, the indifference curve must be concave to the origin *throughout*. The proof of this concavity is indeed much more conclusive than that of the convexity of the ordinary (q) indifference curve. For now, assuming that prices can change continuously, every point on the diagram is a possible point – one that may actually be taken up in some possible circumstances. There must be an indifference curve, and a bonus line, through every point; unless they coincide at that point, every other point on the indifference curve must lie within the bonus line. Whence the conclusion follows.[21]

That the p-indifference curve (or indirect indifference curve, as some may prefer to call it)[22] should bend the opposite way from the familiar q-curve is perhaps a little disconcerting. But it is a property

---

[20] If the same sorts of goods are purchased at A as at B, there can be no question that the series of price-sets is capable of being extended beyond the A-axis into the negative quadrant, so that the indifference curve through A lies below the A bonus line on both sides. If there are goods in B which are not in A, we cannot assert tangency at A; the rest of the construction (including the curvature of the indifference curve) does, however, remain unaffected.

[21] Concavity of the p-indifference curve is an expression of the substitution Theorem (*RDT*, chs. 7, 12); convexity of the q-indifference curve expresses the principle of Diminishing Marginal Valuation. As shown in *RDT* (ch. 9), the latter principle is subject to more exception than the former.

[22] The utility function, in which utility is made to depend upon income and prices, instead of depending on quantities directly, has been called by Houthakker the 'indirect utility function' (H. S. Houthakker, 'Compensated changes in quantities and qualities consumed', *RES*, XIX, 1951–2, p. 157). My p-indifference curves are its contour lines.

that belongs to the nature of the case; as far as I can see it is quite unavoidable.

12. Fig. 3.2 can of course be completed by drawing bonus line and indifference curve based on B. When that has been done, the rules about the relations between price-indices and utility-indices can be read off at once, just as we read them off from the q-diagram.

Defining the new $OB/O\alpha$ and $O\beta/OA$ as new utility-indices, we must in this case take $OB/O\alpha$ as the Laspeyres index (because of the criss-crossing). Call it λ. Then $\lambda \geqslant P$ (since α now lies inside a); and if π is the Paasche utility index $L \geqslant \pi$ (since β now lies inside b). Thus the relations of λ and π to L and P are the same as those of l and p. Since λ and π must be greater or less than unity together (so long as we maintain the integration assumption), exactly the same rules, and the same classification into cases, will hold here as in the q-theory.

This is, of course, as it should be. For what we are trying to do, by either method, is to reduce the movement from A to B (actual A to actual B) to a movement from one indifference level to another. l and p, λ and π, are all of them measures of the relation between these indifference levels. If there is an integrated want-system, they must all of them cohere with one another, rising or falling together. Subject to this general harmony, it does, however, remain possible that one pair may move in a less eccentric manner than the other. There is a point which can be made about this.

There is indeed some reason to expect that there will be a bias in this matter; and that it will be a bias on the price side. If our two *positions*, A and B, are positions of the same economy, but are far enough apart in time to give opportunity for 'long period' adjustments in supply, relative price changes should be kept, by these supply adjustments, fairly small; even when the economy is growing, by capital accumulation and technical progress, this should still be true. If they are positions of different economies at the same time, international trade makes for some degrees of price-harmony. I am unable to see that there are any similar forces that make for quantity-harmony. It is characteristic of economic growth that consumption expands along Engel curves, which rarely show a unity elasticity. The budgets of the representative consumers of different countries differ profoundly, quite apart from differences in wealth, for climatic reasons alone. It may indeed be maintained that for these reasons there is at bottom something unnatural about q-comparisons; p-comparisons do not merely sound better sense, they are better sense, in the kind of world in which we live.

IV.   Relaxing the Integration Assumption

13. We now begin our attempt to relax the classical assumptions. The first to be considered is the Integration Assumption. I shall begin by taking that, not in its most general form, but in the special form of the Assumption of the Representative Consumer, to which it largely corresponds. This assumption (once we are conscious of it) is one of the most obvious limitations of the classical analysis; can we get rid of it?

What we have hitherto been doing is to frame our critical question in the following manner. If income at A, and income at B, had been equally divided among a number of identical consumers, each with an integrated want-system that was revealed by his market behaviour (identical on the average with actual market behaviour), how much would they (each of them) have gained by moving from the one situation to the other? That, as we have seen, is in principle an answerable question; but it may fairly be argued that it is not the question that we want to have answered. The incomes of different consumers are in fact different and their wants may be different; we are therefore, by this procedure, taking an economy of one kind (with unequal distribution) and transforming it into an economy of another kind (with equal distribution) in order to make the situations comparable. It is natural to ask whether we are unable to make a comparison which does not involve any such transformation.

This (as I now see it) is the root of the question which was being asked by the 'New Welfare Economists' of the late nineteen-thirties. They were indeed over-confident in their belief that they had found a means of direct comparison which will always work. But I still maintain that they did find a means of direct comparison which will often work – a means which enables us to go some way (though we shall go on disputing whether it is a great way) beyond the confines of classical analysis.

Here again it is essential to be clear what we are trying to do. As I insisted at an earlier point in this article,[23] it is not possible to allow for every sort of individual idiosyncrasy. All we can do is to admit the existence of different classes in the population, with a representative individual in each class. Let us say that there are N_1 representative consumers of type I, N_2 of type II, and so on. The number of types can be as many as we like, but (for the present) we retain the

---

[23] p. 65 above.

assumption of a fully integrated want-system for each of these typical consumers.

It is evidently possible, when we decide to group the population in this way, to take each class separately, and to apply the Classical analysis to that class, in isolation from the rest. Instead of asking 'what is the change in the Average Real Income of the Nation as a whole?', we can confine our attention to subsidiary questions, such as 'what is the change in the Average Real Income of coal-miners?' But there are occasions – indeed, there are many occasions – in which we do want to give a meaning to the change in the Real Income of the whole community; we cannot ultimately avoid the larger question. And it is, of course, true that the smaller question, when we look at it closely, reproduces, on a smaller scale, the same difficulties.

If we have knowledge, not only of total quantities consumed, but also of the distribution of consumption between classes, we are clearly at liberty to serve up our results in the form of a statement that the real income of class I has risen so much, that of class II has risen so much, and so on. We should, however, be able to say something about the change in real income of the community as a whole without requiring such knowledge, or (perhaps) without directly using such knowledge. We are still trying to give a meaning to the price-weighted index-numbers of consumption as a whole; only we want to avoid the introduction of assumptions about distribution that are patently false.

14.   Once again we proceed by seeking equivalents. We interpose between A and B a position α which is cardinally comparable with B, and equivalent, in want-satisfying power, to A. As before, the cardinal comparison can be effected in either of our two manners, so that we still have a q-theory and a p-theory at our choice. The essential change, which differentiates our new construction from its predecessors, concerns the other leg, the equivalence by indifference.

It was (we can now see), the Great Discovery of the New Welfare Economics, that the notion of indifference is capable of being extended, with suitable precautions, from the behaviour of a single (or representative) individual to that of a not necessarily homogeneous group. Starting from a set of quantities (q_1) that are distributed in a given manner among such a group, we can define a series of other sets which are capable of being distributed, *without waste*, in such a way as to keep *each* individual on the same level as he reached initially. The qualification 'without waste' is important. If, for the actual set of commodities acquired at A, there is substituted, for each individual separately, another set which satisfies the indifference condition, it will in general be possible for some at least to improve their position by mutual exchanges, so that, after the exchanges, the indifference condition no longer holds. The totals of goods that have then been provided turn out to be more than sufficient to keep every individual on the same indifference level. A set which is *collectively indifferent* to (q_1) must be capable of being distributed so as to leave each individual on his initial indifference level, without leaving any opportunity for advantageous exchange. The indifferent positions are all of them optimum positions in this limited sense.

That collective indifference curves (or hyper-surfaces) in this sense can in general be constructed is made ocularly evident by that adaptation of the celebrated box diagram which we owe to Kaldor. It is sufficient to take the case of two persons and two commodities. If individual *I* is at position *P*, with respect to axes $O_1 X_1$ and $O_1 Y_1$, while *II* is at position *P* with respect to axes $O_2 X_2$ and $O_2 Y_2$, the superposition of the two *P*'s (with axes reversed) as shown in Fig. 3.3, enables us to read off the total quantities at the disposal of the pair by considering the coordinates of the second origin (O_2) with respect to the *I* axes. It is at once apparent that if the indifference curves through *P* do not touch, the total quantities can be reduced $(O_2$ can be moved south-west), while each individual remains on the same indifference level. If we insist that the tangency condition is to

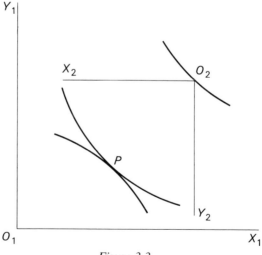

Figure 3.3

be maintained throughout, we can move the II curve round on the I curve, keeping contact; the locus of O_2, with respect to the I axes, will then be the collective indifference curve. It is evident that it has the same shape as an ordinary indifference curve. And clearly we may extend the same method of compounding to any number of persons and any number of commodities.

If the quantities acquired at our A are being acquired on a market, with identical prices to different consumers (so that the Revelation Assumption holds), the tangency condition (or optimum condition of exchange) is automatically satisfied at that position. We can accordingly draw collective indifference curves through A, with the optimum condition assumed to be satisfied along the curve.

15. All this being understood, let us go back to the q-theory. As in the classical version (Fig. 3.1), we can measure A- and B-bundles along the two axes. But we must now be clear that the bundles are put together in a 'macro'-manner; commodities are combined in the proportions in which they are consumed *in the economy as a whole*. Initially *total* consumption is represented by OA A-bundles. Oa is the number of B-bundles which have the same money value (at A prices) as OA A-bundles; OB/Oa is the Laspeyres price-weighted index, as before. $A\alpha$ is the *collective* indifference curve (between A- and B-bundles) that passes through A. In view of the way in which that curve has been built up, we may take it that it is convex to the axes (under similar restrictions as held in the classical case), and that it touches Aa at A. All this is identically the same as it was in Fig. 3.1; I have therefore thought it unnecessary to redraw the diagram.

The only way in which there may be a difference between the diagram, so interpreted, and that which we drew originally, concerns the relation between the two indifference curves $A\alpha$ and $B\beta$. In the classical version, $A\alpha$ and $B\beta$ were two indifference curves of the same consumer; given that he had an integrated want-system, it followed that the one curve must lie wholly within the other. Here (it is, of course, the Great Discovery of the Critics of the New Welfare Economics) there is no reason, in general, why intersections should be ruled out. It is not necessary that the utility measures, which result from the present construction, should *cohere*, as they were bound to cohere in the classical version. The collective indifference curves are not parts of an integrated want-system; the proof of coherence, which was previously given, therefore falls to the ground.

This must be accepted; but we need not therefore admit defeat. We are doing no more than generalising the classical theory, which remains valid as a special case of the present construction; what was true there cannot always be untrue here. We must clearly be prepared to insert additional qualifications as we generalise; it should, however, be possible to establish more precisely what those qualifications are.

To begin with, it is evident that we have already gained something by the concentration, on which we have insisted, on particular measures of the utility gain. Even if our two measures are in fact coherent, so that B lies outside α, and β lies outside A, we are clearly no longer entitled (once we lose the general proof of non-intersection) to assume that some other commodity-mix could not be found, measured along which the relation of the two indifference levels would be reversed. But, so long as we confine our attention to the relation between the two positions A and B, what might happen in quite other conditions may be judged irrelevant. If coherence between the A- and B-based utility measures could be established we should have all that it is fair to ask.

If B lies inside α while β is outside A, so that the utility measures **l** and **p** are not coherent, the collective indifference curves $A\alpha$ and $B\beta$ must intersect between the axes (Fig. 3.4). We can establish the conditions which are necessary for this to happen by considering the properties of a point of intersection E. E, it must be emphasised, is an actual set of quantities of commodities; since it lies on the curve $A\alpha$, it must be capable of being distributed so as to make every individual exactly as well off as he is at A; and since it lies on the curve $B\beta$, it must be capable of being distributed so as to make every individual exactly as well off as he is at B. But if A and B do not lie

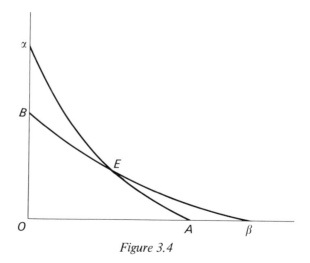

Figure 3.4

on the same curve (in which case there is no problem), it will only be possible for E to have these properties if the E goods are differently distributed, according as E is thought of as lying on the one curve or the other. And since each E distribution is a wasteless distribution (in view of the optimum property of the collective curves), E goods can only be differently distributed if E incomes are differently distributed; the redistribution must be to the advantage of some individuals (or classes) and to the disadvantage of others. There is in fact no longer a single indifference curve passing through each point on the diagram; there is a 'fan' of indifference curves through each point corresponding to different distributions. Along any single curve distribution (in this sense) must be taken to be the same; thus it is not possible for the two curves to intersect unless distributions at A and at B are significantly different.

This, I think, is by now well understood; but it is possible, by our apparatus, to take the matter a little further. We know that if distribution is the same at A and at B, there can be no intersection. Accordingly, when there is a change in distribution, we may break up the whole change that is under consideration into two steps. In the first step, there is a change in distribution, but no change in quantities; at the second there is a change in quantities, but no change in distribution. (That there is no change in distribution needs to mean no more than that the real incomes of all classes move in the same direction.) Since the total quantities consumed are unaffected by the first step in this division, there is no movement, at that first step, away from the position A on the diagram. But since there is a change in distribution, the position of the indifference curve $A\alpha$ will, in general, be varied. Suppose that it moves to $A\alpha'$ (Fig. 3.5). Then, since at the second step there is no change in distribution, $A\alpha'$ and $B\beta$ cannot intersect. Consequently, if $A\alpha$ and $B\beta$ do intersect, while $A\alpha'$ and $B\beta$ cannot intersect, there must not only be some movement from $A\alpha$ to $A\alpha'$; there must be a movement in a particular direction. The perverse case, in which the curves intersect, can only arise if there is a change in distribution which swings the indifference curve in a particular direction.

What that direction is, can be seen in the following manner. When the curve $A\alpha$ is swung downwards to $A\alpha'$, its tangent at A will also (not quite certainly, but most probably) be swung downwards, to a position such as that shown by Aa' on Fig. 3.5. What this signifies, in economic terms, is that the change in distribution, with total consumption of all commodities unchanged, will ordinarily require a change in prices. Let us call the quantity-index, of (q_2) to (q_1), which is weighted by these new prices, $\mathbf{L_0}$. Then if $Oa' < Oa$, OB/Oa'

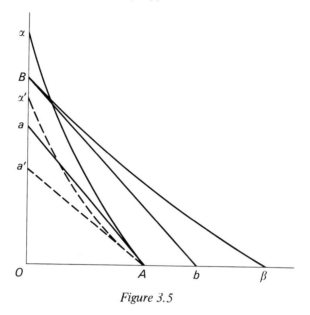

Figure 3.5

$> OB/Oa$, and $L_0 > L$. The change in prices, which results from the change in distribution, must accordingly move the quantity-index in the opposite direction to that in which it is 'normally' moved by the change in quantities; this is the same kind of distributional effect as makes for unstable equilibrium in the (Walrasian) theory of simple exchange, and it is not in the least surprising to find that it gives trouble in this context too.[24]

16. I have worked out this analysis at length in terms of the q-theory, since that theory proceeds with ordinary indifference curves, instead of the inverted kind, which will be less familiar to the reader. Exactly the same principles could, however, have been expressed in p-terms, and it may well be that in its p-version the argument is more compelling. It seems unnecessary to write out the p-version at similar length; an outline will be sufficient.

A collective indifference curve, of the p-variety, will indicate the sum of the incomes, spendable at a given set of prices, which would enable each consumer to reach a position indifferent with that which he occupied in his initial position. Since the individual p-curve is constructed with the set of prices as an independent variable, the rule of compounding is simpler than that which applied to the q-curves.

---

[24] But see addendum to this article in *CEET* I, pp. 183-5.

The individual p-curve is the locus of (x, y) when $x + y$ is the income which will admit of the attainment of a position indifferent with the initial position, when prices are defined by a parameter represented by y/x. The collective indifference curve is accordingly formed by adding the individual curves along each vector; the slope of the vector (y/x) determines the price-set, and the coordinates of the corresponding point on the collective curve are then found by summing Σx and Σy over all individuals. It is evident that the collective curve must have the same shape as the individual curves (being concave to the origin, as in Fig. 3.2 above): and it can be shown that it will touch the bonus line in the same manner.[25] Thus the p-diagram, just like the q-diagram, can be reinterpreted in a collective sense: in neither case is there any change in the diagram, except that in both cases we lose the direct proof that the two indifference curves $A\alpha$ and $B\beta$ cannot intersect.

It is at once apparent that if the curves intersect, there must be a change in the distribution of income between the positions that are being compared. For the point of intersection (E) now represents a particular total of incomes spendable at given prices; if it is to be indifferent with A along $A\alpha$, and with B along $B\beta$, and they are not indifferent with each other, the two E's must be in some way different, and the only difference that can now exist is a difference in distribution. Therefore, as before, we can construct a 'fan' of indifference curves through each point of the diagram. And, as before, we can split up the total change into (1) a distribution change, which swings the indifference curve around the point where the change in distribution is made, and (2) a pure change in aggregate quantities (or rather of prices and aggregate income) without change in distribution, the latter being a change where there can be no incoherence.

As usual, however, we must be careful about criss-crossing. Instead of beginning with the distribution change, and taking the 'quantity' change afterwards, we shall get the correct comparability with our q-procedure, if this time we work the other way about, and swing the $B\beta$ curve around B. It is also important to notice that the intermediate position, when prices and aggregate income have changed to their B-values, but distribution remains as at A, will not normally engender the same demands for commodities as exist at B. This

---

[25] If $Y = (p.q)$, summed over all commodities and persons, $dY = (p.dq) + (q.dp)$. Along an indifference level, $(p.dq) = 0$ for each individual; accordingly, when each individual remains on the same indifference level, $dY = (q.dp)$. The change in the price of each commodity being the same for each individual, this establishes the required tangency.

does not matter, since the intermediate position is only a step in the argument; we do not have to inquire whether it is realisable on the supply side. That 'unreal' quantities are consumed in the intermediate position of the p-theory signifies no more than that 'unreal' prices operate in the intermediate position of the q-theory. We are simply asking what *would* happen if prices and aggregate income were the same as at B and distribution were different.

As before, a swing in the indifference curve $B\beta$ will ordinarily entail a swing in its tangent, the bonus line Bb. When we take proper care over the translation, this emerges as the same result as before, that L_0 (the price-weighted index corrected for the distribution effect) should be greater than L, if there is to be an intersection. The two methods of analysis lead to the same formal result, which is, of course, as it should be.

17. The conclusion at which we have arrived, and which we have now confirmed, is capable of being illustrated in quite simple terms. Let us suppose (in imitation of a previous argument) that we are dealing with a case in which both of the observed indices (L and P) show a rise of roundabout 5 per cent. If we were prepared to make the classical assumption of a representative consumer, we could then conclude that the Laspeyres utility-indices (l and λ) would register a rise of at least 5 per cent, while the Paasche indices (p and π), though they must rise by not more than 5 per cent, must also mark a rise. If we were correct in our 'hunch' that prices are likely to move more harmoniously than quantities, we could also expect that the p-indices would move less eccentrically than the q-indices, so that λ and π might not differ very much from the 5 per cent rise which is observed. How much difference is made to these results when we drop the classical assumption, so as to allow for the possibility of distributional change?

It is still true, from necessary inequalities that still hold (from the shapes of the curves) that λ and l must show at least a 5 per cent rise. What is not excluded, as it was excluded on the previous interpretation, is the possibility that π and p might register a fall. But it is, of course, by no means necessary that they should do so. They might be moved in either direction by the distributional effect; and it is, of course, entirely possible (if the changes in distribution were of a random character) that they might not be moved at all. It is a quite particular sort of distributional effect which causes a movement in the dangerous direction; while if π and p would be significantly above unity, when no account was taken of the distributional change, the 'perverse' effect must be large if it is to upset the coherence. It would appear, from what has been said, that π is more likely than p to have this protection; its chance of maintaining coherence, whatever (in reason) happens to distribution, may therefore be better.

If there is a perverse distributional effect, and it is considerable, equality between the observed indices (L and P) is likely (as we have seen) to imply that if there had been no change in distribution, L would have been a good deal greater than P, being brought back into equality with P by the distributional effect.[26] This, I think, is the kind of condition which might be capable of being identified econometrically. If we knew whether it is of frequent occurrence, or whether (as I suspect) it is a rare case, we should be much further on.

18. That concludes what I have to say on the main problem of this section. All that remains is to give a brief indication of some other ways in which the same technique of generalisation could be used. One may mention, in passing, that liberation from the classical necessity of equal division incidentally frees us from absurdities about indivisibility.[27] We are no longer obliged to slice the okapi, provided that we are willing to reckon the okapi 'consumer' as forming a class by himself! Full allowance for *lumpy* consumption would indeed require some careful adjustment of the continuity assumptions which are hidden away in our curves. But I have not considered it necessary to pay much attention to this, since the breaches of continuity could not be considerable in relation to our 'macro' aggregates, and the essentials of our analysis have been expressed in terms of inequalities, not of equations.

The remaining point which I do want to bring up is quite different.

We have allowed for heterogeneity among consumers, but have so far maintained the assumption that the wants of each individual consumer are fully integrated. Suppose we want to drop that assumption: is there anything we can do about it? I do not think there is anything we can do about it, in general; if our individuals' want-systems have *no* inner consistency, the question of measuring Real Income (by a utility measure) loses all sense. There is, however,

---

[26] It may be well, at this point, to remind the reader that it is L which is tied to π or p by the curvature of the indifference curve. The same (distributional) movement that turns a (π) (>1) into a (π) (<1) will bring L_0 *down* to L.

[27] See above, p. 69.

a possibility of Partial Integration: the individual can make choices (consistent choices) among certain sets of goods, considered as means to the attainment of Objectives,[28] but among the Objectives themselves he can make no consistent choice. Of course, with a limited income at his disposal, he cannot satisfy his desire for one Objective more without satisfying that for another less; but it is possible that the choice between these wider alternatives may be too difficult to be made in a consistent manner.

Suppose that consumers' wants (or the wants of *some* consumers) are of this kind.[29] We can still apply the analysis which we have just been working out. We must simply treat each 'non-integrated' consumer as a bundle of separate 'consumers'. We can do this, for at no point in the preceding analysis have we implied that the 'individuals', out of whose wants the collective curves were compounded, were physically (or personally) separate from one another. Their role has been merely that of distinct want-systems. There is no reason why one person should not combine a number of distinct want-systems; nor (indeed) why a number of persons (such as a family) should not have a single want-system in common.

What I claim to have shown is that the interpretation of rising Real Income as gain in want-satisfying power can be applied to heterogeneous wants, as to homogeneous. That there is an exception, where the application will not work, is admitted; but the distribution exception is no more important (and may be much less important) than that which persists in the homogeneous case, from the possibility that, after all, wants may have changed.

V.   Relaxing the Revelation Assumption

19.   When we contemplate the task of extending the classical analysis, so as to deal with those sectors of the Social Income where the Assumption of Revealed Wants does not readily apply, we find an array of very large problems confronting us, consideration of which could lead us very far afield. A serious treatment of the

---

[28] *RDT*, ch. 17.

[29] That they should be of this character is one of the most plausible alternatives to the classical assumption of an integrated scale of preference. It is also the most plausible interpretation of mathematical 'non-integrability'. As is shown in *RDT*, ch. 4, a failure of transitivity must either imply circular ordering (which does not seem to be interesting economically) or a breakdown of the *gearing* condition which brings alternatives into contact with one another. It is the latter possibility which can be dealt with in the above manner (for which my debt to Dr Morishima must again be acknowledged).

investment sector would involve us in capital theory; a serious treatment of the public sector would take us near to political theory; at the tail end of an already lengthy article the temptation to roam in such directions must be resisted. I shall therefore confine myself here to a few formal points, which are reasonably relevant to the matters with which we have been so far concerned.

As soon as we extend our concept of Real Income to cover goods which are made available to the consumer (or user) in some other way than simple purchase, there are several aspects of the preceding analysis which require to be re-examined. We must doubtless proceed, in large measure, by fitting the non-marketed goods into some shadow or simulacrum of a market structure – considering that someone, somehow, is paying for them, and looking for evidence on which we can base an estimate of what is being paid. But it is a hopeless endeavour to assimilate these hypothetical 'markets' in every way to ordinary free markets. As soon as we pass beyond the ordinary free market, our problem is not only one of finding boxes into which the difficult parts of the Social Income can be fitted; it is also a question of the way in which these hypothetical markets can be supposed to work.

It is fortunate that this latter question can be examined, at least to some extent, without raising the major question of the valuation of those goods which by their nature are recalcitrant to simple pricing. The goods which are distributed in some other way than disposal on a free market may be such special goods, but they can be quite ordinary goods, which might be distributed through a market, though they happen not to be so. Cases of ordinary goods that are distributed in special manners are provided by some goods that are consumed by their own producers,[30] and (of course) by goods that are distributed by a system of rationing.

For such goods as are not disposed of on a free market, two of the conditions on which we have been relying break down. Though we

---

[30] The phenomenon, it should be understood, is that of goods that are neither bought nor sold by those who produce them. If I grow potatoes, but not enough for my consumption, so that I buy some potatoes on the market, it is clearly correct to value my whole consumption at the price which I pay, since my position is the same as if I sold my crop at that price, and then bought back what I wanted to consume at that price also. If I grow potatoes, but more than enough for my consumption, so that I sell some on the market, it is similarly correct to value my whole crop at the price which I *get* – for identically the same reason. In both of these cases the price-system is working normally. But if I neither buy nor sell, though we may value my crop at something intermediate between the prices at which I could buy or sell, this intermediate price is not a market price and does not behave like one, since it rises (along my marginal cost curve) with my consumption.

may find a convention to enable us to put 'prices' on the goods in question, these prices cannot play the parts which we have been ascribing to them. It is not possible for the individual to adjust his consumption, so that he chooses his most preferred position with the income and prices that are given to him; he cannot substitute one commodity for another at a given price-ratio, but either the 'price'-ratio varies with his consumption, or (as in the case of rationing) he cannot substitute at all. It further follows that the marginal rates of substitution between pairs of commodities are not brought into equality between different consumers. Distribution ceases (in general) to be an optimum distribution, in the limited sense in which we have been using that term.

So long as we could suppose our consumers to be acquiring their consumables on uniform-price markets, it did look (I have repeatedly emphasised) as if the p-utility measure gave us a better meaning for the concept of Real Income – a meaning which is more in accordance with the sorts of questions we want to have answered, and which is more likely, in application, to give us a measure that can be expected to behave in a reasonable way. But as soon as we pass to the consideration of cases where the price-system is not working, or not working 'properly', this primacy of the p-measure seems to disappear. It is indeed very hard to see how we can use the p-measure when consumption ceases to be determined by income and by the prices confronting the consumer. The p-measure belongs to the free market; the possibility of measuring Real Income in that way is one of the many services which the existence of a market provides for economics.

What, however, of the q-measure? The q-measure is not so obviously dependent on the price-system, so that we may perhaps have done well to keep that alternative in play, ready for use when we need it. But the theory of the q-measure, as it has been given, has also relied upon the price-system; if it is to transcend the price-system, it will require, at the least, some adjustment. What are we to mean by the collective indifference curve through A, when A is not to be automatically regarded as a distributive optimum? Unless we impose some rule about the distribution of goods between individuals as we go along the curve, the curve is not determined; but the rule which we previously employed, of wasteless distribution all along the curve, is not available, when A itself is not an optimum position.

Consider the following problem. At A certain goods are being produced, but are being distributed (by a bad rationing system) in a non-optimum manner; at B *identically the same goods* are being produced, but are being distributed in a more efficient way, so that (taking a strong case, to bring out the point) everyone is better off. There is (let us grant it to the Cardinalist, to the very heart of whose case I fancy we have now come) a gain in Utility; is there a gain in Real Income? For my own part, I want to say that there is a gain in Real Income; but it is clear that we have got to stretch things quite far in order to be able to say it.

We cannot apply our usual (q) technique to this case unless we can find a rule which shall tell us how other quantities of goods than those actually available are to be distributed on the A- and B-plans respectively. Only by such a rule can we identify anything corresponding to our intermediate positions – sets of goods distributed on the B-plan which are (collectively) indifferent with A, and sets distributed on the A-plan (collectively) indifferent with B. It seems only too likely that there will be no such rule to be found. Nevertheless, if it is once granted that the B-plan is not merely more efficient than the A-plan, but is itself an optimum distribution, things become better. We can then construct a number ($O\alpha$) of bundles that can be (optimally) distributed so as to make each individual as well off as he is at A; and the ratio $OB/O\alpha$ then gives us *one* measure for the gain from optimalisation. Thus we can here get *one* measure, though we are not able to find a partner to check it.

This being so, the only way of comparing two non-optimum distributions will be to make an independent comparison of each with an optimum distribution of the same goods. But the optimum distribution which is to be taken as a standard of reference is not fully defined, and there is no certainty that the relation between A and B will look the same from the point of view of one optimum distribution C as from another. Here (as elsewhere) no great confidence can be placed in indirect comparisons. It must be admitted that the problem of comparing non-optimum distributions is on the edge of being insoluble; into these shadows the light which is cast by our present methods is dim indeed.

VI.   Conclusion

20.   It is tempting (but this temptation also must be resisted) to conclude by discussing the bearing of the principles we have been elaborating on crucial topics of Welfare Economics – to which field the latter part of our analysis has been coming very close. I will merely say that in my view the typical 'Welfare' problem can also be reduced to a comparison between two *positions*: only one of them now being an actual position, the other being a proposed

alternative. The choice between such alternatives can be analysed by an adaptation of the methods which have been here described. It is a useful analysis, provided that it is sensible to divide the change from actual A to proposed B into productional and distributional components, distinguishing between the change in Aggregate Real Income which is involved and the change in the Distribution of that Income. That such a division is not always possible, is confirmed by what has been said here. But I think that what I have said does help to show the reason why, in the sort of world in which we live, it does usually seem possible to make it. In a world where it can be made, the economist has more of a job to do than he would have in a society where interests were more diametrically opposed.

But it may be argued that the distinction between the production and the distribution of Real Income is cleaner and tidier when Real Income is measured in terms of cost, instead of being measured by the utility measure with which we have been here concerned. Our concept of Real Income may be regarded as an identification of the collective indifference surface which passes through the point of current output; our problem of measurement has been a problem of estimating some relevant parameters of that surface. We have granted that the collective indifferent surface is liable to be moved by changes in distribution; if the movement is important, the line between production and distribution components cannot, on this line of analysis, be clear cut. It could apparently be made much sharper if we measured in terms of the alternative outputs producible from the currently applied resources – taking our measure on the 'obstacle' side, as Pareto would have called it, not on the side of 'tastes'. For though resources applied may change when distribution changes, it is reasonable to abstract from that effect. We can then consider that a change in distribution requires no more than a movement along the *same* curve of obstacles (or 'production possibility curve', as Samuelson would call it).

Close analysis of the cost measure does, however, raise corresponding difficulties to those which have perplexed us over the utility measure; they can be classified in a rather similar way. On the 'integration' side, we have a major difficulty on what I have called *coherence*. We have granted that the collective indifference curves, based on our positions A and B, *may* intersect; but we have to take great pains over our definition of the cost measure if we are not to find ourselves with a construction where intersections of the corresponding curves are almost inevitable. It may indeed be true that it is only in the case of a regularly growing economy, and then only if we insist that the comparison is to run in terms of long-period cost (in Marshall's sense of that term) that the cost method has any hope of providing a coherent measure. When we apply it to the measurement of fluctuations (or retrogressions) it is worse than the utility measure.

On the 'revelation' side, the assumption that prices correspond to marginal utilities is one that (over a large part of the field) is fairly digestible; but who could swallow, without the gravest reservations, the corresponding assumption about marginal cost? There seems to be no more, in this place at least, that needs to be said.

I hope, on another occasion, to investigate some of these problems of the cost measure much more fully.[31] They are merely mentioned here, as a justification for my belief that in analysing the utility measure so elaborately, I have not been wasting time.[32]

---

[31] See essay 4, below.
[32] The reader is referred to Hicks' addendum to this paper, *CEET* I, pp. 183-8].

4

Valuation of Social Income – the Cost Approach

This paper, though promised at the end of the study of the utility approach (in 1958, essay 3 above), did not get written until 20 years later, and first appeared in *Wealth and Welfare, CEET* I (1981).

What can be done in a study of the cost approach is very limited. One can construct, on the utility side, a method of measurement, and of interpretation of that measurement, which, when applied to an economy where consumers' markets are fairly free, is practicable, and should (not always, but often) make good sense. So there is light at the end of one's tunnel. On the cost side, by contrast, no such coherent theory is attainable. Not even in the freest of free economies can the factor costs, or cost-coefficients, which should play the part on this side that is played by market prices on the other, be readily discovered, or even unambiguously defined. And even if they were to be identified, the meaning that could be given to them would be very restricted. Thus any results which emerge from a study of the cost approach must be largely negative.

But this does not mean that such a study is useless. For if the cost approach is bad in theory, in practice it appears to be triumphant. It is not just that national income statisticians present their tables *at factor cost*. That can well be defended as the most convenient way of presenting their information; it does not necessarily imply that the statistical factor costs (which must include many sorts of transitory gains, as well as monopoly gains, while excluding externalities) are reliable representatives of factor costs in an economic sense. Yet in the application of social accounting, whenever a question arises of the diversion of 'resources' from one objective to another, as from consumption to investment, or from private use to public, the temptation to treat them as if they were true economic costs is very strong. It is incumbent on the theorist to show to what extent, to what extremely limited extent, that can be done.

That is one reason why a study of the cost approach is desirable, but there is another. If there is no market for consumer's goods, or for final products in a wider sense, the utility method cannot be applied. Cost valuation might be, at least in principle. Thus it turns out that cost valuation has relevance to non-market economies, while utility valuation does not. It is therefore entirely logical for Marxian economists to reject utility valuation, and so to think, more single-mindedly than non-Marxian economists can do, in terms of cost. So cost valuation theory has affinities with Marxian theory; this is especially true of the *real cost* version of cost valuation theory with which I shall begin. But I shall make no attempt to follow out these Marxian affinities, for it would be a distraction from my main purpose to do so. I merely note that they exist.

I. The Real Cost Version

1. I take the real cost version in its simplest form, the cost of producing a particular product being the 'quantity of resources' required to produce it. It is indeed not possible to put a figure on this 'quantity' unless a way can be found of reducing the various inputs, commonly required, to a common measure. I begin by assuming that this can be done, so that all costs are *ultimately* reducible to quantities of 'homogeneous labour'.

A cost measurement of output is then straightforward. Commodities $(1, 2, \ldots, n)$ are being produced. Each commodity has a given and unchanging specification; it is physically defined. q_i is the output of the ith commodity. c_i, the labour coefficient, is the quantity of labour that is required for the production of a unit of the ith commodity. Then Σcq is the total quantity of labour required.

In another situation, outputs are (q') and coefficients (c'). The ratio $\Sigma c'q'/\Sigma cq$, being the ratio between the total quantities of labour employed, is an input index. But $\Sigma cq'/\Sigma cq$, in which the coefficients are kept unchanged, since it is formed with constant weights, is an output index. What it measures, in economic terms, is the change in labour input which *would have been required* if the new outputs had been produced with old coefficients, that it to say, with the old technique. This, so long as we accept the homogeneous labour assumption, is a concept with a clear economic meaning.

Just as in price-quantity index theory, where to the quantity index corresponds a price-index, so here there is a corresponding index, where quantities are kept constant but coefficients are varied. It is natural to take this as an index of productivity. Since

$$\Sigma cq'/\Sigma cq = (\Sigma c'q'/\Sigma cq)\,(\Sigma cq'/\Sigma c'q')$$

Index of output = Index of input × Index of productivity, as we should like. (It will be noticed that as in price-quantity theory, to a Laspeyres output index corresponds a Paasche productivity index; there is the usual criss-crossing.)

So far, then, the conventional quantity- and price-index theory has been exactly duplicated. But in order to use the c's as weights, we need to know the c's. And how should we know the c's?

The q's, we may take it, are quantities of final outputs – outputs of consumption goods, or other outputs that are directly required, as by a public authority. Production, we may suppose, is carried on in firms. By a firm we mean no more than a producing unit; nothing is said about ownership. We can thus assume that all costs are costs of the relevant firms; there are no externalities.

If all the firms were fully integrated, producing nothing but final outputs, and having no input but labour, the c's would be directly revealed as costs of the firms. But it is clearly more interesting to take it that there are intermediate products, produced by some firms and disposed of to others.

The place of intermediate products in a model of this kind, with homogeneous labour, has been elaborately analysed by distinguished modern economists, Leontief[1] and Sraffa[2] in particular. There is not much of their work which we shall need to use, but it will be useful to follow them, for a few steps.

It has emerged from their work that it is most important to distinguish between the case in which each firm produces one product only, final or intermediate, and the case in which there are products which have to be produced together (joint supply). I begin, as they do, with the no-joint-supply case.

2.   The cost of production, per unit, of each final product (FP) may then be decomposed into cost of labour required + costs of intermediate products (IPs) required. Let us call these IPs, directly required for production of FPs, first-order IPs.

The cost of each first-order IP may then be similarly decomposed into cost of labour required + cost of IPs required. Call these IPs, required for production of first-order IPs, second-order IPs. (It is

[1] W. Leontief, *Studies in the Structure of the American Economy* (1953).
[2] P. Sraffa, *Production of Commodities by means of Commodities* (1960).

important to notice that there is no reason why some particular IPs should not appear in each class, some first-order and some second-order IPs being physically identical.)

The cost of the first-order IPs which appeared in the first decomposition could then be decomposed by the second, giving

Cost of FP = Cost of labour directly required

+ Cost of labour required for first-order IPs

+ Cost of second-order IPs required

These second-order costs can then be decomposed in a similar manner, and so on, for as many rounds as we like.

It will be noticed, as one follows out this reduction, that, so long as some labour is required for the production of each order of IPs, the labour cost which has been identified in the cost of the FP must increase at each round. It would be wrong to conclude from this that the *proportion* of the cost of the FP which has been attributed to labour must increase; for we do not, as yet, have any means of reducing the cost of the residual IPs to a cost that is expressible in terms of labour. But suppose that we look on to a round of some high order, say the one-hundredth. And suppose, for the moment, that the costs, per unit, of the hundredth-order IPs, expressed in terms of labour, are taken arbitrarily. Then, with these costs taken arbitrarily, we can work back through the previous 99 rounds, and we shall find that the *proportion* of the cost of the FP which has been identified as (direct or indirect) labour cost will always be less at a lower round than at a higher. That is so, whatever is the arbitrary figure which has been chosen for the high-order IPs.

That the proportion of the total cost which is (directly or indirectly) attributable to labour must increase at each round may thus be taken to be a general rule. But this does not itself show that labour cost must ultimately swallow up the whole cost, or even come near to swallowing up the whole cost; for the labour proportion might go on rising, yet never exceed a limit of less than 100 per cent, a limit which is approached asymptotically. This could certainly not happen if at some round, of however high an order, the whole of the IPs required in the residue had no costs but labour costs; for at that point the sequence would have to stop, the whole cost of the FP being reduced to labour cost.[3] But it is unnecessary to invoke that possibility.

---

[3] It has long been my opinion that this simple way out is implied in the work of many of the older economists. It would not make bad sense in their time. .

For suppose that there is a limit, approached asymptotically, at (say) 70 per cent. Then after a large number of rounds nearly 70 per cent would be identified as labour cost; but however more rounds were taken, hardly any more would be absorbed. This must imply that of the IPs of high order, hardly any of their costs would be labour costs; so, by going far enough, what was left would form a perpetual-motion machine, running with negligible assistance from labour. If, as seems reasonable, that is ruled out, a sufficient number of rounds must cause effectively the whole cost to be reduced to labour cost.

3.   That may thus be granted; even so, the succession of rounds must take much time. How can we make sense of the story if (as is surely proper) the quantities of FPs which are to enter into our index are to be quantities produced *during a period*? The succession must surely extend outside the period, into a past that is quite remote. Why should the quantities of IPs, and of labour, that have been required for the production of particular IPs have remained the same, over all that time? If we have to assume that they have remained the same, our measurement of Output, by the method that is under discussion, is confined in application to stationary economics – to economies, at least, that are technically stationary. (For the quantities produced have not entered into the calculation of the cost-coefficients; these quantities could vary, but it would still have to be true that the techniques of production must be unchanging.)

That would be very cramping; is there any way out? There is a possible way out, which seems to be implied in the work of those who have developed such models; it is to assert that the sequence is logical, not temporal. We do not look at the actual production of the IPs which were used as inputs for the production of the FPs of the current period. All we need is that each of these IPs (which, it will be remembered, have been physically defined) should be such as to be still in production in the current period. We then represent the past production, which formed part of the actual history of the current FPs, by its analogue in the current period. We cannot do even this without some concession to stationariness of technique since there must be no change of specification between the past IPs and the current IPs which are to stand proxy for them. I do not myself think that it would be wise to grant even that; but let us see what happens if we grant it.

The way is then open to the algebra which has become conventional. There are now, in the whole system, *m* IPs. Let γ_j be the (calculated) cost, in terms of labour, of a unit of the jth IP. Let a_{jk} be the amount of the kth IP which is used to make a unit of the jth; let b_j be the amount of labour directly required to make that unit. Then

$$\gamma_j = b_j + \Sigma a_{jk}\,\gamma_k \tag{1}$$

where the sum may be taken over all m IPs, though some (perhaps most) of the a_{jk} in any particular equation will be zero.

We have equations of the type shown in (1) for each of the IPs, m equations in all; so (in principle) these equations can be solved for the γ_j's ($j = 1, 2, \ldots, m$). Then, having got the γ's, we can determine the c's. For each FP ($i = 1, 2, \ldots, n$) we have an equation

$$c_i = b_i + \Sigma a_{ij}\,\gamma_j \tag{2}$$

where the sum is taken over all m IPs, b_i is the labour directly required for the ith FP and a_{ij} is the requirement of the jth IP for the ith FP. From these n equations, the n c_i's are very simply determined.

Nevertheless, as is well known, there are difficulties. How do we know, if the a_{jk} are taken arbitrarily (even though they are all non-negative) that the equations (1) will have a solution in positive γ's? (One may say positive, not just non-negative, if the b_j are all taken to be positive.) It has been shown that the mathematical condition for this is that the technique which is expressed in the a_{jk} should be *productive*, not, either as a whole, or in any sub-group, absorbing more IPs as inputs than it produces as outputs. If the state of technique is constant over time (there is technical stationariness) it may be granted that this condition must be satisfied, since a technique which was not productive in this sense could not maintain itself.[4] When the system is reduced to a set of m equations, we are, as has been seen, impelled to this interpretation. But in the more general case, when the techniques that were used in the higher rounds are not necessarily the same as those used in the lower, or necessarily coherent with them, we have to fall back on a sequential determination. This, as has been shown, requires no such condition for the generation of positive costs, in terms of labour.

[4] In mathematical terms, the condition for a solution of equations (1) with positive γ's is that the dominant root of the (a_{ij}) matrix should be positive and less than unity. If the dominant root were greater than unity, sequential determination would show costs that continually rose, without converging upon a finite limit. (Thus our, surely reasonable, assumption that the 'hundredth order' IPs have *some* definite cost would be falsified.) If the dominant root were equal to unity, positive quantities of IPs could be produced without any labour – the 'perpetual-motion machine'.

4. It has been worth while to pay this amount of attention to the simple model of disintegrated production with one homogeneous factor and no joint supply, since it is the only case in which a cost approach can be carried through as if a cost-index had the same properties as a price-weighted index. In all other cases, as we shall see, there are further complications. I shall proceed, at the next stage, while maintaining the hypothesis of the single homogeneous factor, to drop the assumption of no joint supply. What then happens can be illustrated by a simple example.

Suppose that our two collections of goods (q) and (q') are identical save for the amounts of two particular goods, which we will label 1 and 2. Suppose that these two goods can only be produced in a fixed proportion, which by suitable choice of units may be made one to one. Thus if 50 units of the first are required, 50 units of the second will have to be produced, whether they are required or not. So the total cost of the 'bundle' will be the same, whatever the number required of the second good, so long as it is less than 50. But if the number required of the second increases beyond 50, the cost of the 'bundle' will increase, without any increase in the requirement for the first good.

It might well be thought that the natural 'economic' way of dealing with this situation would be to insist that goods 1 and 2 must be taken together. If they have to be produced in a fixed proportion, they cannot be required in a different proportion; the requirement of so many units of the one *implies* the requirement of at least as many units of the other. When it is final products that are jointly produced, this device may be satisfactory; but it does not deal with the whole of the problem. For it doeŝ not deal with joint production of intermediate goods. This may be seen by a simple extension of our example.

The two final goods (now to be labelled FP_1 and FP_2) are now *not* jointly produced; they do not have to be produced in a fixed proportion. But each requires for its production, in addition to some direct labour, a certain amount of an intermediate good, which is 'specific' to that production – it is not used elsewhere. Let the good which is specific to FP_1 be called IP_1 and that which is specific to FP_2 be called IP_2. And consider what happens when IP_1 and IP_2 are jointly supplied.

As before, we may choose units so that the fixed proportion between IP_1 and IP_2 is one to one; and we may also select units of the final products so that one unit of IP_1 is required for one unit of FP_1 and one unit of IP_2 for one unit of FP_2. Then if the requirements for FP_1 and FP_2 are equal, everything fits; but if they are unequal, we cannot avoid difficulty by adjusting requirements. For 50 of FP_1 together with 40 of FP_2 will require less labour than 50 of FP_1 together with 50 of FP_2. Each collection, it is true, requires 50 of IP_1 and (in consequence) 50 of IP_2; the indirect input of labour, in the production of the intermediate products, is the same. But the direct input of labour, in the production of the final products, can well be different. The total costs of the two collections will then be different. There is no device by which we can pretend that they are the same.

The consequences of this for labour cost valuation are drastic. It remains quite true that when the direct labour coefficients are given, and the input coefficients of the intermediate products are given, the total cost of a collection $(q_1, \ldots, q_n)$ in terms of labour (still supposed homogeneous) can be determined. But it cannot be expressed as an aggregate Σcq with constant c's. The c's themselves depend upon the q's required.

Consider this in terms of our example. We may define labour units so that one unit of labour is required for the production of one unit of IP_1 together with one unit of IP_2; and we will suppose that in that production no other input save this labour is required. As stated above, one unit of IP_1 is required for one unit of FP_1; and one unit of IP_2 for one unit of FP_2. Let f_1 be the requirement of direct labour for one unit of FP_1, and f_2 for one unit of FP_2. Then, for the total cost of the collection (q_1, q_2) we have

$$f_1 q_1 + f_2 q_2 + q_1 = (f_1 + 1) q_1 + f_2 q_2 \qquad \text{(when } q_1 > q_2)$$
$$f_1 q_1 + f_2 q_2 + q_2 = f_1 q_1 + (f_2 + 1) q_2 \qquad \text{(when } q_2 > q_1)$$

Thus, when the line $q_1 = q_2$ is crossed, c_1 changes from $f_1 + 1$ to f_1 and c_2 changes from f_2 to $f_2 + 1$.

The result is that the interpretation of the cost-weighed output index as measuring the change in labour input which would be required if the new quantities had to be produced with the old techniques breaks down. So long as labour is homogeneous, and is the only input that is not an output, there will still be particular c-coefficients for every collection (q). Thus Σcq is still meaningful; but what of the $\Sigma cq'$ which is to be set against it? $\Sigma cq'$ is defined as the quantity of labour which would have been required if the new outputs (q') had had to be produced with the old coefficients (c). But we now see that it may be *impossible*, even under labour cost assumptions, to produce the new outputs with the old coefficients; if, between the old outputs and the new, there is a crossing of a boundary, the c-coefficients will have to be changed. Thus if we follow the regular index-number practice, of using the costs in the old situation for valuing, so as to get a Laspeyres index, we are not making a comparison which has economic sense. For the cross-position, in which costs are (c) and outputs (q'), is a position which could not possibly arise.

If, on the other hand, we substitute the coefficients (c^*), which properly belong, on old techniques, to the outputs (q'), the index $\Sigma c^* q' / \Sigma cq$ is no longer an index of output. For it is affected by the change in the c's as well as by the change in the q's.

5. That happens, just because of joint supply. It may nevertheless appear that the conditions we have been supposing, which have been shown to lead to the joint-supply complication, are rather special; when we are thinking of valuing a social output consisting of many commodities, a few idiosyncrasies of this sort should be readily absorbable. But this is because we have implicitly been taking it that the IPs which are jointly supplied are IPs that are both produced and used within the current period. There is, however, an important case, an extremely important case, where this does not hold. It is the case of fixed capital equipment. Fixed capital goods are intermediate products which continue to be used over quite a time. So the FPs in the production of which such a good is an input are not just the FPs of the current period but also FPs of other periods, which from the point of view of the current period may be past or may be future. So the inputs of the services of such a good into the FPs of the current period and those into the FPs of the other periods are jointly supplied.

In the case of 'horizontal' or contemporaneous jointness, that was considered in the preceding section, there was no question about the ascertainment of the total cost of producing outputs (q_1, q_2) of final products when taken together. The only trouble was that when a boundary was crossed, the identification of the particular IP, some part of the production of which must be wasted, would change. Thus the cost of the jointly produced IP would be imputed, sometimes to the one FP, sometimes to the other. Both of the FPs would nevertheless form part of the aggregate which we are seeking to measure.

In the case of intertemporal complementarity that is no longer so. q_1 is then an output of the current period, which forms part of the aggregate in question, but q_2 is not. But as we have seen, it will be impossible to derive a labour coefficient c_1, for the output q_1, without having knowledge of q_2.

To demand that for every fixed capital good, we should have knowledge of its whole history, including the outputs of all the FPs, which it has assisted to produce in the past, is quite a large order; to demand that we should have similar knowledge of future FPs is plainly impossible. Thus the introduction of fixed capital equipment is bound to upset a labour cost valuation, unless we can replace this unavailable information by an acceptable proxy.

The readiest choice for such a proxy would be to introduce a convention that the outputs in the 'other' periods are to be supposed to be in some sense 'normal'. It would then follow that if output in the current period was less than normal, we would have $q_1 < q_2$, so that the cost of the fixed capital would not enter into the cost of q_1. This would lead to the principle (which for some purposes may be quite acceptable) of valuing, when output is at less than normal capacity, at no more than 'variable' cost. It will, however, be noticed that the logical consequence of this procedure is that the whole of the capital cost must be supposed to be thrown on other periods. That is quite disturbing; but it is more disturbing to find that if the output in the current period is greater than normal, the *whole* of the capital cost must be supposed to be thrown on to the current period. Yet it is that which seems to follow.

It will further be noticed that if the output in the current period is actually normal (so that $q_1 = q_2$) we have, on this principle, no means of imputing the capital cost to one period or to another. In the 'horizontal' case that did not matter (as long as $q_1 = q_2$), since the total cost could still be determined; but here, since we have to make an imputation to the current period, it does matter. The businessman, or accountant, when he is confronted with this problem (it is in fact the same problem) has found no way out except to make an arbitrary division, on some simple rule. It does not appear that economic analysis, using a real cost approach, has any better answer.

6. I have thought it useful to go so far as this, maintaining the fundamental assumption of homogeneous labour, in order to show that, even while we maintain it, valuation at real cost, particularly because of the problem of fixed capital, encounters formidable difficulties. It is of course obvious that if one refuses to accept this fundamental assumption, a breakdown will occur much sooner. If there are many sorts of labour (many sorts of inputs which are 'original', not being IPs) a cost reduction can do no more than express the costs of final products as so much of this and so much of that; we can get no further, unless we have some means of expressing the 'value' of one original input in terms of another.

The issue has nevertheless been much confused, historically, by the difficulty of avoiding associations with ethical, legal, and political concepts of equality, which are here quite irrelevant. If all men are equal, why should labour not be homogeneous? It must be insisted, in reply, that our problem of measurement has nothing to do with control or with distribution. Nothing has been said about who gets the final products; nothing indeed about the ownership of products, final or intermediate. The issue, in the terms in which we have taken it up, arises in just the same way in the most centrally planned economy (or even the most autocratic economy) as under extreme *laisser faire*. So we have no right to express one kind of labour in terms of another by reference to wages. That way out is also closed.

Yet it is tempting to look for a way out by supposing that there is an 'unskilled' labour that is homogeneous; skilled labour is this simple labour plus something extra (training). This extra can then be treated as an intermediate product ('human capital'). Whether such simple labour can in fact be identified is an arguable matter, but there is no need to argue it. For even if the simple labour assumption is granted, the solution will not work. For human capital is fixed capital, in the sense of the preceding discussion. The problems of imputation which it raises are exactly parallel. How much of the costs of training should be imputed to the current period? It is just the old trouble.

I therefore conclude that there is no way of valuing, in terms of real cost, which does not run into difficulties. It remains to be seen if we can make more progress in another direction.

II. The Opportunity Cost Version

1. It is well known that there are just two cases when it is permissible to treat a collection of goods $(q_1, \ldots, q_n)$ as if they were a single commodity. One is that when the ratios (q_i/q_j) remain unchanged throughout the comparisons that are being considered; the other is that in which the various goods remain convertible into one another at constant rates throughout the comparisons. In either case we have an unequivocal measure of the change in the aggregate from one situation to another. In the former all components will have changed in the same proportion, so the aggregate must have changed in that same proportion. In the latter we can unambiguously express the components in terms of a common measure; the aggregates are therefore measurable, and comparable.

In the problems of valuation that are being considered in these essays, we have neither of these advantages. We may nevertheless proceed by attempting to get as near as we can to one or other of these unambiguous measures; either to the one or to the other; for the two are essentially different, so the methods of approximation, to the one and to the other, are essentially different.

This has already appeared in essay 3, on the utility approach. We there had two methods, by direct utility and by indirect utility. The former looked at quantity-proportions; the latter measured by the income (or total expenditure) which would be required if the quantities of goods were to be purchased at fixed prices, thus being convertible, one into another, through the market. Here, on the cost approach, we have already met the convertibility method, for it is nothing else than that with which we began – the 'labour theory of value' model with its constant coefficients. The total (labour) cost of the collection (q) plays in that procedure exactly the same role as total income in the indirect utility theory. We have seen where that leads us. We have now to examine what can be done on the other tack.

2.   It will be convenient to use the same expository device as was used in a corresponding place[5] in essay 3. We take the initial outputs (q) and suppose that each q_i is divided into a large number of units, say m units. (m is to be the same for each commodity.) Take one unit of each commodity, and combine them into a 'bundle'. Then in the initial situation (the A-situation) total output consist of m such bundles; since the commodities are combined in this bundle in A-proportions, I call it an A-bundle.

A-bundles are measured along the horizontal axis of a diagram (Fig. 4.1). The m bundles that are actually produced in the A-situation are marked off by a length OA; so we may regard the A-situation as represented by the point A. We similarly divide the quantities produced in the other (B) situation into m bundles, and mark numbers of these B-bundles on the vertical axis. The point B (where $OB = m$, so that it is geometrically equal to OA) will then represent the quantities produced in the B-situation. Any other points (x, y) on the diagram can then be interpreted as representing a collection of quantities which is such that it can be put together by combining x A-bundles and y B-bundles. Of course it is no more than some special collections of goods which are capable of being put together in this

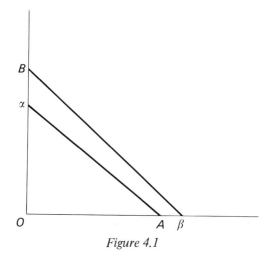

Figure 4.1

way; the diagram represents no more than a small proportion of those which could possibly be produced. But these special collections are in fact the only collections which we need to consider.

A labour theory model, with constant c-coefficients, can readily be represented on such a diagram (Fig. 4.1). Those points on the diagram which represent collections that are capable of being produced from the A-quantity of labour will then lie on a straight line through A. For these points are related by the equation

$$\Sigma c\left[(x/m)\,q + (y/m)\,q'\right] = \Sigma cq$$

or

$$x\,\Sigma cq + y\,\Sigma cq' = m\,\Sigma cq$$

the equation of a straight line ($A\alpha$) on Fig. 4.1. We find $O\alpha$ by setting $x = O$ in this equation. Then, remembering that $OB = m$, we see that the (Laspeyres) index $\Sigma cq'/\Sigma cq$ is represented by $OB/O\alpha$. Alternatively, since OB has been made equal to OA, it is represented by the slope of the line $A\alpha$.

As for the Paasche index ($\Sigma c'q'/\Sigma c'q$), it is similarly represented by $O\beta/OB$, where $B\beta$ is the corresponding line through B. Or, as before, it is the slope of the line $B\beta$.

In a pure labour theory model, because of the constancy of the c-coefficients, all points on the *straight* line $A\alpha$ are possible positions in the A-situation; all points on the *straight* line $B\beta$ are possible positions in the B-situation. But that is all of the labour theory model which is preserved in the new representation. What happens, under more general assumptions, can also be represented, without difficulty, on the same diagram.

For the ratio $OB/O\alpha$, which has just been identified with the Laspeyres index, does not need to be interpreted as the relative change in the quantity of labour which would be required, with A-labour coefficients, to produce B-outputs. It could just as well be interpreted as the relative increase in the actual production of B-bundles, in the B-situation, over the number of B-bundles which could have been produced, with A-techniques, from the A-quantity of labour. That indeed is the natural interpretation of the diagram. $O\alpha$ and OB are both of them measured along the vertical axis, in B-bundles. The quantity of labour at A and at α can be compared without raising any question of measurability of labour, since it is the same in both situations. The same principle can therefore be used even when we admit that products are produced by the cooperation of resources other than labour, or if we take labour to be hetero-geneous. All that is necessary is that A and that α should represent collections of products which are capable of being produced, in the same technical conditions, from the same quantities of all kinds of factors of production.

We are then measuring outputs, not with reference to the quantities of factors of production employed to produce them (which no longer require to be reducible to a single homogeneous factor), but by the quantities of outputs for which those inputs might alternatively have been used. That is to say, we measure output by what has been called its Opportunity Cost.

3. One of the advantages of going over to an Opportunity Cost measurement is that we are no longer obliged to burrow into the past in the search for some 'original' homogeneous input. We can take the initial capital – the material capital and the human capital embodied in skills – as it was at the beginning of the period, in all its complexity and heterogeneity, as the unchanged input on the basis of which the alternative outputs are to be compared. We do not need to go back into the past, but we cannot in the same way avoid consideration of the future, of what is to happen when the period under study is over. I shall, however, for the moment postpone these temporal problems, taking first some 'static' questions which come up independently of them.

When the curves $A\alpha$, $B\beta$, on which the Opportunity Cost measure-ment turns, are considered statically, they may easily be mistaken for the familiar *production-possibility* curves of Samuelson; but to make that identification would, I think be incorrect. For production-possibility curves are naturally to be taken as connecting optimum positions – positions in which the system is operating at maximum efficiency. But there is surely no reason why we should wish to assume that an actual position (A and B are actual positions) is a position of maximum efficiency. α and β, of course, are not actual positions; but to assume that they are optimum positions, while A and B are not optimum positions, would make nonsense of the whole comparison. That must surely be avoided.

I can see only one way of avoiding it. We must say that the difference between the actual position and the optimum position (with products produced in the same proportions) is a difference in what may be called 'organisation'. Closer study of what can be meant by organisation is a task for allocation theory with which I am not concerned in this paper; here I shall leave it rather vague. We just have to suppose that the organisation (whatever it is) which produces the outputs A from the given resources, could produce other outputs from those same resources, if demand conditions (here meaning no more than requirement conditions) were different. The points that are joined by the curve $A\alpha$ will thus represent the outputs which could have been produced from the given resources if organisation were unchanged. The ascertainment of such positions looks like being a difficult matter; but is it any different from the questions that are regularly asked in positive economics (and econometrics)? How would the system, as we have it, react to changes in demand?

If the curves $A\alpha$, $B\beta$, are not production-possibility curves, we shall need a name for them. I shall simply call them *level curves*. This is a name with good mathematical precedent, and it here seems appropriate. For the sets of quantities that are on the same level curve are such as, on the test we are using, would generate the same *level* of aggregate output.

Under the labour theory assumption, the level curves are straight lines. On more general assumptions they will of course not need to be straight. They may bend either way, or even follow a serpentine course, with several bends. (The joint supply case, which was considered in the first part of this paper, would generate a level curve with two straight segments, not in line with one another.) None of these possibilities can be excluded.

If the level curves were production-possibility curves, connecting optimum positions, we could conclude, in the conventional manner, that the normal effect of heterogeneity of inputs would be to cause the curve to be outward-bending. For then, as we substitute B-bundles for A-bundles (which implies increasing the production of things more heavily represented in B, and diminishing the production of things more heavily represented in A), we should begin by transferring those factors that have the highest marginal product B-wise, relatively to their marginal product A-wise; and then proceed, step by step, to the transfer of factors with ever lower comparative advantage B-wise. Thus the total production of B-bundles, when the transfer is completed, will be smaller than it would have been if the whole substitution could have been carried through at the initial rate. Which is what is shown by outward-bending.

It may happen, on the other hand, when there are scale economies, that a partial change over from one product-mix to another is less productive than one which is more complete. The economies may show themselves in industries which are relatively large in A, or in those which are relatively large in B, or in both. A complete change-over would enable industries that are large in B to achieve economies of scale, or industries that were large in A to release large quantities of factors (perhaps because they are shut down altogether, as may happen if some of the products in the A-bundle are unrepresented in the B-bundle). With a partial change-over resources would be kept in the A-large industries, but would there be underemployed. In such cases as these there would be inward-bending.

It will be noticed that the conditions making for outward-bending are different in kind from those making for inward-bending; so there is no reason why both should not be present together. If so, either the one would cancel the other, so that there would be a reversion towards linearity; or it might be that the one was stronger at the one end, and the other at the other end, so that the curve would be doubly bent.

Any of these things could happen, even with production-possibility curves and their optimum positions; they cover the whole range of cases that are possible geometrically, so that, when we turn to the level curve interpretation, there is in that sense nothing to add. There may be new reasons why there should be underemployed resources; but (as we have just seen) it is not excluded, when the product-mix is given, that even in an optimum position there should be such. If, when the product-mix is changed, underemployment is lessened, that makes the transition easier. That is so, whatever the cause of the underemployment.

4. Thus it appears that the level curve may go from A to α by any one of a variety of routes; but how much does that matter? The shapes of the curves would appear to be a quite secondary considera-

tion; the important thing is the position of the point α, which determines the ratio $OB/O\alpha$ (which is equal to the slope of the *straight* line $A\alpha$) the index with which we are concerned. All that significantly survives from a consideration of bendings is the need for distinguishing between this slope (the *complete* substitution rate between the bundles, we may call it) and the slope of the curve at A, which is the *marginal* substitution rate, in a natural extension of the ordinary sense of that term.

It is tempting to see the relation between these two substitution rates as equivalent to that between average cost and marginal; but the equivalence is not exact. It is curious that the theory of the firm has never given us a good terminology for the costs that are intermediate between marginal and average – the costs that are significant, not for a small change in output (marginal cost properly defined) nor for a complete setting-up or closing-down (which is where average cost comes in), but for a large change in output, which is nevertheless not such as to involve complete cessation, in either of two situations that are being compared. The cost that has then to be taken is the sum of the marginal costs of the units by which output is increased, or diminished, averaged over the change in output. This is the general concept of cost which we here require.[6]

Formally, that is what we have to do; but the right costs in this sense must be most difficult to estimate. The substantial simplification that was made in the 'labour theory' model was that the costs to be used as weights were independent of the particular change in outputs occurring. In a world of variable costs that ceases to be true. Though a meaningful comparison can in principle be made, the costs to be used as weights depend upon the size of the change in outputs; we ought to take different weights, for each change in outputs that we have to examine. In practice, of course, that cannot be done. We are bound to use costs that look appropriate for any reasonable change, and to hope that they apply, without too much inexactitude, to the change that is in question. So we slip back, in practice, to something that is equivalent to an acceptance of a labour theory. It does not seem to be avoidable.

5. It is of course quite possible that this does not matter very much. It may do no more than cause a certain imprecision in the index, causing it to exaggerate the change a little in some cases, damp

---

[6] Such costs can be reckoned, for purposes of computation, in terms of any factor; changes in the relative scarcities of other factors being allowed for in the calculation of the marginal costs of the successive units of output.

it down a little in others. The statistical laws of averaging are a protection to the economist who commits no worse crime than a fuzziness about weights. As is well known,[7] 'errors' in the weights that are used in the computation is of an index-number do not make much difference, so long as there is no systematic association between the errors and the variations in the quantities that are being averaged.

But the trouble may go much deeper. Even in the 'labour theory' case it is possible that a change in coefficients between A and B may cause A- and B-based indexes to become very different; it is even possible that the level lines may intersect, so that what appears on the one test to be a rise in output may appear as a fall on the other. There is nothing in principle unacceptable about this; we must always admit that there is a possibility of indeterminate cases. Their occasional existence need not imply a breakdown of the whole system of measurement.

It does nevertheless appear to be essential, if the measure we are examining is to be of any interest, that indeterminate cases should not be too frequent; and so long as we hold to labour theory assumptions, it seems reasonable to suppose that they will be uncommon. But can we be sure that the same will hold when we generalise to a multiplicity of factors? Is there not a danger that indeterminateness will then become the rule; determinateness the exception. A condition of this kind I call *incoherence*.

The resources from which production is derived are in general supposed to be different between A and B. If the differences are purely quantitative, so that A disposes of the same kinds of resources as B, just more or less of each sort, multiplicity of resources seems itself to be no reason why Opportunity Cost comparisons should not be possible; there could well be sufficient coherence. That, I think, must be what is supposed to happen with the comparisons that are made of National Product, of the same country, in successive years. (One may have reservations about it even in that application; but perhaps they are not serious.) The position is very different with

---

[7] The index $\Sigma p_i q_i' / \Sigma p_i q_i$ could also be written $\Sigma k_i y_i$, where $k_i = p_i q_i / \Sigma p_i q_i$ and $y_i = q_i'/q_i$. With a different set of weights, the k are changed to $k + \delta k$, but the y are unchanged. So the difference that is made to the index is $\Sigma(\delta k_i) y_i$. But $\Sigma k = 1$, and $\Sigma(k + \delta k) = 1$, so $\Sigma(\delta k) = 0$. If $\bar{y}$ is the arithmetical mean of the y's,

$$\Sigma(\delta k_i) y_i = \Sigma(\delta k_i)(y_i - \bar{y})$$

which is the co-variance of the (δk)'s and the y's. So if these are uncorrelated, the index is unaffected by the change in weights.

international comparisons, where the resources available, in the one country and the other, will often be different, indeed very different, qualitatively. There are some resources which are present in Japan but not in Saudi Arabia; some which are present in Saudi Arabia but not in Japan. So there are products included in the Japanese bundle which cannot be produced in Arabia; and there is oil, which is produced in Arabia, but cannot be produced in Japan. So the number of Japanese bundles which could be produced in Arabia is zero; and the number of Arabian bundles which could be produced in Japan is zero. So the level lines will lie along the axes, both α and β coinciding with the origin. There is *perfect incoherence*; the Opportunity Cost comparison breaks down completely.

That is rather obvious; but there is a more insidious, though no less important case, that is represented in Fig. 4.2. Here there is a sufficient quantity of B-oriented resources, present in A, for it to be possible to shift production to a certain extent in a B-direction (and vice-versa for B); but in each case the supply is insufficient for movement in the direction of the other bundle to proceed, at all easily, very far. If this happened, there could be enough substitutability for the establishment of marginal costs (so that a marginal substitution rate could be determined); but if we took that marginal rate to represent a complete rate (or even if we made a moderate correction so as to get something nearer to a complete rate) we might think that we had found a coherent measure, when there was in fact almost perfect incoherence. Even in the comparison of successive years within a single country, that could happen.

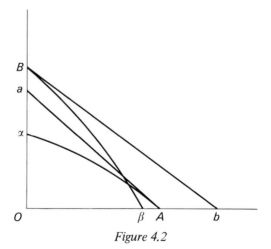

Figure 4.2

For suppose that the country's resources were highly specialised (specialised labour and specialised equipment) and that between one year and the next (here *A* and *B*) there was a substantial change in the make-up of these specialised resources. The product-mix that could be produced from those resources would then be substantially changed. We need not suppose that no other mix than that actually produced in *B* could be produced in *B*; the resources need not be so specific as that. The range that could be produced, with anything like full utilisation of the specific resources, might nevertheless be quite narrow. If we impose an artificial mix (as in our construction we do), making the one year combine its products in the proportions of the other, it is perfectly possible that this could only be done if capacity were underutilised, perhaps quite considerably. The economy could move a little way in the direction of the 'wrong' product-mix without much underutilisation, but not the whole way. That is the situation disclosed in Fig. 4.2.

It would seem to follow that even in application to the growth of a single economy, over time, the transformations that are occurring must not be too rapid. We can make reliable comparisons between situations that are fairly similar, but not between such as differ very much. It is just the same as with international comparisons.

The question nevertheless arises: is it not possible that comparability might be restored, in application to the single economy, by admitting the possibility of converting the specialised resources into other shapes, so that they lose their cramping specialisation. It is true, after all, that in the long run many are replaced. But that is not a matter which can usefully be discussed without giving closer attention than we have done so far, in what has been said of the Opportunity Cost version, to the productive system as a process in time.

6. The period, during which our outputs (q) emerge, has an end and a beginning. It begins with a capital stock, inherited from the past, to which a flow of labour is applied; thus the inputs of the year include both stock and flow. There is a corresponding distinction on the output side, between the flow output of final products and the capital stock left over at the end. It is conventional to replace the latter by *net investment*, the increment of capital between the beginning and the end; but this, though it looks like a flow, is not a flow *during* the period. It is an output of the period *as a whole*.

All products, it will be remembered, have given specifications; so the terminal stock, of the period, as well as the initial stock, are physically defined. Net investment must therefore consist of additions to the stocks of some goods, and subtractions from the stock of some others. It thus comprises negative items as well as positive; but how, in an Opportunity Cost comparison, can that be allowed?

It will be impossible, logically impossible, to produce *B*-bundles from *A*-resources, if the *B*-bundle contains negative items – unless the capital stock, from which the *A*-process starts, contains sufficient amounts of the identical goods which in the *B*-process are used up. Only so will negative items be possible, for there can be no negative output of any good, unless there is an initial stock of that good, from which the negative item is a subtraction. It thus appears that we cannot make an Opportunity Cost comparison, where that is interpreted to take account of net investment, unless the initial stocks of the processes which are being compared are quite similar. If they are not very nearly similar, the comparison cannot be made.

This is indeed no more than a reinforcement of what we have already found. We have already seen that an Opportunity Cost comparison between the outputs of widely different economics is very likely to result in incoherence. What seems to occur, when we shift our stance so as to think of comparisons of processes, is that an old danger of incoherence has become more acute.

It may, however, be asked: is not this new incoherence one that could be avoided? It could be avoided if we adopted von Neumann's device, now familiar to economists, reckoning the *whole* of the terminal capital as part of output. When output is taken in this *inclusive* sense, to include both the flow of finished products and the whole of the terminal capital, it is something very different from anything that statisticians would seek to measure. It will nevertheless be useful to give it a little attention. For it is a better concept *theoretically*; so it is a useful device for translating the static analysis of preceding sections into more temporal terms.

What accordingly is to be meant, on this von Neumann interpretation, by a 'cross-over', such as was represented by the point α on Figs. 4.1 and 4.2? $O\alpha$ is now to be the inclusive output, combined in *B*-proportions, which can be produced by *A*-techniques from *A*-resources. The *A*-resources are to include the stock of initial capital and the flow of labour, available in *A*. The *B*-proportions are to apply, not only to the flow component, but also to the terminal stock. Thus it is necessary, in the 'cross-process', as we may call it, that an initial capital, combined in *A*-proportions, should be transmuted, at the end of the period (to be an equal period) into a capital that is combined in *B*-proportions, having turned out flow outputs, also combined in B-proportions, on the way. If the Opportunity Cost method of comparison is to be possible – if there is not to be perfect incoherence – such a transformation must be possible. It is easy to think of cases where it will be quite impossible. If the A-inputs include land (land in the Ricardian sense, 'original and indestructible') and if the B-inputs include land that is qualitatively different, it will be impossible that an inclusive output, combined in B-proportions, should be produced from A-resources. So in applications where there are such differences (as will usually be the case with international comparisons) land will have to be excluded. There will of course be no difficulty about excluding land, in the case of comparisons between the performance of a single country over different periods of time.

If land is excluded, the comparison of inclusive outputs looks better. If the initial capitals in A and in B are not too different, the traverse from A to α could possibly be made.

Even so, it must take time. And it is to be made in the same time as the *straight* processes A and B. So if the length of the period, production during which we are comparing, is very short, the cross-process must be impossible; there will be no time to convert the initial stock into the prescribed form. As we lengthen the period, it becomes progressively easier. So we find, as we have already been suspecting, that there is a sense in which an Opportunity Cost comparison is more feasible over a long period than over a short.

Consider, however, the application, which we are very likely to want to make, to the comparison of performance within successive periods of the same economy. If the period is very short (say one month) the initial capitals (at the beginning of 'March' and the beginning of 'April') will be very similar; that makes the comparisons easier. But to transform the capital of March 1 into one that has the same mix as that of April 30, and do it by March 31, is likely to be quite unfeasible; there is not time to make the change. If we take an annual period – comparing, say, 1973 with 1974 – the transformation is easier, but the initial stocks are further apart. We seem to lose in one way what we gain in the other.

But perhaps there is a way out. Suppose we compare the performance of the same economy in two quinquennia, one of which begins no more than one year after the other. As an example, compare performance in 1969–73 with performance in 1970–4. The nearness of the opening dates keeps the opening stocks fairly similar, while the length of the period makes transformation easier. OB is now inclusive output in 1970–4; $O\alpha$ is inclusive output in 1969–73, as it would have to have been if it had been laid down that the capital stock at the end of 1973 was to have the same mix as that actually attained at the end of 1974. If that were to be achieved, some processes would have had to be speeded up and some, no doubt, slowed down; but there is time to do it. The quinquennium does give some elasticity – as those who work in terms of five-year plans are well aware!

Though the suggestion of overlapping has emerged through working in terms of inclusive output, it could be applied to net output also. Comparison of net outputs also looks more feasible if it is made in terms of fairly long, overlapping, periods.

7. Overlapping helps; but there remain further troubles. It is not easy to make sense of long-period comparisons, such as that to which we have come, unless one can allow oneself to suppose that the techniques of production have remained unchanged during the period (the actual period). For if there have been changes within the period where in the cross-process do we place them? To make a fair comparison, when techniques are changing, will be quite difficult.

There is a comparable difficulty, on which there is more to be said, concerning the flow component of output (the output of consumption goods, or of final products). It is only as we lengthen the period that this issue comes up, but when we do so it is of fundamental importance. What do we assume about the time-shape of the flow outputs? If A and B are actual performances of some particular economy, during appropriate quinquennia, the flow outputs of A and of B will have particular time-shapes; they may have a steady growth rate, or they may be fluctuating in some particular manner. But what are we to say about the time-shape of the flow output of the cross-process? This is a hypothetical process, on which we appear to be at liberty to impose what time-shape we choose. But what should we choose?

It might seem logical to insist that since the outputs of the various final products are to be produced in α in B-proportions, the α stream of flow outputs should have the same time-shape (being divided between sub-periods in the same proportions) as the actual flow of outputs in B. But on this interpretation, little, or nothing, is gained by the lengthening of the process. The cross-process will have to *begin* by producing flow outputs in a manner which is ill-suited to the resources available to it; and it will have to maintain this uncomfortable, and therefore low, rate of output over the whole of the quinquennium. It is nearly true to say that the quinquennium would have been reduced to a sequence of shorter periods, for each of which comparison, as we have seen, is likely to be unfeasible. We should have made no progress.

One could, on the other hand, make no prescription about time-shape, but allow the cross-process to produce flow outputs on whatever time-shape was most convenient to it. Feasibility would then be improved, but is it not too much improved? It must be supposed that the actual processes do not produce flow outputs in just the time-shape that is most convenient to them; they cannot in fact be organised on the basis that an addition to 'consumption' at one date is just as good as an equal addition at another. It makes nonsense to suppose that an economy which produces plenty in year 5 at the expense of a famine in year 1 is doing as well as one in which the same total is more evenly distributed. If therefore the actual processes are tied down, in their time-shapes, by something other than pure productive convenience, while the cross-processes are not thus tied down, we are giving an unfair advantage to the cross-processes. We are not making a fair comparison.

Is there any third alternative? We might invoke the concept of 'organisation' which was invoked above for another purpose, saying that the time-shape of the outputs that are produced from the actual process is a matter of the organisation of that process; and that the cross-process is to have the same organisation. But this is no more than an evasion of the difficulty; it gives no firm guidance. It is not a way out.

8. The fact is that we have come, at the end of this discussion of the Opportunity Cost version – and by implication, as we shall see, also at the end of the Real Cost version – to a quite basic issue. Are products that are physically identical, but are forthcoming at different dates, to be treated as identical, or as different products? If we insist on treating them as different products, we put an intolerable strain on the Opportunity Cost measure; for it is impossible to suppose that in an actual economy, the timing of whose manufacturing processes is largely fore-ordained by the structure of its fixed capital, while its agricultural processes have to be fitted into a seasonal pattern, there can be enough substitution over time to prevent incoherence. But if we treat them as identical, what are we doing but imposing rates of equivalence between them, rates which are not the result of cost relations but are imposed from outside? If we have to impose rates from outside, it is by no means evident that these are the rates which we should impose.

It is almost impossible, as was seen in the above case of the famine in year 1 and the glut in year 5, not to find the rates over time, which we should be imposing, by going back to wants, and therefore going over to a utility measure. But a utility measure, as was shown in essay 3, is very unhappy unless it can refer to a market, on which wants are revealed, and the more perfect the market the better.[8] For intertemporal exchanges we do not have a perfect market, so a utility measure cannot be expected, in this intertemporal application, to perform very well. Intertemporal exchanges do nevertheless occur; rates of interest do exist.

It may well have been found surprising that in what was said above about the Real Cost version, nothing was said about rates of interest. Has it not been traditional among economists, at least among the more 'orthodox' economists, to include the cost of *waiting* among their *real costs*? The inclusion has indeed been controversial, and the controversy has not been free of prejudice. There is nevertheless a point to be made, on both sides.

It was characteristic of the Real Cost approach that it strove, indeed quite desperately strove, to reduce all costs of production to something homogeneous. It was not easy to reduce all costs into terms of homogeneous labour; but perhaps, with an effort, it could be done. But it could only be done if an assumption crept in: that the labour applied at one time was not just physically indistinguishable, but also economically interchangeable, with labour applied at another time. If the reduction to labour cost is performed in the sequential manner, which we found in our discussion of the reduction to make better sense, the question of the identity between present labour and past labour does appear, when the question is raised, to be rather relevant. If one assumes the two to be identical, is one not (as before) imposing an equivalence *from outside*?

This is largely concealed if we make the transformation into the simultaneous equation form, which is so mathematically appealing that it has become conventional. For we then replace the past labour which has actually produced the IPs that are used in current production of FPs, by the current labour that is producing IPs that are physically identical. Thus there appears to be no question of imposing identity upon past labour and current labour; current labour is the only labour that is involved. But surely this means that it is simply in another way that we have performed the trick – by imposing identity upon current IPs and past IPs!

[8] See above, p. 90.

I am not suggesting, it should have been made clear, that Opportunity Cost is an easy way out. It is not easy to make the long-term comparisons, which seemed at first to have better prospects of coherence than short-term comparisons, without some imposition of identity of products over time. We may possibly do better by having recourse to utility valuation, but that also has its difficulties. There is no wholly adequate solution.

All imposition of identity over time makes analysis more static. It is easy to say hard things about economic statics; but, as has amply appeared from the preceding analysis, we cannot dispense with staticising altogether. That is just as true of the Opportunity Cost version as of the Real Cost version. We cannot avoid staticising; we should yet be continually aware how dangerous it is. When we find that in a particular application it is particularly dangerous, we should look for ways of diminishing our dependence on it. That is as much as can be hoped for; but perhaps it is enough.

E

Part II
Welfare Economics

The concepts developed in Part I, concerning the explanation of consumer behaviour and the measurement of income are used by Hicks to provide a foundation for his welfare economics. Hicks' contribution to welfare economics consists of the seminal paper launching the 'New Welfare Economics' in 1939, his measurement of consumer surplus papers, his income papers discussed above, and a series of more reflective papers in later years. In this section, the first paper is reproduced, along with his later 'Preference and Welfare' (1974) to which has been added 'A Manifesto' (1958).

The 1939 'Foundations of Welfare Economics' begins with a defence of welfare economics against the still dominant positivism, to which Hicks himself had formally adhered, as he explains in sections 1 and 2 of the paper. There follows (sections 3 and 4) a formal statement of the optimal conditions in static terms, but admitting of economies of scale, which has not since been bettered. On scale economies, the reader is referred to Hicks' later essay 'Optimisation and Specialisation' which appeared for the first time in *Wealth and Welfare, CEET* I (1981).

5

The Foundations
of Welfare Economics

This essay first appeared in *Economic Journal*, December (1939).

1. The subject of this paper is a matter of very fundamental importance, both for economic theory and for the proper attitude of economists towards economic policy. That being so, it is not surprising that it should have been a matter of controversy, controversy which has even tended to widen into a profound difference of opinion. During the nineteenth century, it was generally considered to be the business of an economist, not only to explain the economic world as it is and as it has been, not only to make prognostications (so far as he was able) about the future course of economic events, but also to lay down principles of economic policy, to say what policies are likely to be conducive to social welfare, and what policies are likely to lead to waste and impoverishment. Today, there is one school of writers which continues to claim that economics can fulfil this second function, but there is another which (formally at least) desires to reject it. According to their view the economics of welfare, the economics of economic policy, is too unscientific in character to be a part of economic *science*. So long as economics is concerned with explanation, it can hope to reach conclusions which will command universal acceptance as soon as they are properly understood; but once it goes beyond that point, and endeavours to prescribe principles of policy, then (so they hold) its conclusions must depend upon the scale of social values held by the particular investigator. Such conclusions can possess no validity for anyone who lives outside the circle in which these values find acceptance. Positive economics can be, and ought to be, the same for all men; one's welfare economics will inevitably be different according as one is a liberal or a socialist, a nationalist or an internationalist, a christian or a pagan.

It cannot be denied that this latter view is in fact widely accepted. If it is intellectually valid, then of course it ought to be accepted; and I must admit that I should have subscribed to it myself not so long ago. But it is rather a dreadful thing to have to accept. No one will question the activity of some of our 'positivists' in the criticism of current institutions; but it can hardly be denied that their authority to advance such criticism *qua* economists is diminished by their abnegation, so that in other hands economic positivism might easily become an excuse for the shirking of live issues, very conducive to the euthanasia of our science.

Fortunately there is no need for us to accept it. The way is open for a theory of economic policy which is immune from the objections brought against previously existing theories.

The standard representative of these existing theories is of course Professor Pigou's *Economics of Welfare*. It is such, not only in its own right, but as the culmination of a great line of economic thought. A whole series of economists, among whom Dupuit, Walras, Marshall and Edgeworth deserve particular mention, had sought to find in utility theory a sure basis for prescriptions of economic policy. In those of its aspects which particularly concern us, the *Economics of Welfare* is essentially a systematisation of this tradition.

I am not so much concerned in this paper with Professor Pigou's conclusions (most of which are very readily acceptable, and are abandoned with reluctance even by the positivists), as with the grounds on which those conclusions are based. It is not surprising that these grounds should have caused so much trouble. Professor Pigou derives his prescriptions from the postulate that the aim of economic policy is to maximise the real value of the social income. In order to arrive at such a *real value*, the quantities of the various commodities produced must be weighted by a *given* set of prices – and the prices actually selected are those ruling on the market in the actual circumstances considered. In order to justify this procedure, a long argument is needed, which occupies most of Part I of the book. There are three steps in this argument which cause difficulty. The first is at the very outset, when the reader is asked to accept a direct correlation between economic welfare and social welfare in general (whatever that may be). This not easy to swallow; in any case it is open to the positivist objection that it reflects a particular social outlook, held by certain classes at certain times, and never likely to be acceptable universally. At the next step, we have to admit the possibility of comparing the satisfactions derived from their wealth by different individuals. (This is where Professor Robbins parts company; for my own part, I go with him.) And then further, even if these things are admitted, a third jump has to be taken.[1] Strictly

---

[1] *Economics of Welfare,* 4th edition, p. 57.

speaking, the quantity to be maximised is the sum of the consumers' surpluses derived from the various commodities in the social dividend. This is too awkward to handle, so it is replaced by the real value of the dividend – which is not the same thing at all.

I do not think that anyone can be blamed for declining to entrust himself to a chain containing three links as weak as these. If there were no alternative foundations for the theory of economic welfare, it would be nothing more than the development of an interesting ethical postulate – the status Professor Robbins allows. Alternative foundations are, however, available. A way round the first difficulty has been shown by Mr Harrod;[2] round the second by Mr Kaldor;[3] while Professor Hotelling, in a most valuable and suggestive paper covering the whole subject, has provided a mathematical analysis in which all these difficulties are in fact overcome.[4]

Therefore my own task is mainly one of synthesis. I propose to set out briefly and simply the main lines of the new welfare economics. It will appear that the main propositions can be established quickly and easily, and at the same time their significance can be made perfectly clear.

2. The *positive* theory of economics exhibits a system in which people co-operate with one another in order to satisfy their wants. We assume each individual ·(each free economic unit[5]) to have a certain scale of preferences, and to regulate his activities in such a way as best to satisfy those preferences. As Pareto put it, in his famous masterpiece of generalisation, the economic problem consists in an opposition of 'tastes' and 'obstacles', each individual endeavouring to satisfy his tastes as far as is possible in view of the obstacles to satisfaction which confront him. Looking at society as a whole, the obstacles are technical obstacles – the limited amount of productive power available, and the technical limits to the amount of production that productive power will yield. Looking at a single individual, the obstacles which prevent him from attaining a fuller satisfaction of his wants are not only technical obstacles but also the wants or tastes of other people. He is prevented from being better off than he is, not only because total production is limited, but also because so

---

[2] 'Scope and method of economics', *EJ*, September 1938, pp. 389-95.

[3] 'Welfare propositions and inter-personal comparisons of utility', *EJ*, September 1939, pp. 549-52. See also Viner *Studies in the Theory of International Trade* (1937), pp. 553-4.

[4] 'The general welfare in relation to problems of taxation and of railway and utility rates', *Econometrica*, July 1938.

[5] It would appear from Mr Harrod's analysis that we ought to be prepared, on occasion, to reckon public and semi-public bodies among our 'individuals'.

much of total production is at the disposal of persons other than himself. The same thing holds, of course, for any group or society of individuals, so long as that group is less than the totality of a closed community.

Now as soon as the economic problem is conceived in this way (and it is in some such way that all modern economists regard it), we are really obliged to go on and to consider as part of our business not only the objective consequences of this pursuit of satisfactions (the quantities of goods produced and exchanged, and the prices at which they are exchanged – the problems of positive economics) but also a further problem. We ought to examine how far these activities are effective in achieving the ends for which they are designed, to be able to examine the efficiency of any particular economic system as a means of adjusting means to ends. We are obliged to go so far, because the subject-matter of our study is something which is defined relatively to its purpose. We are not like geologists, comparing rocks laid down by natural forces; we are like archaeologists, comparing flint implements made by man for a purpose, one of whose functions must be to compare the relative efficiency of these implements, and by tracing the ups and downs of that efficiency, to trace out the tortuous course of human evolution.

The task of examining the efficiency – in this sense – of any given economic organisation is thus one which we should like to regard as an integral part of economics. But before we can accept it as such, we have to face the second difficulty which lies in our way, the difficulty of inter-personal comparisons. Although the economic system can be regarded as a mechanism for adjusting means to ends, the ends in question are ordinarily not a single system of ends, but as many independent systems as there are 'individuals' in the community. This appears to introduce a hopeless arbitrariness into the testing of efficiency. You cannot take a temperature when you have to use, not one thermometer, but an immense number of different thermometers, working on different principles, and with no necessary correlation between their registrations. How is this difficulty to be overcome?

We may list three possible ways of dealing with it, two of which have to be rejected as unsatisfactory. One is to replace the given thermometers (the scales of preference of the individuals) by a new thermometer of one's own. The investigator himself decides what he thinks to be good for society, and praises or condemns the system he is studying by that test. This is the method which is rightly condemned as unscientific. It is the way of the prophet and the social reformer, not of the economist.

Secondly, one may seek for some way of aggregating the reports of the different thermometers. This is the traditional method of Marshall, Edgeworth and Pigou. The fundamental reason why it cannot be accepted is that it is impossible to arrive at an aggregate without 'weighting' the component parts; and in this case there is no relevant reason why we should choose one system of weights rather than another. (The equal weights, 1, 1, 1, ... are just one possible system of weights like the rest.) As a matter of fact, when they are composing their aggregate, Marshall and Pigou pay no attention to variations of the marginal utility of money between rich and poor – a point which, on their own principles, ought plausibly to be taken into account.[6] Thus although their method can produce results, the significance of those results remains quite uncertain.

The third method is Mr Kaldor's. It consists in concentrating attention upon those cases which have been admitted, even by some of the positivists,[7] to be an exception to their general rule that the impossibility of inter-personal comparisons prevents any estimation of the general efficiency of the economic system. Mr Kaldor's contribution is to have shown that these cases are not the mere trifling exception they appear to be at first sight, but that they do actually offer a sufficient foundation for at least the more important part of welfare economics.

3.   Let us go back to the Paretian scheme referred to a little while ago. For society as a whole, the only *obstacles* to satisfaction are the limited quantity of physical resources, and the limited quantities of products which can be got from those resources. For the individual, however, the wants of other people have to be reckoned among the obstacles which limit the satisfaction of his wants. There are usually some ways in which he can improve his position without damaging the satisfactions of other people; there are other ways in which an improvement in his position (an upward movement on his scale of preferences) involves a downward movement for other people on their scales. Now these latter movements, which make some people better off and some people worse off, cannot be reckoned as involving an increase in 'social satisfaction' unless we have some means of reducing the satisfactions of different individuals to a common measure – and no unambiguous means for such reduction seems to exist. But the former movements, which benefit some people with-

---

[6] Cf. Kahn, 'Notes on ideal output', *EJ*, 1935, p. 2.
[7] Cf., for example, G. Myrdal, *Das politische Element in der nationalökonomischen Doktrinbildung* (1929), p. 288.

out damaging others, stand in another category. From any point of view, they do represent an increase in economic welfare – or better, an increase in the efficiency of the system as a means of satisfying wants, that is to say, in the efficiency of the system *tout court*.

Let us then define an *optimum* organisation of the economic system as one in which every individual is as well off as he can be made, subject to the condition that no reorganisation permitted shall make any individual worse off. This is not an unambiguous definition of an optimum organisation; it does not enable us to say that with given resources and given scales of preference, there will be one optimum position and one only. That is not so; there will be an indefinite number of different possible optima, distinguished from one another by differences in the *distribution* of social wealth.[8] In spite of this, we are able to lay down the conditions which must be fulfilled in order that a particular organisation should be optimum, and so we can test whether an actual organisation is optimum or not. If it is not optimum, then there is a definite sense in which its efficiency can be increased. Some at least of the individuals in the system can have their wants satisfied better, without anyone having to make a sacrifice in order to achieve that end.

The significance of this definition may be illustrated by taking the familiar case of comparative costs in inter-regional trade. Suppose that the supplies of two commodities are each derived from two regions, each region producing each commodity. Suppose that each commodity, in each region, is produced under diminishing returns, and that no migration of factors between the regions is possible. Then, as is well known, the technical possibilities of production in each region can be represented by a *substitution curve*.[9] The abscissa of each point on this curve represents a certain quantity of the one commodity, and the corresponding ordinate represents the maximum amount of the other whose production is consistent with the production of that amount of the first. A and B (Fig. 5.1) represent the substitution curves of the two regions. Under the assumed diminishing returns, each substitution curve will be concave to the origin.

---

[8] If we start from a given organisation which is not optimum, there will be several different optima which can be reached subject to the condition of no one being damaged, since the 'increment of wealth' can be divided in different ways. In addition to these there will be many other optima which cannot be reached from the initial position, since they involve some people being worse off than they were initially. These are optimum positions all the same, although they could only be reached by a 'permitted reorganisation' if we begin from some other starting-point.

[9] G. Haberler, *Theory of International Trade* (1936), p. 176.

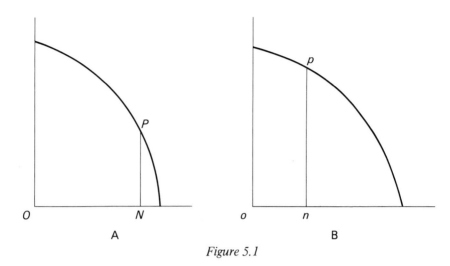

Figure 5.1

Suppose we start with a case where the quantities of the goods produced in the two regions are ON, PN and on, pn. Then, taking the two regions together, the total amounts produced of the two commodities are $ON + on$, $PN + pn$. These total amounts might be plotted on a third diagram, but a more instructive method of compounding is to 'sit' the one curve on the other, keeping the axes parallel, as in Fig. 5.2. It will be observed that the curve B is reversed before being superposed,[10] so that it is the co-ordinates of o with respect to the A-axes which represent the total amounts produced. This reversal has a definite advantage, since it shows us at once what condition must be fulfilled in order for the distribution of production between the regions to be optimum. If, when the diagrams are superposed, the curves intersect, a reorganisation of production will enable the outputs of both products (in the two areas taken together) to be increased. It is only when the curves touch (as in the dotted position) that an optimum organisation is realised.

When two curves touch, their slopes are the same; and the slope of a substitution curve measures the ratio between the marginal costs of the two products. It is thus a condition of optimum organisation that the marginal costs of the two commodities should be in the same ratio in the two regions. If this condition is not satisfied, the position is not an optimum; for the production of both commodities can be increased by a suitable re-arrangement.

[10] I owe this device to Mr Kaldor.

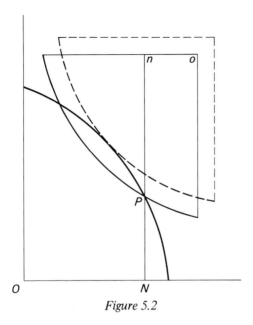

Figure 5.2

An exactly similar construction can be used for the case of exchange between two individuals. Here again we can construct a substitution curve (an indifference curve, as it is more commonly called), showing the various quantities of two commodities which would yield a particular individual the same amount of satisfaction. His whole scale of preferences can be represented by a series of such curves. Now if the first individual only moves from one position on his scale to another position by exchanging goods with the second, every movement of the first individual implies a movement of the second in the opposite direction. We can then draw the second individual's indifference map upon the same diagram as the first's, but his curves will naturally all turn the other way.[11]

Once again, if the amounts possessed by the two parties are such that their indifference curves through that point intersect, the position cannot be an optimum. For it will be possible for either party to reach a preferred position (a position on a higher indifference curve) while the other party remains on the same indifference curve as before. One party can be made better off without the other being worse off, so the position is not an optimum position. The position will only be an optimum if the curves touch – in this case, if the ratio

[11] A. L. Bowley, *Mathematical Groundwork of Economics* (1924), Fig. 1.

of the marginal utilities of the two commodities is the same for both parties.

4.   The general conditions for the attainment of an optimum organisation may now be set out in a formal manner.[12]

The first set of conditions are *marginal* conditions. They state – in the terminology I prefer – that the marginal rate of substitution[13] between any two commodities must be the same for every individual (who consumes them both) and for every producing unit (which produces them both) in the whole economy. In the older terminology, the ratio of the marginal utilities of the two commodities must be the same for every individual; the ratio of the marginal costs must be the same for every producing unit; and these ratios must be equal. Exactly similar conditions must hold between factor and product, and factor and factor, as between product and product. Thus the marginal product of labour in terms of a particular product must equal the marginal disutility of labour in terms of that product. And so on.

If these conditions are not fulfilled, some 'tightening-up' (of the kind illustrated in our diagrams) will always be possible.

The second set of conditions are *stability* conditions. Their rôle is to ensure that the position established is one of maximum, not minimum, satisfaction. They can be defined in terms of the curvature of the substitution curves; but it does not seem necessary to elaborate them here, because their importance for the theory of the optimum is largely eclipsed by that of the third set of conditions – which we may call the *total* conditions.[14]

The function of the total conditions is to ensure that no improvement can be brought about by the complete abandonment of the production or consumption of some one commodity, either in one producing or consuming unit, or generally; and that no improvement can be secured by the introduction of new commodities, which could

---

[12] It should be observed that it is not at all necessary to raise the awkward problems about the definition of real income, which gave so much trouble to Professor Pigou. We can *proceed directly* to the analysis of the optimum. This is, of course, not to deny that a definition of real social income is wanted for other (statistical) purposes, and that the issues raised in the search for that definition are very cognate to those in question here. In my ideal *Principles of Economics* the theory of economic welfare and the theory of the social income would be the subjects of consecutive chapters – but they would not get into the same chapter.

[13] See *VC*, pp. 20, 86.

[14] Compare the triple classification of the conditions of equilibrium in positive economics, given in *VC*, chap. 6.

have been produced or consumed, but were not being produced or consumed, either partially or generally, in the initial situation. Similar conditions must hold for factors – thus conditions referring to the mobility of labour (occupational or local) arise in the form of total conditions. The working of both these latter sets of conditions can be readily understood by reference to our diagrams. In Fig. 5.2 (the inter-regional trade case) both the stability condition and the total condition were in fact assumed to be satisfied – as a consequence of the assumption of diminishing returns. Complications arise from increasing returns. In Fig. 5.3 the marginal condition is satisfied, but neither of the other conditions. In Fig. 5.4 we have both the marginal condition and the stability condition, but not the total condition. In both these cases, it is only possible for an optimum position to be reached if production of one commodity is abandoned in one of the regions. (Optimum positions are such as those indicated by the dotted curves.) There must be specialisation in the inter-regional case; more generally, there must be a change in the kinds of goods produced or consumed somewhere.

5. These are the general conditions for optimum organisation; they are universally valid, being applicable to every conceivable type of society. No economic system has ever existed, nor (we may be sure) will any ever exist, to which they are irrelevant.[15] But for us the most

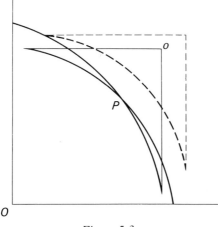

Figure 5.3

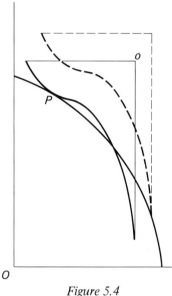

Figure 5.4

interesting application which they offer still lies in their use as a means of criticising or testing the efficiency of production by private enterprise.[16] It is this which I shall take as my topic for the remainder of this paper.

When we are dealing with the system of private enterprise, there is one point which requires special attention, although it is (in a sense) nothing but the practical aspect of that theoretical difficulty which has concerned us all along. Under private enterprise, any ordinary change in economic policy involves a change in the price-system, and any change in prices benefits those on one side of the market, and damages those on the other. Thus no simple economic reform can be a permitted reorganisation in our sense, because it always inflicts a loss of some sort upon some people. Nevertheless, this does not

[16] Another important application of Welfare Economics, which should perhaps be distinguished from this, is the application to Public Finance. Welfare Economics, defined as we have defined it, cannot lay down what is *the* optimum method of raising a given revenue – the 'least sacrifice' method, as taxation theorists would call it. That is impossible without inter-personal comparisons. It can, however, distinguish between those methods of raising revenue which are consistent with optimum production and those which are not. In practice, this would seem to be a quite sufficient achievement.

On these questions of optimum taxation Professor Hotelling (*op. cit.*) has thrown particular light.

prevent us from applying our criteria to the case of private enterprise, because we can always suppose that special measures are taken through the public revenue to compensate those people who are damaged. A 'permitted reorganisation' must thus be taken from now on to mean a reorganisation which will allow of compensation being paid, and which will yet show a net advantage. The position is not optimum so long as such reorganisation is possible.

The critique of private enterprise naturally begins by pointing out the one conceivable case in which an optimum position may be attained by perfect *laisser faire*. This occurs when competition is *perfect* in all industries, so that every producer and every consumer takes for granted the prices of all those things he buys or sells, and contents himself with adjusting quantities to these (for him) given prices. If these conditions are realised, the *perfection* of the consumers' market ensures that each individual consumer equalises his marginal rate of substitution between every pair of goods to the ratio of their market prices; and the *perfection* of the producers' market ensures that each producer makes the marginal cost of every article he sells equal to its price. Thus the marginal conditions for the optimum must be satisfied. The fact that such universal perfect competition is only possible under universal diminishing returns[17] ensures that the stability and total conditions for the optimum must be satisfied too. Thus, so it appears, an optimum position must be reached.

There are, however, certain reasons why an optimum position may not be attained, even in these favourable circumstances of universal perfect competition and universal *laisser faire*. The first is one which has been rightly emphasised by Professor Pigou.[18] It is of enormous importance that only some of the ways by which human beings affect one another's prosperity are controlled through the mechanism of the price-system. We are all of us affected by the economic activities of other people in ways for which we do not pay, or are not paid. Thus it is not necessarily to the social advantage (even in the narrow sense in which we are using that term) that a person should be able to acquire a particular product so long as he is willing to pay a price equal to the marginal cost of that product. This condition

---

[17] Since these particular technical conditions are necessary in order for universal perfect competition to be a possible state of affairs, the true basis for the criticism of monopolistic output is always to compare it with optimum output, not with competitive output (which may easily be a meaningless term in the state of affairs assumed). Whatever the technical conditions, an optimum output always exists.

[18] *Op. cit.,* pp. 172 ff.

ensures that he can acquire it without making anyone else worse off because that person has to bear a part of the ordinary costs of production of that commodity; but there are other ways in which other people may be injured (or benefited). The ultimate implications of this exception are indeed very large. Hidden under this heading are some of the gravest philosophical issues about the relationship between the individual and society.

This qualification is generally admitted; but there are other qualifications, of a more dynamic character, whose place in the theory is less generally appreciated. When they are taken strictly, the optimum conditions can only be interpreted *ex post*; it is only *after the event* that we can say whether an optimum organisation has in fact been achieved. Now even under perfect competition, producers only equate prices to marginal costs *ex ante*; it is anticipated marginal costs which are made equal to anticipated prices, so that if any of these anticipations are wrong, actual prices will not equal actual marginal costs, and the position achieved, though planned to be an optimum, will not turn out as such in fact. Of course, the utmost which can be done by wise economic policy is to secure equality *ex ante* – the planned optimum; but it is as well to remind ourselves that this does not necessarily imply a realised optimum, in order that we should be quite clear about the part played by foresight in economic efficiency.

Nor is this all; if the optimum conditions are interpreted *ex post*, they can make no allowance for risk, since risk is a phenomenon due to uncertainty of the *future*. On the other hand, the policy of the individual producer, being *ex ante*, is greatly influenced by risk; consequently prices always tend to exceed the relevant marginal costs by a risk-premium. Consequently production is carried less far in the more risky industries than is theoretically desirable.

If foresight is very bad, there may be little harm in this; for the refusal to embark resources in risky enterprises may prevent much mal-investment and waste. Indeed, so long as it confines itself to deflecting resources from more risky to less risky sorts of *production*, we may not need to have much quarrel with the risk factor in practice; the trouble is that it may go beyond this. Liquidity-preference is only a form of risk-aversion; and the effect of liquidity-preference on the general activity of industry is well known. When liquidity-preference manifests itself in a large amount of 'involuntary unemployment', a monetary policy directed to the reduction of interest rates, and even a public works policy which calculates the profitability of public enterprise at an 'artificially' low rate of interest, may be measures which promote movement in the direction of the optimum as we have defined it.[19]

6. I do not propose to say very much in this paper about the welfare economics of monopoly and imperfect compeitition, for this is altogether too large a subject to be capable of useful treatment on the scale here available. A very large part of the established theory of imperfect competition falls under the head of welfare economics, and it is actually much the strongest part of the theory which does so. Considered as a branch of positive economics, the theory of imperfect competition is even now not very convincing; the assumption that the individual producer has a clear idea of the demand curve confronting him has been justifiably questioned, and the presence of intractable elements of oligopoly in most markets has been justifiably suspected.[20] When it is considered as a branch of welfare economics, the theory of imperfect competition has a much clearer status. Oligopoly and monopolistic competition fall into their places as reasons for the inequality between price and marginal cost, whose consequences are then a most fertile field for study along welfare lines.

It is perhaps rather to be regretted that modern theories of imperfect competition have not been cast more overtly into this form; for the general apparatus of welfare economics would have made it possible to state some of the most important propositions in a more guarded way than usual. Take, for example, the very important question of the optimum number of firms in an imperfectly competitive industry, which is so near the centre of modern discussion. Since (*ex hypothesi*) the different firms are producing products which are economically distinguishable, the question is one of those which falls under the heading of our *third* set of optimum conditions – the *total* conditions; we have to ask whether a reduction

---

[19] In spite of the close dependence of actual interest rates upon risk factors (expressed by Mr Keynes in his liquidity-preference theory), it must not be supposed that the payment of interest is itself inconsistent with optimum organisation. For a convincing demonstration of this, see Lindahl, 'The place of capital in the theory of price' (*Ekonomisk Tidskrift,* 1929, appearing in English as Part III of his *Studies in the Theory of Money and Capital*). The economy with perfect foresight and perfect competition, elaborately analysed by Professor Lindahl, is automatically an economy with optimum organisation and yet it has a rate of interest (of course a pure time-preference rate). The time-preference element in interest is that element which is consistent with the optimum, the liquidity-preference element is that which is not.

[20] Cf. Hall and Hitch, *Price Theory and Business Behaviour,* Oxford Economic Papers, Number 2 (1939).

in the number of products would be conducive to a movement towards the optimum.

Suppose then that a particular firm is closed down. The loss involved in its cessation is measured by the compensation which would have to be given to consumers to make up for their loss of the opportunity to consume the missing product, *plus* the compensation which would have to be given to producers to make up for the excess of their earnings in this use over what they could earn in other uses. The loss is therefore measured by Marshall's *Surplus* (Consumers' Surplus[21] *plus* Producers' Surplus). Under conditions of perfect competition, this loss is a net loss. For when the factors are transferred to other uses, they will have to be scattered about at the margins of those uses; and (since the earnings of a factor equal the value of its marginal product) the additional production made possible by the use of the factors in these new places is equal in value to the earnings of the factors (already accounted for). Under perfect competition, the marginal productivity law ensures that there is no producers' surplus generated at the new margins; while, since the marginal unit of any commodity is worth no more than what is paid for it, there can be no consumers' surplus either. Thus there is nothing to set against the initial loss; there cannot be a movement towards the optimum if the number of products is reduced.

But if competition is imperfect, there is something to set on the other side. The earnings of a factor are now less than the value of its marginal product by an amount which varies with the degree of monopolistic exploitation; and therefore the increment to production which can be secured by using the factors at other margins is worth more than the earnings of the factors. There is a producers' surplus, even at the margin, and this producers' surplus may outweigh the initial loss. The general condition for a particular firm to be such that its existence is compatible with the optimum is that the sum of the consumers' and producers' surpluses generated by its activities must be greater than the producers' surplus which would be generated by employing its factors (and exploiting them) elsewhere.

[21] This use of Consumers' Surplus is not open to any of the objections which have been brought against Marshall's concept; it does not involve either interpersonal comparisons or the measurement of utility. Consumers' surplus is the measure of the compensation which consumers would need in order to maintain them at the same level of satisfaction as before, after the supply of the commodity had been withdrawn. It is, however, not exactly equal to the area under the ordinary demand curve (see *VC*, Appendix to Ch. II). This inequality (usually only a slight inequality) was responsible for the difficulties about the aggregation of consumers' surpluses which troubled Professor Pigou.

The rule usually given is a special case of this general rule. If entry to the industry is 'free', price equals average cost, and the producers' surplus generated by the firm as a whole can be neglected. If the products of the different firms are very close substitutes, or merely distinguished by 'irrational preferences', consumers' surplus can perhaps be neglected as well. With these simplifications, the number of firms in an imperfectly competitive industry is always excessive, so long as price is greater than marginal cost anywhere in the industry. (Or, if we can retain the identity of price with average cost, the number of firms is excessive until average cost is reduced to a minimum.)[22]

These, however, are simplifications; it is not always true that the number of firms in an imperfectly competitive industry is excessive, though very often it may be. Before recommending in practice a policy of shutting down redundant firms, we ought to be sure that the full condition is satisfied; and we ought to be very sure that the discarded factors will in fact be transferred to more productive uses. In a world where the most the economist can hope for is that he will be listened to occasionally, that is not always so certain.

7.   By adopting the line of analysis set out in this paper, it is possible to put welfare economics on a secure basis, and to render it immune from positivist criticism. That is a great gain in itself; but, as often happens in such cases, other gains are secured with it. The main practical advantage of our line of approach is that it fixes attention upon the question of compensation. Every simple economic reform inflicts a loss upon some people; the reforms we have studied are marked out by the characteristic that they will allow of compensation to balance that loss, and they will still show a net advantage. Yet when such reforms have been carried through in historical fact, the advance has usually been made amid the clash of opposing interests, so that compensation has not been given, and economic progress has accumulated a roll of victims, sufficient to give all sound policy a bad name.

[22 Hicks comments in *CEET* I, 1981: I wish I had laid more stress on this point about average cost. That the output of a firm should be carried to the point where its average cost is minimised is not, in general, a necessary condition of optimality. Take the case of a drug, which is necessary to maintain the life of a small number of persons, who suffer from some uncommon disease. They must have a certain amount per period; it cannot be to the social interest, however defined, to deprive them of it; but to produce more than is required must be wasteful. It might well be that a larger amount could be produced at lower average cost; but there would still be no point in producing it.]

I do not contend that there is any ground for saying that compensation ought always to be given; whether or not compensation should be given in any particular case is a question of distribution, upon which there cannot be identity of interest, and so there cannot be any generally acceptable principle. This being so, it will often happen in some particular case that the economist will find himself not at all anxious for compensation to be given;[23] but his personal feeling in that direction will be based either upon the non-economic ground that the persons damaged do not deserve much consideration, or upon the only quasi-economic ground that the loss inflicted on them is nothing but the materialisation of a risk they may be expected to have allowed for. Nevertheless we must expect that there will be many other cases where the redistribution, resulting from a sound measure carried through without compensation, would be regarded by him as deplorable; and then, if he considers the measure in isolation from the question of compensation, he will pay no more than lip-service to its productive efficiency, and probably reject it in practice. From this it is only a step to the state of mind which judges measures solely by reference to their distributive justice, without reference to their bearing on efficiency. If measures making for efficiency are to have a fair chance, it is extremely desirable that they should be freed from distributive complications as much as possible.

We can make this separation in our own minds if we accustom ourselves, whenever we can, to thinking of every economic reform in close conjunction with some measure of compensation, designed to render it approximately innocuous from the distributive point of view. Since almost every conceivable kind of compensation (rearrangement of taxation, for example) must itself be expected to have some influence on production, the task of the welfare economist is not completed until he has envisaged the total effects of both sides of the proposed reform; he should not give his blessing to the reform until he has considered these total effects and judged them to be good. If, as will often happen, the best methods of compensation feasible involve some loss in productive efficiency, this loss will have to be taken into account. In practice, it is not unlikely that we shall have to reject on these grounds many measures which would be approved of by the traditional analysis, but which would only be

---

[23] The typical hard-boiled attitude is, of course, to reject all compensation on the ground that such risks *ought* to have been allowed for. In view of the importance of foresight for economic efficiency, there is something in this; when applied to ordinary changes in data which promote productivity (such as inventions) it is probably a decisive consideration; nevertheless, if it is always regarded as decisive, the case for an active pursuit of economic efficiency in other ways is seriously weakened.

reckoned by that analysis as offering a small gain. (It is not very surprising to find that some of the fine points in welfare theory are nothing but snares.)

Further investigations of such matters would lead us far beyond the 'Foundations' which have been the subject of this paper. I have accomplished my end if I have demonstrated the right of Welfare Economics – the 'Utilitarian Calculus' of Edgeworth – to be considered as an integral part of economic theory, capable of the same logical precision and the same significant elaboration as its twin brother, Positive Economics, the 'Economical Calculus'.

ADDENDUM

In spite of the allowance for some 'dynamic' considerations which is on pp. 138-9 in this paper, the general tendency of the analysis is static. This carries with it the apparent implication that the gains and losses, and the compensations, on which the discussion has turned, are all of them permanent. It would have been a great improvement if I had made an explicit distinction between permanent and temporary gains and losses. I did this in a passage in *Capital and Growth* (1965), pp. 202-3, from which I quote.

As soon as we make that distinction, we can add to the (probably almost empty) category of changes in which some gain but none lose, a more interesting category of changes which are such that losses are temporary while gains are permanent. Compensation for temporary losses is more feasible than compensation for permanent losses. The former, indeed, is such that it can often be introduced by agreement; while the latter (suggestive of those 'compensations' given by the Courts for the loss of a limb, or the break-up of a marriage) has something inherently inadequate about it. A Compensation Principle, that was restricted in application to compensation for temporary losses, looks distinctly more acceptable than one which did not make this distinction.

The question may nevertheless arise; how are permanent and temporary gains and losses to be weighed against one another? It does not necessarily arise in an acute form, but it may do so. Suppose, to take the simplest possible case, that a particular *primary* change (as we may call it) confers a permanent benefit on A, and a temporary loss on B. If B's loss is offset by a temporary measure of compensation (at A's expense), A is left with a permanent gain, secured at a temporary cost; the only question which then arises is whether the 'investment', from A's point of view, is worth while. But if the time-shape of the compensation that is offered does not match that of the loss (and this is a matter on which there may well be differences of opinion) B's time-preferences as well as A's must be considered. To some extent it may be possible to avoid *this* inter-personal comparison by reference to opportunities for lending (and borrowing) on a market; but we cannot take it for granted that the opportunities for such intertemporal transactions that are open to A and to B are the same. ... Perhaps it is true that imperfection of the capital market is the most fundamental of all kinds of market imperfection.

6

Preference and Welfare

This has been put together from two sources. The first of them is a paper, with this title, which first appeared in a volume of essays in honour of Professor A. K. Dasgupta (OUP, Calcutta, 1974). It is a retrospective survey of the author's work in the field with which the preceding five papers in this volume have been concerned. Much of it was used, later on, for the 'Introduction' to *CEET* I.

The other is a little note, also included in *CEET* I, entitled 'A Manifesto'. It was written earlier (1958), but it seems to be appropriate as a concluding section, since it enlarges upon the vistas, beyond conventional welfare economics, which open up when the subject is looked at in the manner here described.

From the theory of demand to the economics of welfare: how does one pass from the one to the other? When I look back over what is now quite a long period on what I have written upon these subjects, I can see that in some important ways I have changed my views. I am not ashamed of that for I think I have been learning. 'The man who never alters his opinions', said Blake in one of his *Prophetic Writings*, 'is like standing water, and breeds reptiles of the mind'. But that makes it all the more necessary that I should explain myself.

I can distinguish, over the whole course of these writings, three phases. In the first, which includes my first value paper,[1] and extends up to *Value and Capital* (1939), I was solely concerned with positive economics. I was actually, at that stage, a disbeliever in welfare economics; I was aware of the weakness of Pigou's foundations, but I had nothing to put in their place. The second phase is that of the 'Kaldor–Hicks New Welfare Economics'. The original suggestion was due to Kaldor; but in three papers, which belong together,[2] I

---

[1] Essay 1 above.
[2] 'Foundations' (essay 5 above), 'Valuation of Social Income' (1940), and 'Rehabilitation of Consumers' Surplus' (1941).

developed Kaldor's suggestion quite a long way. I am still on the whole rather proud of those articles; I think that they did make a contribution which, after a fashion, stands. But not in the form it was there given. That, I now grant, was blasted by critics, by Scitovsky, by Samuelson, by Little and by others. So it was up to me to do the work over again.

I have never quite managed to do it again. I wrote a book called *A Revision of Demand Theory* (1956) which contains a restatement of the positive theory of my first phase, revised in the light (mainly) of Samuelson. I wrote a paper on 'Measurement of Real Income' (1958),[3] which may be regarded as an introduction to a restatement of welfare economics. But it is not more than that; the consequences of what I was saying, for welfare economics proper, were not fully drawn. The rest is fragments.[4] In what follows I shall try to do something to pull them together.

I

I begin with the positive side (the first phase and its 1956 *Revision*). It was not explained, in the Hicks–Allen article, what has prompted us to make our enquiry. It began in fact from econometrics. Henry Schultz, a pioneer of econometrics, had endeavoured to calculate some cross-elasticities – demand for X against price of Y. He thought it followed from Marshallian demand theory that these cross-elasticities should be symmetric. The slopes of the 'cross demand curves' (X against Y and Y against X) should be the same, since each should be equal to the cross second derivative of a utility function. But this, by his econometrics, did not seem to be verified. What we did was to take the 'neo-classical' demand theory (as it might now be called) in a Paretian, instead of a Marshallian, form; and to show that it gave no reason why Schultz's symmetry should hold. Schultz had left out the *income effects*, which for direct elasticities may indeed be negligible, as Marshall (in effect) supposed them to be; but for cross-elasticities there is no reason why they should be negligible. It is only with strong substitutes, or strong complements, that they are likely to be swamped by the substitution term.

---

[3] 'The Utility Approach' (essay 3 above).
[4] That is how things were in 1974. Some later writings have made the statement a little better rounded. All are included in *CEET* I. There are (1) 'The Scope and Status of Welfare Economics', (2) 'Optimisation and Specialisation' and (3) 'The Cost Approach' (essay 4 above).

It has seemed worth while to tell this story, since it illustrates the atmosphere in which, in the thirties, we were working. We took the 'neo-classical' utility theory for granted. We preferred the Paretian form, with ordinal rather than cardinal utility, not so much because the cardinal assumption seemed unnecessary, as because (with a very little mathematics) the consequences came out more clearly and more precisely. But it was fundamentally the same theory, however expressed. We worked it out with the intention that it should be used by econometrists in formulating the questions which they were to ask of the facts.

There is not a great deal of difference between this approach and the 'revealed preference' of Samuelson. The latter is perhaps no more than a sharper statement of what we (and of course many others at that time) appeared to be doing. The facts that are presented to the econometrist register the consequences of human behaviour; his task is to use them to deduce some characteristics of the 'wants' or 'preferences' or 'utility functions' that motivate them. It is taken for granted that these 'wants' exist.

I have never (I think) myself been a 'revealed preference' man. The effect on me of Samuelson's sharper statement was to make me wonder whether (still for the econometric purpose) one needed to go so far. Then I convinced myself that it is not at all necessary. So when I came to the corresponding point in my 1956 *Revision*, I was much more cautious. This is what I said:[5]

The econometrist, who seeks to make a demand study, has before him something like the following situation. He is contemplating certain factual data, generally in the form of a time-series, showing the amounts of some commodity (or commodities) which have been purchased by a particular group of people during certain specified periods of time. His object is to find an explanation of these statistics, a hypothesis which will account for them. Common sense at once suggests a number of possible explanation ...

First of all, there are the entirely non-economic (or, perhaps it would be better to say, non-price) explanations - changes in population, age-distribution of population, social habits due to developments in housing and education, and so on... The second group will consist of price-explanations, explanations in terms of prices... Explanations in terms of the lagged effects of price-changes ... I would keep over for a third head...

... the first thing which is asked of the econometrist is that he should estimate the effects which can be attributed to the various stimuli of the current-price type ... But in order for him to be able to make such estimates, he needs a technique for separating out the current-price effects from the others... The econometric purpose of the theory of demand is to give assistance in making this separation.

The kind of theory which is needed for this purpose is one which will tell us something about the ways in which consumers would be likely to react if variations in current prices and incomes were the only causes of changes in consumption. This is precisely what the theory of demand, considered from the econometric point of view, has to do. It proceeds by postulating an *ideal consumer*, who by definition is only affected by current market conditions, and asks how we should expect such a consumer to behave.

In order to get any answer to this question, we have to make some assumption about the principles governing his behaviour. The assumption of behaviour according to a scale of preferences comes in here as the simplest hypothesis, not necessarily the only possible hypothesis, but the one which, initially at least, seems to be the most sensible hypothesis to try.

Perhaps I should have qualified this last remark by saying that for the data to which econometrics is usually applied, it seems the most sensible hypothesis. It might not be sensible for other data. With that amendment, I think I will stand by the passage just quoted. It falls, it will be noticed, a long way short of 'revealed preference'.

II

The justification, just given, for the use of the Preference hypothesis in demand theory, relates solely to its use for econometrics. If it is to be used for another purpose, whatever that is, it will have to be justified all over again.

At the stage of the New Welfare Economics that was of course not realised. I do not think it is surprising (considering dates) that it was not realised; so I do not think one need apologise for the omission. But as soon as one had decided to take the cool line, just described, about the econometric theory, the 'Foundations of Welfare Economics' have to be looked at again.

There was one of the thing which had come up, at the stage of the New Welfare Economics, which provied to be a help. Welfare economics is commonly thought of as a normative (or shall we say quasi-ethical?) subject; though Pigou, it may be remembered, did not wish it to be taken in that way. To jump from econometrics to quasi-ethics is rather frightening; many a horse can jib, and has jibbed, at that leap. It is fortunate, therefore, that it need not be taken directly; there is a way round with a foothold on the way.

There is one topic, which in a treatise of welfare economics could hardly be avoided, but which does not look like being normative at all. This is the theory of the macroeconomic concepts (as commonly used in quite positive analysis), of which it is sufficient in this place to take the social product, in any of its senses, as an example. What do we mean by the social product, by the real social product, and by its growth rate, that is so bandied about? That, Pigou thought (and I came to believe that he was quite right in thinking), is the first of the questions which in 'Welfare Economics' comes up to be discussed.

We know how statisticians calculate it – by adding up the quantities of products produced, valued at market prices (Σpq). This, to get the real product, is then deflated by an index-number of prices. I leave on one side the statistical difficulties, and the theoretical difficulties associated with the carry-over from one period to another. Here we have just to ask, Why should we value at market prices? And what should we use as substitutes for market prices, if for any of the things we want to include in the social product, a market price does not happen to be available?

If we lived in the kind of world that was contemplated by Ricardo, and by Marx, in some of their work, the answer might seem to be easy. If labour (homogeneous labour) were the only factor of production, and there were no economies of scale, prices (one might expect) would be proportional to quantities of labour embodied. If we used a labour standard, measuring prices in terms of labour, Σpq would be the total quantity of labour employed. The change in employment, from year 0 to year 1, would be shown as $\Sigma p_0 q_0$ to $\Sigma p_1 q_1$. This, to the statistician, would be the change in the value of the social product; to get the real social product, he would deflate by an index-number of prices; thus getting, for the proportionate change in the real product, $\Sigma p_1 q_1 / \Sigma p_1 q_0$.

There is no difficulty, in a labour theory world, about the meaning of $\Sigma p_1 q_0$. It is the labour that would be required, in the conditions of year 1, to produce (q_0), the actual products of year 0. So what the statistician would show, when he calculated that there had been a rise in the social product from year 0 to year 1, would be that the outputs of year 0 could be produced in year 1 with less labour than was actually employed in year 1. This might come about, it will be noticed, either because there had been an increase in the labour actually employed, or (even without any increase in labour employed) it might come about by an increase in productivity.

It will also be noticed that even in this labour theory world there are two measures of changes in product – $\Sigma p_1 q_1 / \Sigma p_1 q_0$ and $\Sigma p_0 q_1 / \Sigma p_0 q_0$ – which do not necessarily agree. Even here, there is an 'index-number problem'.

We do not live in a labour theory world, but in our statistics, and in the interpretation we put upon them, we often pretend that we do. When the statistician tells us that the National Product of Japan has increased by 15 per cent from one year to the next, we look first to see what has happened to labour (and perhaps to capital) employed; we then ascribe the rest to an increase in 'productivity'. In a labour theory world that kind of thing would be unobjectionable; can it be carried over to more complex conditions?

To some extent, I believe, it can. In the labour theory world we were measuring the change in the (heterogeneous) product by reducing it to terms of homogeneous labour; when the factors of production are heterogeneous that cannot be done. The reduction must fail. What does remain possible is that we might be able to get an answer to a substantially equivalent question.

Take the 'bundle' of goods that is produced in year 0, and divide the output of each good into n_0 equal parts, n_0 being the same for each separate good. Then put together one of each of these parts, one for each good, to form a 'unit bundle'. The social product of year 0 can then be regarded as consisting of n_0 unit bundles – unit (0) bundles, as we may call them, since the goods are combined, in each of these unit bundles, in the proportions in which they are combined in the production of year 0. Then consider how many of these (0) bundles could have been produced, with the resources, and with the productivity, of year 1. Let this be n_1. Then n_1/n_0 is a possible measure of the change in real social product from year 0 to year 1. It will be noticed that one of the measures which we got in the labour theory world could be defined in exactly this manner.

As there, it is not the only measure; instead of considering how many (0) bundles could have been produced in (1) conditions, we might have considered how many (1) bundles could have been produced in (0) conditions. As there (and indeed as always) there is an 'index-number problem'. Now it may be that this index-number problem is not very serious; in an economy which was advancing fairly uniformly, it might not be very serious. But when the advance is non-uniform, it can be serious indeed. A 'cost comparison', as it may be called, works well enough in a labour theory world, because in that world all factors of production are perfect substitutes for one another. In reality they are far from being perfect substitutes; in the long run a good deal of substitution is possible, but in the short run much less. Thus it is only too likely that cost comparisons, in terms of short-run costs (and it is surely short-run costs which should be taken when one is comparing one *year* with another), will give inconsistent results. The outputs of year 1 will be more than would be attainable, in year 0, with the resources of year 0; *and* the outputs of year 0 will be more than would be attainable, in year 1, with the resources of year 1. This can happen, and is quite likely to happen, even though the statistical comparisons, using price-weights, appear to give results that are quite coherent. All may be well if the economy is advancing fairly uniformly; but when there is advance in some sectors and contraction in others, there is almost certain to be trouble.

There is much more than this to be said about the 'cost' measure of the social product; but I am only concerned with it here to show that it will not do for us all that we should like. It needs, at the least, to be supported in another manner.

III

Instead of looking for a 'cost' interpretation of the (Σpq) social product, we may look for an interpretation on the demand, or 'utility' side. This is the point at which (by the route we are here following) we enter welfare economics. Yet we are not, so far, asking any normative question. We are simply looking for an alternative interpretation of social product.

It is best (I now believe) to proceed in a way which is parallel to the path we followed on the cost side. We begin with a *base theory*,[6] which plays much the same part as was played by the labour theory on the cost side; we then relax its assumptions, seeing how far we can go.

Just as the labour theory neglected differences between factors, so the base theory neglects differences among consumers. There are many (say N) consumers, but they are identical consumers, with the same wants and the same incomes. By them the whole of the social product is bought on a market and is consumed.

So, in the base theory, if prices are (p) and outputs (q), Σpq is the income of consumers; $(1/N)(\Sigma pq)$ is the income of the consumer. If $\Sigma p_1 q_1 > \Sigma p_1 q_0$, the consumer's income, in year (1), is more than sufficient for him to purchase the goods which he bought, being able to buy, in year (0); we would then want to say that his wants are better satisfied. But if we say that, we are taking it for

---

[6] In my 'Measurement of Real Income', *Oxford Economic Papers* (1958) I called this *base* theory *classical* theory. That, I was aware, was not a good term; and it has got worse as time has gone on. 'Base theory' is not ideal, but it is rather better.

granted that his wants, in the two years, are the same. We cannot draw that conclusion, without assuming that wants have not changed.

Thus here again, as in the econometric theory, we need a definition of constant wants. There may be other (usable) definitions; but it will at least make for economy in the exposition of our economics if we agree to use the same definition for each purpose, not overlooking the fact that they are quite different purposes. We do not have to lay down – we are in no position to lay down – that this is the way in which consumers, in practice, behave. The assumption of behaviour according to a fixed scale of preferences is no more than an easy way of defining 'constant wants', as needed for a 'utility' theory of social product comparisons.

I shall not trouble to set out the base theory, running in these terms. It seems unnecessary to do so, since in one form or another, it is set out in so many text-books. (My own preferred version is my 1958 *Measurement* article.) I will merely remark that when as supposed, we have a given set of indifference 'curves' for the consumer, there are three levels of income, spendable at the prices of year 1, which are identifiable. First there is actual income, Y_{11} $(=\Sigma p_1 q_1)$; secondly, there is the income which would be just sufficient for the purchase of the goods which were purchased in year 0, $Y_{10} (=\Sigma p_1 q_0)$; and thirdly, there is the income which would permit of the attainment of the same indifference level as was attained in year 0 but nothing more – call this y_{10}. Suppose that he had income Y_{10}, while prices as stated, were (p_1). He would then be able to purchase the same collection of goods. He chose that collection at (p_0); but at (p_1) he may be able to find an expenditure pattern which suits him better. Thus with income Y_{10}, he may be better satisfied than he was in year 0; he cannot be worse satisfied. Thus $Y_{10} \geqslant y_{10}$.

The rise in the social product, which the statistician would measure as Y_{11}/Y_{10}, may thus be compared with an 'indifference defined' rise, Y_{11}/y_{10}. When the consumer is free to choose, the latter will ordinarily be larger.

It will be noticed that just as there are two statistical measures (Laspeyres and Paasche) according as we move from year 0 to year 1, or from year 1 to year 0, so there are two indifference-defined measures. But while it is perfectly possible for the two statistical measures to give inconsistent results – one showing a rise in the social product and the other a fall – it is not possible, *in the base theory*, for the two indifference-defined measures to give inconsistent results. One of the indifference levels must be higher than the other (if they are not the same) wherever it is encountered. Though the extent of the change may seem different, according as it is measured in the one way or in the other, there must always be the same *direction* of change. All this, however, is just *base theory*, corresponding (as explained) to the labour theory on the cost side. As on the cost side, we may wish, and no doubt will wish, to go further. There are many ways in which we might seem to go further; some (which I shall not examine), which involve relaxing the extreme dependence of the base theory on the *market*, may well be important. I cannot however neglect the principal way in which it has so far been attempted to go further, that which is associated with the New Welfare Economics. What was then sought to be done was to drop the assumption of identical consumers. Everything else was retained; in particular, each consumer was taken to have a given scale of preferences, just as in the base theory.

We were still concerned, it must be insisted, with the measurement of the social product. We were measuring production, not distribution; so it was not to be expected that any change in distribution, which might have occurred between our two years, would show up. (It does not show up in the statistical comparison – Y_{11}/Y_{10}, as we have been writing it – these incomes being now understood as totals, over the body of consumers as a whole.) Our question, in substance, was whether there was anything remaining, when consumers have different wants and different incomes, which corresponds to the 'indifference-defined' income, y_{10}. We found that there is. It would still be possible to define the minimum income, spendable at prices (p_1) which could be distributed in such a way as to make it possible for each consumer to attain the same indifference level as he attained in year 0. One can go as far as this with the 'utility' theory of the social product.

That was our discovery; but it was almost at once confronted by another discovery (due, in the first place, to Scitovsky[7]) that when the indifference-defined measure is re-interpreted in this manner, the consistency (which in the base theory it was able to boast) does not necessarily hold. It does not *necessarily* hold; but when one follows through the conditions which have to be satisfied, in order that it should not hold, it appears that they are rather stringent. There must have been a significant change in distribution between the two years that are beng compared; that is evident, but it is not enough. The change in distribution must be such as to have an important effect

[7] T. Scitovsky, 'Welfare Propositions in Economics', *Review of Economic Studies* (1941-2).

on the (relative) demands for products; and it must also be such as to affect the relative demands in a particular way. It must generate an 'income effect' which works against the 'orthodox' substitution effect, and which is strong enough to offset it. This may happen; but there are many comparisons for which it does not seem at all likely to happen. We should usually be able to tell whether it was likely to happen. Otherwise, the extended theory will work in the same way as the base theory.

IV

So much (in this place) for measurement. But a theory of measurement, however far it is developed (and I can well believe that it may be developed much further), gets us no more than a part of the way across. We are still short of the 'normative' theory. All we have got is a jumping-off point for the further leap.

This is the point at which we have to face the key question: why should we be interested in the social product, however measured? It is not enough to say that it is an analytical convenience; it is obvious that that is no sufficient answer. People are interested in the social product; the growth rate of GNP is an economic magnitude on which politicians and journalists have come to set great store. But they do so only because economists have taught them to do so; the justification of the social product – its wider justification – is our responsibility.

We should of course be easy about it if we could bring ourselves to believe that an increase in the social product is without qualification a good thing. But few economists, surely, would dare to say that. 'Human sacrifice on the altar of GNP', ran a recent headline in the London *Times*, referring (not surprisingly) to 'pollution' in Tokyo. But it is not only because of 'pollution' and suchlike externalities that we have to put something less than full faith in the social product as a measure of 'welfare'. In the light of what has been revealed in our discussion of measurement, it is already impossible to say that an increase in the social product increases 'welfare'. It cannot be unequivocally good to change from A to B, if it is also unequivocally good to change from B to A. With every measure that we have examined – every measure that is based upon assumptions which even begin to be realistic – there are cases in which that might happen.

If the social product – the use of the social product – is to be justified, it must be in a different way. Since there are different measures, the uses of these measures may not be the same. By one measure we can distinguish one kind of advantage, by another another. It is useful to distinguish advantages, even though there is no reason why any of the advantages which we may thus distinguish should in all cases be overriding.

Once this is grasped, we need have no compunction in applying the measurement theory in a normative (or quasi-normative!) manner. There is always a problem of measurement, even in relation to such application. When a project is recommended 'on economic grounds', we usually mean that we think that its adoption would increase the social product, in some such sense as those that have been defined. We are still comparing two situations (or perhaps two 'programmes'), one the actual (or that which we think would be actual if 'nothing' were done), the other that which we think would result if our proposal were accepted. We may still use measurement theory as a means of estimating the expected gain. But we do no more that state the gain in terms that are appropriate to the method of measurement.

Thus it is to each of the measures of social product which we have identified, there corresponds a test of *efficiency*. We can use these tests as a basis for the criticism of economic arrangements, from the various points of view.

In the labour theory world, the social product depends on labour employed, and upon the productivity of labour in each use. The social product could be increased, without employing more labour, by increasing productivity, even by increasing productivity in just one particular use. If, in each use, productivity was as great as it could be, with existing technical knowledge, the system could be regarded as having reached an economic optimum, being *economically* perfectly efficient. But if, for some reason, there were uses in which productivity was less than 'perfect', the social product could be increased by removing the obstruction. In a labour theory world product being measured in terms of cost) there would be no more to be said.

In a labour theory world there is no problem of allocation. There can be perfect efficiency, in the cost sense, whatever the distribution of labour among industries. As soon as we admit multiplicity of factors, allocation comes in. By redistributing resources between industries, it may be possible to increase production in the cost sense; more can be produced of some things without less of others. The Ricardian theory of international trade is the classical example.) There must be optimum allocation if the economic optimum, even in the cost sense, is to be attained.

It is still implied, if we are content to use this cost test, that to have more of some things and no less of others is a *good thing*. Nothing is said, at this stage, about the characteristics of the things that are to be produced. The additional things which we might get, by moving towards this optimum, might be things which no one wanted – or might even be things which were obviously 'bad'. An efficiency test, which goes no further than this, has its uses; but it does not get us very far.

To get any further, we must turn to demand – to wants and their satisfaction. We may begin with what corresponds to our 'base theory'. Differences between consumers are neglected, so that production is regarded as directed towards satisfying the wants of a representative consumer, a consumer who, as before, has given preferences. Perfect efficiency will then be definable as a condition in which no change in organisation will enable the wants of the consumer to be satisfied better – a rather inclusive economic optimum, many might think! Such an optimum will require that cost efficiency conditions should be satisfied, for the range of commodities that are actually produced; it will also require that the outputs of these commodities should be 'right' (marginal utilities proportional to marginal costs, or however we like to state that condition). And it will further require that the list of commodities produced should be right – that there can be no gain in satisfaction by the introduction of new commodities, or by the withdrawal of old, so as to concentrate upon a 'better' list.

Already, at this stage, we meet the famous crux. The consumer's wants have been defined in terms of market behaviour – market behaviour at uniform prices. But it is perfectly possible, and indeed likely, that in a market with uniform prices this economic optimum cannot be attained. There may well be a net gain from the introduction of some particular commodity; but if there are economies of scale in its production, sale at a price which generates optimum output will involve producers in a loss. Some means must then be found by which consumers can compensate producers for their losses, if the optimum is to be attained. No such means can be found within the uniform price-system.

When we allow for differences among consumers, the compensation problem remains; it is indeed much intensified. For it then becomes necessary for different consumers to make different compensations. The 'experiments' which would be necessary to discover the 'right' compensations – or even sufficiently right compensations – look quite impracticable; and, what is more important for our present purpose, there is no kind of market behaviour which can 'reveal' them. They must be covered by what, in effect, is a *tax* – whoever levies it.

It does not follows that the route, by which we have arrived at the compensation test, is without value. It has clarified ideas; and it has thrown light on what can be done, can usefully be done, in practical cases.

This can now be said with much more confidence that it could be said in the days of the New Welfare Economics. The rise of 'cost-benefit' has demonstrated the practical fruitfulness of these ideas. We may claim to have assisted these practical investigators in formulating their problem. They do not, of course, estimate their 'gains' and 'losses' by market experiments. They proceed, as in practice it is necessary to do, by seeking what compensation (either way) can be regarded as 'fair'. For that purpose they use market information, both direct and indirect market information, but they also use other kinds of information – any kind of relevant information on which they can lay their hands.

In doing so, they are pushing on – rightly pushing on – beyond the formal theory, with which I have so far been mainly concerned. But for that formal theory what they do has a lesson. I have tried to show that welfare economics, as I would not regard it, is composed of a series of steps, steps by which we try to take more and more of the things which concern us into account. None of our 'optima' marks a top of that staircase. We must always be prepared to push on, if we can, a little further.

Welfare economics is an open-ended subject.

V

It will be useful, when attempting to carry on that line of thought, to have a name for those who would not accept this open-endedness – those who believe that when an economist has found a 'solution' to a practical problem in terms of conventional optima, he has done his job. So, in this concluding section, which is frankly polemical, I shall call them *welfarists*. That the economic problem is one of an adaptation of means to ends is of course agreed. What I do not admit is their use of economics to specify the ends, to choose them so as to suit an economist's convenience.

One is doing just that, if one takes it that ends can be adequately specified in terms of 'utility functions' or 'indifference maps' that are 'revealed on the market' or could be so revealed under suitable conditions. That we need such constructions as these I am not at all denying. Our basic concepts, production and distribution themselves, make no adequate sense without them; I have indeed devoted a good deal of attention to investigating the connection, and I hope that it has been somewhat clarified as a result of my own work. But, even in the course of these investigations, I have become more and more conscious of the artificiality of these assumptions. They are simplifications, by which we beat reality into a form which makes it tractable to economic analysis; they are not more than that. In our role as economic technicians, we cannot do without them; but as soon as we aspire to be something more than technicians, we must see them for the shaky supports that they are.

I cannot therefore now feel that it is enough to admit, with that very moderate welfarist Dennis Robertson, that 'the economist must be prepared to see some suggested course of action which he thinks would promote economic welfare turned down – his own judgement perhaps consenting, perhaps not – for overriding reasons'.[8] This is still no more than an admission that there are 'parts' of welfare which are not included in economic welfare, and that the two sorts of ends may conflict. The economist, as such, is still allowed, and even encouraged, to keep within his 'own' frontiers; if he has shown that a particular course of action is to be recommended, *for economic reasons*, he has done his job. I would now say that if he limits his function in that manner, he does not rise to his responsibilities. It is impossible to make 'economic' proposals that do not have 'non-economic aspects', as the welfarist would call them; when the economist makes a recommendation, he is responsible for it in the round; all aspects of that recommendation, whether he chooses to label them economic or not, are his concern.

It will be sufficient to take one strong example. One of the issues that can be dealt with most elaborately by welfarist methods is that of monopoly and competition: the theory of the social optimum which would be reached in a (practically unattainable) condition of all-round perfect competition, and of the departures from the optimum which must occur under any form in which a system of free enterprise can in practice be organised, is one of the chief ways in which the welfarist approach has left its mark. I do not question that we have learned a great deal from these discussions; but they leave me with an obstinate feeling that they have failed to penetrate to the centre of the problem with which they are concerned. I did indeed, at one time, suppose that the unacceptability (to me) of the

---

[8] *Lectures on Economic Principles*, i, p. 29.

practical conclusions which seem to follow from such a work as Mrs Robinson's *Economics of Imperfect Competition* was due to the narrowness of the 'production and distribution' or cost-minimisation standards that were being applied; if one widened it out, in a more faithfully Pigouvian manner, so as to take account of gains and losses in consumers' surplus, the conclusions which followed would be less paradoxical. I still think that this extension is a help; the more Robertsonian conclusions, which then emerge, are easier to swallow; but I do not know feel that this extension goes far enough. It does not, even yet, carry the discussion fully over into the territory where it largely belongs.

Why is it, for instance, that anti-monopoly legislation (and litigation) get so little help, as they evidently do, from the textbook theory? Surely the answer is that the main issues of principle – security on the one side, freedom and equity on the other, the issues that lawyers, and law-makers, can understanding – have got left right out. They cannot be adequately translated even into the terms of surpluses.

One crucial example of this inadequacy, which deserves more extended treatment, is the Welfarist incomprehension of the role of advertisement. To the Welfarist, advertisement appears as sheer waste; but from the other side, although the abuses to which it is liable would of course be admitted, freedom of advertisement is the opposite number to freedom of the press. It is the hallmark of economic freedom, just as the other is of political freedom.

I do indeed recognise the core of truth in the doctine of 'consumer sovereignty' – that there is an ultimate sense of 'want' in which it is wise to assume that the consumer himself knows best what his wants are. But at the same time I would insist that he can do with a good deal of help in making the right choices for the satisfaction of his wants. His need for such help does indeed become of increasing importance with the growth of modern technology. A peasant people, which had been living for generations in much the same economic conditions, will have built up (by trial and error) a fair knowledge of how to take advantage of the limited opportunities available to it, and will have incorporated that knowledge in its social tradition. It is learned at the mother's knee, and handed down in the family. Modern people have no such inherited knowledge, with respect to the new opportunities available to them. They have to acquire it in other ways, and may not find it easy to acquire it. In spite of their greater opportunities, they may not use their opportunities anything like so well.

The best ways of utilising new opportunities may not be known to anyone; they may be in process of discovery. Nevertheless, at any particular time, there is in existence a body of such knowledge; there is therefore a problem of diffusing it. This, it is clear, is in a wide sense an educational problem; it can be dealt with, and is to some extent dealt with through the normal educational system. Diffusion of that kind is, however, a slow process, though not so slow as might appear at first, since children can (and do) educate their parents on these matters. It does not, however, eliminate the need for a form of adult education.

The chief means of adult education (to this end) which has hitherto been discovered is advertisement. When advertisement is considered in this light, it is seen to have a more active social (and economic) function that economists have always been prepared to allow to it. It is, I think, always allowed that informative advertising has an economic function. But when advertisement is regarded as a form of adult education, it becomes apparent that it will not be effective if it is merely informative – or, as we might well say, bleakly informative. The attention of the consumer has to be attracted, and his interest aroused. In order to perform its social function, advertisement has to be attractive and (let us not be afraid to say) persuasive.

If it has this real and important function, why does advertisement (even among economists) have on the whole a bad name? The reason, I would suggest, consists in the tying together of the two distinct services – that of providing the article, and of providing the information upon which the decision to buy is based.

It is easy to see why they get tied together; the producer himself is often in the best position to provide the information. But the identity of source has a natural tendency to bias. Even when it does not lead to bias – when the information provided is fair and generally informative – the expenditure upon advertisement may well be excessive, since it is determined in a way which is unrelated to its social function.

There is a real problem here, which must be encountered, sooner or later, by any economy which uses modern techniques and which is based upon division of labour. Those who are specialised to particular forms of production have an interest in seeing that the demand for their services is as large as it can be made. In some economies this is expressible in terms of the profit motive, but (granted specialisation, which is itself so essential a characteristic of efficient production) it must always be present in some form or other. One way of expanding demand is by inproving quality, another by lowering price; but a third is, inevitably, by persuasion. Some amount of such persuasion is socially advantageous; but it is more advantageous to the producer of the particular article than it is to the consumer of it. Thus, if the producer controls it, it may always be taken too far.

To return to the general issue. The liberal, or non-interference, principles of the classical (Smithian or Ricardian) economists were not, in the first place, economic principles; they were an application to economics of principles that were thought to apply over a much wider field. The contention that economic freedom made for economic efficiency was no more than a secondary support. As the nineteenth century wore on, the increasing specialisation of economics led to an increasing emphasis on the economic argument. Then it was discovered – it was rightly discovered – that the economic case for non-interference is riddled with exceptions: exceptions which may well have become more important in fact in the course of technological progress, and which certainly become of greater importance as the demands which were made on the economic system, in the direction of stability as well as of growth, became more exacting. Accordingly, since the other side of the case, which had at one time been the more important side, had been so largely forgotten, what had begun as an economic argument for non-interference became an economic argument for the opposite. I do not question that on its own assumptions that argument, in its latter form, was very largely right.

What I do question is whether we are justified in forgetting, as completely as most of us have done, the other side of the argument. Not that I wish to regard that 'non-economic' side as overriding; all that I claim for it is a place, and a regular place. I do not suppose that if we gave it this due attention, we should find ourselves subscribing, on that side, to all of the liberal principles of a century ago. We have not been helped to maintain our balance by the exaggerations to which the surviving adherents of those principles – for whom all controls are a 'Road to Serfdom' – have been prone. It is useless to close one's eyes to the defects of competition, because one is so much in love with an ideal competitive system, set up in heaven. Neither side should give way to the other; but there is no reason why there should not be scope for marginal adjustments, in great things as well as small.

If there is room for marginal adjustments, there is also room for a 'law of diminishing marginal significance' (or whatever we like to call it) that transcends the economic field. As wealth increases, wealth itself becomes (or should become) less important. At low levels of income, it is right to concentrate on economics; the first need of man is to fill his belly; politics are at best a distraction, at worst no better than communal drug-taking. But as wealth increases, there is room for other (and better) standards. It is no accident that the principles of liberal democracy were the work of those classes, first aristocratic, the bourgeois, who were the first to rise clean above subsistence, so that they had opportunity to turn round and time to think. That is no reason to be ashamed of those principles. The same opportunities – they are in large measure the same opportunities – are now being spread, in the more fortunate countries of the world, far and wide throughout society. We are not so 'affluent' that the need for more wealth has disappeared; but it has become *relatively* less urgent. The problems of combining security with freedom, equity with responsibility, come thereby more strongly to the fore.

But though there is a general presumption, when we look at things in this way, that the attainment of the liberal goods is facilitated by increases in wealth (that is as much as I would now retain of the harmony between economic and non-economic welfare that was assumed by Pigou), it would be too much to maintain that *all* increases in wealth must have so favourable an effect. It is possible, by policy, to increase wealth but to diminish freedom; it is possible, again, that the growth of knowledge, though it must in some sense increase wealth or the possibility of wealth (with some kind of a surplus of economic gains over losses), many diminish the opportunities for freedom. Technological progress is ethically neutral; what it gives with one hand, it can take with the other. The opportunities for freedom have, without doubt, not been enhanced by progress in the military arts; I see no reason why we should count upon progress in other techniques to be uniformly beneficent. Much of the concentration of power in the hands of large organisations, which is the major threat to freedom within Western societies, is technological, not sociological, in its origin.

I have accordingly no intention, in abandoning economic welfarism, of falling into the 'fiat libertas, ruat caelum' which some latter-day liberals seem to see as the only alternative. What I do maintain is that the liberal goods are goods; that they are values which, however, must be weighed up against other values. The freedom and the justice that are possible of attainment are not the same in all societies, at all times, and in all places; they are themselves conditioned by external environment, and (in the short period at least) by what has occurred in the past. Yet we can recognise these limitations, and still feel that these ends are worthier ends than those which are represented in a production index. It is better to think of economic activity as means to these ends, than as means to different ends, which are entirely its own.

Part III
Macroeconomics and Money

Part III contains five selections from Hicks' work on macroeconomics and money, all of which appeared in *CEET* II, *Money, Interest and Wages*. These selections fall under three headings: money, Keynesian theory and dynamics.

On money, Hicks wrote in 1935 'A Suggestion for Simplifying the Theory of Money' (essay 7 below), in which he applied his consumer theory (essay 1 above) to the theory of the demand for money. It is a statement of the 'microfoundations' of monetary theory. For subsequent comment on the paper, the reader is referred to his 'Two Triads' in *Critical Essays in Monetary Theory* (*CEMT*), to his comments on the origin of the paper in 'LSE and the Robbins Circle' in *CEET* II, and his 1962 paper on 'Liquidity'. The extension of monetary theory to a purely credit economy, of Wicksellian rather than Keynesian origin, is considered in essay 11 below, 'The Credit Economy'. For a fuller appreciation of that paper, the reader is referred to 'The Foundations of Monetary Theory' in *CEET* II, of which it forms a part, and to the third part of the 'Two Triads'.

Perhaps one of Hicks' most remembered papers, 'Mr Keynes and the Classics' is reproduced as essay 8 below. It launched the *IS–LM* diagram as an interpretation of Keynes' *General Theory*. The origin and development of that paper I have dealt with in my introduction. The reader is also referred to Hicks' other related papers: 'The General Theory: A First Impression' (1936) and 'The Classics Again' in *CEMT*. Hicks himself is rather less fond of that diagram, and thus his recent 1979 paper, '*IS–LM*' an Explanation', is included here as essay 10, giving his own re-interpretation.

The third area included here is dynamics. In 'Methods of Dynamic Analysis' (essay 9), the ideas of parts 3 and 4 of *Value and Capital* and *A Contribution to the Theory of the Trade Cycle* are developed, and a classification of models as between fix- and flex-price on the one hand, and *ex ante* and *ex post* on the other is proposed. The classification is explained in this paper, and needs no prefatory remarks. The reader is referred to *Capital and Growth* for further extensions.

7

A Suggestion for Simplifying the Theory of Money

This paper first appeared in *Economica*, February (1935).

I

After the thunderstorms of recent years, it is with peculiar diffidence and even apprehension that one ventures to open one's mouth on the subject of money.[1] In my own case these feelings are particularly intense, because I feel myself to be very much of a novice at the subject. My education has been mostly in the non-monetary parts of economics, and I have only come to be interested in money because I found that I could not keep it out of my non-monetary problems. Yet I am encouraged on reflection to hope that this may not prove a bad approach to the subject: that some things at least which are not very evident on direct inspection may become clearer from a cross-light of this sort.

It is, of course, very largely by such cross-fertilisation that economics progresses, and at least one department of non-monetary economics has hardly emerged from a very intimate affair with monetary theory. I do not, however, propose to resume this particular liaison. One understands that most economists have now read Böhm-Bawerk; yet whatever that union has bred, it has not been concord. I should prefer to seek illumination from another point of view – from a branch of economics which is more elementary, but, I think, in consequence better developed – the theory of value.

To anyone who comes over from the theory of value to the theory of money, there are a number of things which are rather startling. Chief of these is the preoccupation of monetary theorists with a certain equation, which states that the price of goods multiplied by the quantity of goods equals the amount of money which is spent on them. This equation crops up again and again, and it has all sorts

[1] The reader is asked to bear in mind the fact that the paper was written to be read aloud, and to excuse certain pieces of mischief.

of ingenious little arithmetical tricks performed on it. Sometimes it comes out as $MV = PT$, and once, in its most stupendous transfiguration, it blossomed into

$$P = \frac{E}{O} + \frac{I' - S}{R}$$

Now we, of the theory of value, are not unfamiliar with this equation, and there was a time when we used to attach as much importance to it as monetary theorists seem to do still. This was in the middle of the last century, when we used to talk about value being 'a ratio between demand and supply'. Even now, we accept the equation, and work it, more or less implicitly, into our systems. But we are rather inclined to take it for granted, since it is rather tautologous, and since we have found that another equation, not alternative to the quantity equation, but complementary with it, is much more significant. This is the equation which states that the relative value of two commodities depends upon their relative marginal utility.

Now, to an *ingénu*, who comes over to monetary theory, it is extremely trying to be deprived of this sheet-anchor. It was marginal utility that really made sense of the theory of value; and to come to a branch of economics which does without marginal utility altogether! No wonder there are such difficulties and such differences! What is wanted is a 'marginal revolution'!

That is my suggestion. But I know that it will meet with apparently crushing objections. I shall be told that the suggestion has been tried out before. It was tried by Wicksell, and though it led to interesting results, it did not lead to a marginal utility theory of money. It was tried by Mises, and led to the conclusion that money is a ghost of gold – because, so it appeared, money as such has no marginal utility.[2] The suggestion has a history, and its history is not encouraging.

[2] A more subtle form of the same difficulty appears in the work of Marshall and his followers. They were aware that money ought to be subjected to marginal utility analysis; but they were so dominated by the classical conception of money as a 'veil' (which is valid enough at a certain level of approximation) that they persisted in regarding the demand for money as a demand for the things which money can buy – 'real balances'. As a result of this, their invocation of marginal utility remained little more than a pious hope. For they were unable to distinguish, on marginal utility lines, between the desire to save and the desire to hoard; and they necessarily overlooked that indeterminateness in the 'real balance' (so important in some applications of monetary theory), which occurs when the prices of consumption goods are expected to change. On the other hand, I must admit that some versions of the Marshallian theory come very close to what I am driving at. Cf. F. Lavington, *English Capital Market*, ch. VI.

This would be enough to frighten one off, were it not for two things. Both in the theory of value and in the theory of money there have been developments in the twenty or thirty years since Wicksell and Mises wrote. And these developments have considerably reduced the barriers that blocked their way.

In the theory of value, the work of Pareto, Wicksteed, and their successors, has broadened and deepened our whole conception of marginal utility. We now realise that the marginal utility analysis is nothing else than a general theory of choice, which is applicable whenever the choice is between alternatives that are capable of quantitative expression. Now money is obviously capable of quantitative expression, and therefore the objection that money has no marginal utility must be wrong. People do choose to have money rather than other things, and therefore, in the relevant sense, money must have a marginal utility.

But merely to call that marginal utility X, and then proceed to draw curves, would not be very helpful. Fortunately the developments in monetary theory to which I alluded come to our rescue.

Mr Keynes's *Treatise*, so far as I have been able to discover, contains at least three theories of money. One of them is the Savings and Investment theory, which, as I hinted, seems to me only a quantity theory much glorified. One of them is a Wicksellian natural rate theory. But the third is altogether much more interesting. It emerges when Mr Keynes begins to talk about the price-level of investment goods; when he shows that this price-level depends upon the relative preference of the investor – to hold bank-deposits or to hold securities. Here at last we have something which to a value theorist looks sensible and interesting! Here at last we have a choice at the margin! And Mr Keynes goes on to put substance into our X, by his doctrine that the relative preference depends upon the 'bearishness' or 'bullishness' of the public, upon their relative desire for liquidity or profit.

My suggestion may, therefore, be re-formulated. It seems to me that this third theory of Mr Keynes really contains the most important of his theoretical contribution; that here, at last, we have something which, on the analogy (the appropriate analogy) of value theory, does begin to offer a chance of making the whole thing easily intelligible; that it is from this point, not from velocity of circulation, natural rate of interest, or Saving and Investment, that we ought to start in constructing the theory of money. But in saying this, I am being more Keynesian than Keynes; I must endeavour to defend my position in detail.

II

The essence of the method I am proposing is that we should take the position of an individual at a particular point of time, and enquire what determines the precise quantity of money which he will desire to hold. But even to this simple formulation of the problem it is necessary to append two footnotes.

1. *Point of Time*. We are dealing with an individual decision to hold money *or* something else, and such a decision is always made at a point of time. It is only by concentrating on decisions made at particular points of time that we can apply the theory of value to the problem at all. A very large amount of current controversy about money seems to me to be due to the attempt, superficially natural, but, in fact, highly inconvenient, to establish a close relation between the demand for money and *income*. Now the simple consideration that the decision to hold money is always made at a point of time shows that the connection between income and the demand for money must always be indirect. And in fact the whole conception of income is so intricate and beset by so many perplexing difficulties, that the establishment of any connection with income ought only to be hoped for at a late stage of investigation.[3]

2. *Money*. What sort of money are we considering? For the present, any sort of money. The following analysis will apply equally whether we think of money as notes, or bank deposits, or even metallic coins. It is true that with a metallic currency there is an ordinary commodity demand for the money substance to be considered, but it is relatively unimportant for most of our purposes. Perhaps it will be best if we take as our standard case that of a pure paper currency in a community where there are no banks. What follows has much wider application in reality. Only I would just ask you to keep this standard case in mind, since by using it as a basis for discussion, we may be able to save time a little.

An individual's decision to hold so much money means that he prefers to hold that amount of money, rather than either less or more. Now what are the precise contents of these displaced alternatives? He could reduce his holding of money in three ways:

(1)   by spending, i.e. buying something, it does not matter what;
(2)   by lending money to someone else;
(3)   by paying off debts which he owes to someone else.

[3] Cf. E. Lindahl, 'The Concept of Income' in *Essays in Honour of Gustav Cassel*.

He can increase his holding of money in three corresponding ways:

(1)   by selling something else which he owns;
(2)   by borrowing from someone else;
(3)   by demanding repayment of money which is owed by someone else.

This classification is, I think, complete. All ways of changing one's holding of money can be reduced to one of these classes or a combination of two of them – purchase or sale, the creation of new debts or the extinction of old.

If a person decides to hold money, it is implied that he prefers to do this than to adopt any of these three alternatives. But how is such a preference possible?

A preference for holding money instead of spending it on consumption goods presents no serious difficulty, for it is obviously the ordinary case of a preference for future satisfactions over present. At any moment, an individual will not usually devote the whole of his available resources to satisfying present wants – a part will be set aside to meet the needs of the future.

The critical question arises when we look for an explanation of the preference for holding money rather than capital goods. For capital goods will ordinarily yield a positive rate of return, which money does not. What has to be explained is the decision to hold assets in the form of barren money, rather than of interest- or profit-yielding securities. And obviously just the same question arises over our second and third types of utilisation. So long as rates of interest are positive, the decision to hold money rather than lend it, or use it to pay off old debts, is apparently an unprofitable one.

This, as I see it, is really the central issue in the pure theory of money. Either we have to give an explanation of the fact that people do hold money when rates of interest are positive, or we have to evade the difficulty somehow. It is the great traditional evasions which have led to Velocities of Circulation, Natural Rates of Interest, *et id genus omne.*[4]

Of course, the great evaders would not have denied that there must be some explanation of the fact. But they would have put it down to 'frictions', and since there was no adequate place for frictions in the rest of their economic theory, a theory of money based

---

[4] I do not wish to deny that these concepts have a use in their appropriate place – that is to say, in particular applications of monetary theory. But it seems to me that they are a nuisance in monetary theory itself, that they offer no help in elucidating the general principles of the working of money.

on frictions did not seem to them a promising field for economic analysis.

This is where I disagree. I think we have to look the frictions in the face, and see if they are really so refractory after all. This will, of course, mean that we cannot allow them to go to sleep under so vague a title.

III

The most obvious sort of friction, and undoubtedly one of the most important, is the cost of transferring assets from one form to another. This is of exactly the same character as the cost of transfer which acts as a certain impediment to change in all parts of the economic system; it doubtless comprises subjective elements as well as elements directly priced. Thus a person is deterred from investing money for short periods, partly because of brokerage charges and stamp duties, partly because it is not worth the bother.

The net advantage to be derived from investing a given quantity of money consists of the interest or profit earned less the cost of investment. It is only if this net advantage is expected to be positive (i.e. if the expected rate of interest ± capital appreciation or depreciation, is greater than the cost of investment) that it will pay to undertake the investment.

Now, since the expected interest increases both with the quantity of money to be invested and with the length of time for which it is expected that the investment will remain untouched, while the costs of investment are independent of the length of time, and (as a whole) will almost certainly increase at a diminishing rate as the quantity of money to be invested increases, it becomes clear that with any given level of costs of investment, it will not pay to invest money for less than a certain period, and in less than certain quantities. It will be profitable to hold assets for short periods, and in relatively small quantities, in monetary form.

Thus, so far as we can see at present, the amount of money a person will desire to hold depends upon three factors: the dates at which he expects to make payments in the future, the cost of investment, and the expected rate of return on investment. The further ahead the future payments, the lower the cost of investment, and the higher the expected rate of return on invested capital – the lower will be the demand for money.

However, this statement is not quite accurate. For although all these factors may react on the demand for money, they may be insufficient to determine it closely. Since the quantity of available money must generally rise to some minimum before it is profitable to invest it at all, and further investment will then proceed by rather discontinuous jumps for a while, we shall expect to find the demand for money on the part of private individuals, excepting the very well-to-do, fairly insensitive to changes of this sort. But this does not mean that they are unimportant. For among those who are likely to be sensitive, we have to reckon, not only the well-to-do, but also all business men who are administering capital which is not solely their own private property. And this will give us, in total, a good deal of sensitivity.

IV

Our first list of factors influencing the demand for money – the expected rate of interest, the cost of investment, and the expected period of investment – does, therefore, isolate some factors which are really operative; but even so, it is not a complete list. For we have also to take into account the fact, which is in reality of such enormous importance, that people's expectations are never precise expectations of the kind we have been assuming. They do not say to themselves 'this £100 I shall not want until June 1st' or 'this investment will yield 3.7 per cent'; or, if they do, it is only a kind of shorthand. Their expectations are always, in fact, surrounded by a certain penumbra of doubt; and the density of that penumbra is of immense importance for the problem we are considering.

The risk-factor comes into our problem in two ways: first, as affecting the expected period of investment; and second, as affecting the expected net yield of investment. There are certain differences between its ways of operation on these two lines; but, as we shall see, the resultant effects are broadly similar.

Where risk is present, the *particular* expectation of a riskless situation is replaced by a band of possibilities, each of which is considered more or less probable. It is convenient to represent these probabilities to oneself, in statistical fashion, by a mean value, and some appropriate measure of dispersion. (No single measure will be wholly satisfactory, but here this difficulty may be overlooked.) Roughly speaking, we may assume that a change in mean value with constant dispersion has much the same sort of effect as a change in the particular expectations we have been discussing before. The peculiar problem of risk therefore reduces to an examination of the consequences of a change in dispersion. Increased dispersion means increased uncertainty.

If, therefore, our individual, instead of knowing (or thinking he knows) that he will not want his £100 till June 1st, becomes afflicted by increased uncertainty; that is to say, while still thinking that June 1st is the most likely date, he now thinks that it will be very possible that he will want it before, although it is also very possible that he will not want it till after; what will be the effect on his conduct? Let us suppose that when the date was certain, the investment was marginal – in the sense that the expected yield only just outweighed the cost of investment. With uncertainty introduced in the way we have described, the investment now offers a chance of larger gain, but it is offset by an equal chance of equivalent loss. In this situation, I think we are justified in assuming that he will become less willing to undertake the investment.

If this is so, uncertainty of the period for which money is free will ordinarily act as a deterrent to investment. It should be observed that uncertainty may be increased, either by a change in objective facts on which estimates are based, or in the psychology of the individual, if his temperament changes in such a way as to make him less inclined to bear risks.

To turn now to the other uncertainty – uncertainty of the yield of investment. Here again we have a penumbra; and here again we seem to be justified in assuming that spreading of the penumbra, increased dispersion of the possibilities of yield, will ordinarily be a deterrent to investment. Indeed, without assuming this to be the normal case, it would be impossible to explain some of the most obvious of the observed facts of the capital market. This sort of risk, therefore, will ordinarily be another factor tending to increase the demand for money.

V

So far the effect of risk seems fairly simple; an increase in the risk of investment will act like a fall in the expected rate of net yield; an increase in the uncertainty of future out-payments will act like a shortening of the time which is expected to elapse before those out-payments; and all will ordinarily tend to increase the demand for money. But although this is what it comes down to in the end, the detailed working of the risk-factor is not so simple; and since these further complications have an important bearing upon monetary problems, we cannot avoid discussing them here.

It is one of the pecularities of risk that the total risk incurred when more than one risky investment is undertaken, does not bear any simple relation to the risk involved in each of the particular investments taken separately. In most cases, the 'law of large numbers' comes into play (quite how, cannot be discussed here), so that the risk incurred by undertaking a number of separate risky investments will be less than that which would have been incurred if the same total capital had been invested altogether in one direction. When the number of separate investments is very large, the total risk may sometimes be reduced very low indeed.

Now in a world where cost of investment was negligible, everyone would be able to take considerable advantage of this sort of risk-reduction. By dividing up his capital into small portions, and spreading his risks, he would be able to insure himself against any large total risk on the whole amount. But in actuality, the cost of investment, making it definitely unprofitable to invest less than a certain minimum amount in any particular direction, closes the possibility of risk-reduction along these lines to all those who do not possess the command over considerable quantities of capital. This has two consequences.

On the one hand, since most people do not possess sufficient resources to enable them to take much advantage of the law of large numbers, and since even the large capitalist cannot annihilate his risks altogether in this manner, there will be a tendency to spread capital over a number of investments, not for this purpose, but for another. By investing only a proportion of total assets in risky enterprises, and investing the remainder in ways which are considered more safe, it will be possible for the individual to adjust his whole risk-situation to that which he most prefers, more closely than he could do by investing in any single enterprise. It will be possible, for example, for him to feel fairly certain that in particular unfavourable eventualities he will not lose more than a certain amount. And, since, both with an eye on future commitments with respect to debt, and future needs for consumption, large losses will lay upon him a proportionately heavier burden than small losses, this sort of adjustment to the sort of chance of loss he is prepared to stand will be very well worth while.

We shall, therefore, expect to find our representative individual distributing his assets among relatively safe and relatively risky investments; and the distribution will be governed, once again, by subjective preference for much or little risk-bearing.

On the other hand, those persons who have command of large quantities of capital, and are able to spread their risks, are not only able to reduce the risk on their own capital fairly low – they are also able to offer very good security for the investment of an extra unit along with the rest. If, therefore, they choose to become borrowers, they are likely to be very safe borrowers. They can, therefore, provide the safe investments which their fellow-citizens need.

In the absence of such safe investments, the ordinary individual would be obliged to keep a very considerable proportion of his assets in monetary form, since money would be the only safe way of holding assets. The appearance of such safe investments will act as a substitute for money in one of its uses, and therefore diminish the demand for money.

This particular function is performed, in a modern community, not only by banks, but also by insurance companies, investment trusts, and, to a certain (perhaps small) extent, even by large concerns of other kinds, through their prior charges. And, of course, to a very large extent indeed, it is performed by government stock of various kinds.

Banks are simply the extreme case of this phenomenon; they are enabled to go further than other concerns in the creation of money substitutes, because the security of their promises to pay is accepted generally enough for it to be possible to make payments in those promises. Bank deposits are, therefore, enabled to substitute money still further, because the cost of investment is reduced by a general belief in the absence of risk.

This is indeed a difference so great as to be properly regarded as a difference in kind; but it is useful to observe that the creation of bank credit is not really different in its economic effects from the fundamentally similar activities of other businesses and other persons. The significant thing is that the person who deposits money with a bank does not notice any change in his liquidity position; he considers the bank deposit to be as liquid as cash. The bank, on the other hand, finds itself more liquid, if it retains the whole amount of the cash deposited; if it does not wish to be more liquid, but seeks (for example) to restore a conventional reserve ratio, it will have to increase its investments. But substantially the same sort of thing happens when anyone, whose credit is much above the average, borrows. Here the borrowing is nearly always a voluntary act on the part of the borrower, which would not be undertaken unless he was willing to become less liquid than before; the fact that he has to pay interest on the loan means that he will be made worse off if he does not spend the proceeds. On the other hand, if the borrower's credit is good, the liquidity of the lender will not be very greatly impaired by his making the loan, so that his demand for money is likely to be at least rather less than it was before the loan was made. Thus the net effect of the loan is likely to be 'inflationary', in the sense that the purchase of capital goods or securities by the borrower is likely to be a more important affair than any sale of capital goods or securities by the lender, made necessary in order for the lender to restore his liquidity position.

Does it follow that all borrowing and lending is inflationary in this sense? I do not think so; for let us take the case when the borrower's credit is very bad, and the lender is only tempted to lend by the offer of a very high rate of interest. Then the impairment of the lender's liquidity position will be very considerable; and he may feel it necessary to sell rather less risky securities to an even greater capital sum in order to restore his liquidity position. Here the net effect would be 'deflationary'.

The practical conclusion of this seems to be that while *voluntary* borrowing and lending is at least a symptom of monetary expansion, and is thus likely to be accompanied by rising prices, 'distress borrowing' is an exception to this rule; and it follows, further, that the sort of stimulation to lending, by persuading people to make loans which they would not have made without persuasion (which was rather a feature of certain phases of the world depression), is a dubious policy – for the lenders, perhaps without realising what they are doing, are very likely to try and restore their liquidity position, and so to offset, and perhaps more than offset, the expansive effects of the loan.

VI

It is now time for us to begin putting together the conclusions we have so far reached. Our method of analysis, it will have appeared, is simply an extension of the ordinary method of value theory. In value theory, we take a private individual's income and expenditure account; we ask which of the items in that account are under the individual's own control, and then how he will adjust these items in order to reach a most preferred position. On the production side, we make a similar analysis of the profit and loss account of the firm. My suggestion is that monetary theory needs to be based again upon a similar analysis, but this time, not of an income account, but of a capital account, a balance sheet. We have to concentrate on the forces which make assets and liabilities what they are.

So as far as banking theory is concerned, this is really the method which is currently adopted; though the essence of the problem is there somewhat obscured by the fact that banks, in their efforts to reach their 'most preferred position' are hampered or assisted by the existence of conventional or legally obligatory reserve ratios. For theoretical purposes, this fact ought only to be introduced at a rather late stage; if that is done, then my suggestion can be expressed by saying that we ought to regard every individual in the community as being, on a small scale, a bank. Monetary theory becomes a sort of generalisation of banking theory.

We shall have to draw up a sort of generalised balance sheet, suitable for all individuals and institutions. It will have to be so generalised that many of the individual items will, in a great many cases, not appear. But that does not matter for our purposes. Such a generalised balance sheet will presumably run much as follows.

Assets	*Liabilities*
Consumption goods – perishable	
Consumption goods – durable	
Money	
Bank deposits	
Short term debts	Short term debts
Long term debts	Long term debts
Stocks and shares	
Productive equipment (including goods in process)	

We have been concerned up to the present with an analysis (very sketchy, I am afraid) of the equilibrium of this balance sheet. This analysis has at least shown that the relative size of the different items on this balance sheet is governed mainly by anticipation of the yield of investments and of risks.[5] It is these anticipations which

---

[5] As we have seen, these risks are as much a matter of the period of investment as of the yield. For certain purposes this is very important. Thus, in the case of that kind of investment which consists in the starting of actual processes of production, the yield which is expected if the process can be carried through may be considerable; but the yield if the process has to be interrupted will be large and negative. Uncertainty of the period for which resources are free will therefore have a very powerful effect in interrupting production. Short-run optimism will usually be enough to start a Stock Exchange boom; but to start an industrial boom relatively long-run optimism is necessary.

play a part here corresponding to the part played by prices in value theory.[6]

Now the fact that our 'equilibrium' is here determined by subjective factors like anticipations, instead of objective factors like prices, means that this purely theoretical study of money can never hope to reach results so tangible and precise as those which value theory in its more limited field can hope to attain. If I am right, the whole problem of applying monetary theory is largely one of deducing changes in anticipations from the changes in objective data which call them forth. Obviously, this is not an easy task, and, above all, it is not one which can be performed in a mechanical fashion. It needs judgment and knowledge of business psychology much more than sustained logical reasoning. The arm-chair economist will be bad at it, but he can at least begin to realise the necessity for it, and learn to co-operate with those who can do it better than he can.

However, I am not fouling my own nest; I do not at all mean to suggest that economic theory comes here to the end of its resources. When once the connection between objective facts and anticipations has been made, theory comes again into its rights; and it will not be able to complain of a lack of opportunities.

Nevertheless, it does seem to me most important that, when considering these further questions, we should be well aware of the gap which lies behind us, and that we should bring out very clearly the assumptions which we are making about the genesis of anticipations. For this does seem to be the only way in which we can overcome the extraordinary theoretical differences of recent years, which are, I think very largely traceable to this source.

VII

Largely, but not entirely; or rather a good proportion of them seem to spring from a closely related source, which is yet not quite identical with the first. When we seek to apply to a changing world any particular sort of individual equilibrium, we need to know how the individual will respond, not only to changes in the price-stimuli, or

---

[6] I am aware that too little is said in this paper about the liabilities side of the above balance sheet. A cursory examination suggests that the same forces which work through the assets side work through the liabilities side in much the same way. But this certainly requires further exploration.

anticipation-stimuli, but also to a change in his total wealth.[7] How will he distribute an increment (or decrement) of wealth – supposing, as we may suppose, that this wealth is measured in monetary terms?

It may be observed that this second problem has an exact counterpart in value theory. Recent work in that field has shown the importance of considering carefully, not only how the individual reacts to price-changes, but also how he reacts to changes in his available expenditure. Total wealth, in our present problem, plays just the same part as total expenditure in the theory of value.

In the theory of money, what we particularly want to know is how the individual's demand for money will respond to a change in his total wealth – that is to say, in the value of his net assets. Not seeing any *a priori* reason why he should react in one way rather than another, monetary theorists have often been content to make use of the simplest possible assumption – that the demand for money will be increased in the same proportion as total net assets have increased.[8] But this is a very arbitrary assumption; and it may be called in question, partly for analytical reasons, and partly because it seems to make the economic system work much too smoothly to account for observed fact. As one example of this excessive smoothness, I may instance the classical theory of international payments; as another, Mr Harrod's views on the 'Expansion of Bank Credit' which have recently been interesting the readers of *Economica* and of the *Economist*.[9] It would hardly be too much to say that one observed fact alone is sufficient to prove that this assumption cannot be universally true (let us hope and pray that it is sometimes true, nevertheless) – the fact of the trade cycle. For if it were true, the monetary system would always exhibit a quite straightforward kind of stability; a diminished demand for money on the part of some people would raise the prices of capital goods and securities, and this would raise the demand for money on the part of the owners of those securities. Similarly an increased demand for money would lower prices, and this would lower the demand for money elsewhere.

---

[7] The amount of money demanded depends upon three groups of factors: (1) the individual's subjective preferences for holding money or other things; (2) his wealth; (3) his anticipations of future prices and risks. Changes in the demand for money affect present prices, but present prices affect the demand for money mainly through their effect on wealth and on price-anticipations.

[8] Of course, they say 'income'. But in this case 'income' can only be strictly interpreted as 'expected income'. And in most of the applications which are made, this works out in the same way as the assumption given above.

[9] The above was written before reading Mr Harrod's rejoinder to Mr Robertson. As I understand him, Mr Harrod is now only maintaining that the expansion of bank credit *may* work smoothly. With that I am in no disagreement.

The whole thing would work out like an ordinary demand and supply diagram. But it is fairly safe to say that we do not find this straightforward stability in practice.

The analytical reason why this sort of analysis is unsatisfactory is the following: the assumption of increased wealth leading to a proportionately increased demand for money is only plausible so long as the value of assets has increased, but other things have remained equal. Now, as we have seen, the other things which are relevant to this case are not prices (as in the theory of value) but anticipations, of the yield of investment and so on. And since these anticipations must be based upon objective facts, and an unexpected increase in wealth implies a change in objective facts, of a sort very likely to be relevant to the anticipations, it is fairly safe to assume that very many of the changes in wealth with which we are concerned will be accompanied by a change in anticipations. If this is so, the assumption of proportionate change in the demand for money loses most of its plausibility.

For if we assume (this is jumping over my gap, so I must emphasise that it is only an assumption) that an increase in wealth will very often be accompanied by an upward revision of expectations of yield, then the change will set in motion at least one tendency which is certain to diminish the demand for money. Taking this into account *as well as* the direct effect of the increase in wealth, the situation begins to look much less clear. For it must be remembered that our provisional assumption about the direct effect was only guess-work; there is no necessary reason why the direct effect should increase the demand for money proportionately or even increase it at all. So, putting the two together, it looks perfectly possible that the demand for money may either increase or diminish.

We are treading on thin ice; but the unpleasant possibilities which now begin to emerge are sufficiently plausible for their examination to be well worth while. What happens, to take a typical case, if the demand for money is independent of changes in wealth, so that neither an increase in wealth nor a diminution will affect the demand for money?

One can conceive of a sort of equilibrium in such a world, but it would be a hopelessly unstable equilibrium. For if any single person tried to increase his money holdings, and the supply of money was not increased, prices would all fall to zero. If any person tried to diminish his money holdings, prices would all become infinite. In fact, of course, if demand were so rigid, the system could only be kept going by a continuous and meticulous adaptation of the supply of money to the demand.

Further, in such a world, very curious results would follow from saving. A sudden increase in saving would leave some people (the owners of securities) with larger money balances than they had expected; other people (the producers of consumption goods) with smaller money balances. If, in their efforts to restore their money holdings, the owners of securities buy more securities, and the producers of consumption goods buy less consumption goods, a swing of prices, consumption goods prices falling, security prices rising, would set in, and might go on indefinitely. It could only be stopped, either by the owners of securities buying the services of producers, or by the producers selling securities. But there is no knowing when this would happen, or where prices would finally settle; for the assumption of a rigid demand for money snaps the connecting link between money and prices.

After this, we shall be fairly inured to shocks. It will not surprise us to be told that wage-changes will avail nothing to stop either an inflation or a deflation, and we shall be able to extend the proposition for ourselves to interference with conventional or monopolistic prices of any kind, in any direction. But we shall be in a hurry to get back to business.

VIII

These exercises in the economics of an utterly unstable world give us something too mad to fit even our modern *Spätkapitalismus*; but the time which economists have spent on them will not have been wasted if they have served as a corrective to the too facile optimism engendered by the first assumption we tried. Obviously, what we want is something between the two – but not, I think, a mere splitting of the difference. This would give the assumption that an increase in wealth always raises the demand for money, but less than proportionately; if we had time, it might be profitable to work out this case in detail. It would allow for the possibility of considerable fluctuations, but they would not be such absurd and hopeless fluctuations as in the case of rigid demand.

However, I think we can do better than that. The assumption which seems to me most plausible, most consistent with the whole trend of our analysis, and at the same time to lead to results which at any rate look realistic, is one which stresses the probable differences in the reactions of different members of the **community**. We have already seen that a considerable proportion of a **community's** monetary stock is always likely to be in the hands of people who are obliged by their relative poverty to be fairly insensitive to changes in anticipations. For these people, therefore, most of the incentive to reduce their demand for money when events turn out more favourably will be missing; there seems no reason why we should not suppose that they will generally react 'positively' to changes in their wealth – that an increase in wealth will raise their demand for money more or less proportionately, a fall in their wealth will diminish it. But we must also allow for the probability that other people are much more *sensitive* – that an increase in wealth is not particularly likely to increase their demand for money, and may very well diminish it.

If this is so, it would follow that where the sensitive trade together, price-fluctuations may start on very slight provocation; and once they are under way, the rather less sensitive would be enticed in. Stock Exchange booms will pass over into industrial booms, if industrial entrepreneurs are also fairly sensitive; and, in exactly the same way, stock exchange depressions will pass into industrial depressions. But the insensitive are always there to act as a flywheel, defeating by their insensitivity both the exaggerated optimism and the exaggerated pessimism of the sensitive class. How this comes about I cannot attempt to explain in detail, though it would be an interesting job, for one might be able to reconcile a good many apparently divergent theories. But it would lead us too deeply into Cycle theory – I will only say that I think the period of fluctuation turns out to depend, in rather complex fashion, upon the distribution of sensitivity and the distribution of production periods between industrial units.

Instead, I may conclude with two general reflections.

If it is the insensitive people who preserve the stability of capitalism, people who are insensitive (you will remember) largely because for them the costs of transferring assets are large relatively to the amount of assets they control, then the development of capitalism by diminishing these costs, is likely to be a direct cause of increasing fluctuations. It reduces costs in two ways: by technical devices (of which banks are only one example), and by instilling a more 'capitalistic' spirit, which looks more closely to profit, and thus reduces subjective costs. In doing these things, capitalism is its own enemy for it imperils that stability without which it breaks down.

Lastly, it seems to follow that when we are looking for policies which make for economic stability, we must not be led aside by a feeling that monetary troubles are due to 'bad' economic policy, in the old sense, that all would go well if we reverted to free trade and *laisser faire*. In so doing, we are no better than the Thebans who ascribed the plague to blood-guiltiness, or the supporters of Mr Roosevelt who expect to reach recovery through reform. There is no reason why policies which tend to economic welfare, statically considered, should also tend to monetary stability. Indeed, the presumption is rather the other way round. A tariff, for example, may be a very good instrument of recovery on occasion, for precisely the reason which free-traders deplore; that it harms a great many people a little for the conspicuous benefit of a few. That may be just the sort of measure we want.

These will be unpalatable conclusions; but I think we must face the possibility that they are true. They offer the economist a pretty hard life, for he, at any rate, will not be able to have a clear conscience either way, over many of the alternatives he is called upon to consider. His ideals will conflict and he will not be able to seek an easy way out by sacrificing either.

8

Mr Keynes and the Classics

This paper was published in *Econometrica*, April (1937).

I

It will be admitted by the least charitable reader that the entertainment value of Mr Keynes's *General Theory of Employment* is considerably enhanced by its satiric aspect. But it is also clear that many readers have been left very bewildered by this Dunciad. Even if they are convinced by Mr Keynes's arguments and humbly acknowledge themselves to have been 'classical economists' in the past, they find it hard to remember that they believed in their unregenerate days the things Mr Keynes says they believed. And there are no doubt others who find their historic doubts a stumbling block, which prevents them from getting as much illumination from the positive theory as they might otherwise have got.

One of the main reasons for this situation is undoubtedly to be found in the fact that Mr Keynes takes as typical of 'Classical economics' the later writings of Professor Pigou, particularly *The Theory of Unemployment*. Now *The Theory of Unemployment* is a fairly new book, and an exceedingly difficult book; so that it is safe to say that it has not yet made much impression on the ordinary teaching of economics. To most people its doctrines seem quite as strange and novel as the doctrines of Mr Keynes himself; so that to be told that he has believed these things himself leaves the ordinary economist quite bewildered.

For example, Professor Pigou's theory runs, to a quite amazing extent, in real terms. Not only is his theory a theory of real wages and unemployment; but numbers of problems which anyone else would have preferred to investigate in money terms are investigated by Professor Pigou in terms of 'wage-goods'. The ordinary classical economist has no part in this *tour de force*.

But if, on behalf of the ordinary classical economist, we declare that he would have preferred to investigate many of those problems in money terms, Mr Keynes will reply that there is no classical theory of money wages and employment. It is quite true that such a theory cannot easily be found in the textbooks. But this is only because most of the textbooks were written at a time when general changes in money wages in a closed system did not present an important problem. There can be little doubt that most economists have thought that they had a pretty fair idea of what the relation between money wages and employment actually was.

In these circumstances, it seems worth while to try to construct a typical 'classical' theory, built on an earlier and cruder model than Professor Pigou's. If we can construct such a theory, and show that it does give results which have in fact been commonly taken for granted, but which do not agree with Mr Keynes's conclusions, then we shall at last have a satisfactory basis of comparison. We may hope to be able to isolate Mr Keynes's innovations, and so to discover what are the real issues in dispute.

Since our purpose is comparison, I shall try to set out my typical classical theory in a form similar to that in which Mr Keynes sets out his own theory; and I shall leave out of account all secondary complications which do not bear closely upon this special question in hand. Thus I assume that I am dealing with a short period in which the quantity of physical equipment of all kinds available can be taken as fixed. I assume homogeneous labour. I assume further that depreciation can be neglected, so that the output of investment goods corresponds to new investment. This is a dangerous simplification, but the important issues raised by Mr Keynes in his chapter on user cost are irrelevant for our purposes.

Let us begin by assuming that w, the rate of money wages per head, can be taken as given.

Let x, y, be the outputs of investment goods and consumption goods respectively, and N_x, N_y, be the numbers of men employed in producing them. Since the amount of physical equipment specialised to each industry is given, $x = f_x(N_x)$ and $y = f_y(N_y)$, where f_x, f_y, are *given* functions.

Let M be the *given* quantity of money.

It is desired to determine N_x and N_y.

First, the price-level of investment goods = their marginal cost = $w(dN_x/dx)$. And the price-level of consumption goods = their marginal cost = $w(dN_y/dy)$.

Income earned in investment trades (value of investment, or simply Investment) = $wx(dN_x/dx)$. Call this I_x.

Income earned in consumption trades = $wy\,(dN_y/dy)$.
Total Income = $wx(dN_x/dx) + wy\,(dN_y/dy)$. Call this I.
I_x is therefore a given function of N_x, I of N_x and N_y. Once I and I_x are determined, N_x and N_y can be determined.

Now let us assume the 'Cambridge Quantity equation' – that there is some definite relation between Income and the demand for money. Then, approximately, and apart from the fact that the demand for money may depend not only upon total Income, but also upon its distribution between people with relatively large and relatively small demands for balances, we can write

$$M = kI.$$

As soon as k is given, total Income is therefore determined.

In order to determine I_x, we need two equations. One tells us that the amount of investment (looked at as demand for capital) depends upon the rate of interest:

$$I_x = C(i).$$

This is what becomes the marginal-efficiency-of-capital schedule in Mr Keynes's work.

Further, Investment = Saving. And saving depends upon the rate of interest and, if you like, Income. $\therefore\ I_x = S(i, I)$. (Since, however, Income is already determined, we do not need to bother about inserting Income here unless we choose.)

Taking them as a system, however, we have three fundamental equations,

$$M = kI, \quad I_x = C(i), \quad I_x = S(i, I),$$

to determine three unknowns, I, I_x, i. As we have found earlier, N_x and N_y can be determined from I and I_x. Total employment, $N_x + N_y$, is therefore determined.

Let us consider some properties of this system. It follows directly from the first equation that as soon as k and M are given, I is completely determined; that is to say, total income depends directly upon the quantity of money. Total employment, however, is not necessarily determined at once from income, since it will usually depend to some extent upon the proportion of income saved, and thus upon the way production is divided between investment and consumption-goods trades. (If it so happened that the elasticities of supply were the same in each of these trades, then a shifting of demand between them would produce compensating movements in N_x and N_y, and consequently no change in total employment.)

An increase in the inducement to invest (i.e. a rightward movement of the schedule of the marginal efficiency of capital, which we have written as $C(i)$), will tend to raise the rate of interest, and so to affect saving. If the amount of saving rises, the amount of investment will rise too; labour will be employed more in the investment trades, less in the consumption trades; this will increase total employment if the elasticity of supply in the investment trades is greater than that in the consumption-goods trades – diminish it if *vice versa*.

An increase in the supply of money will necessarily raise total income, for people will increase their spending and lending until incomes have risen sufficiently to restore k to its former level. The rise in income will tend to increase employment, both in making consumption goods and in making investment goods. The total effect on employment depends upon the ratio between the expansions of these industries; and that depends upon the proportion of their increased incomes which people desire to save, which also governs the rate of interest.

So far we have assumed the rate of money wages to be given; but so long as we assume that k is independent of the level of wages, there is no difficulty about this problem either. A rise in the rate of money wages will necessarily diminish employment and raise real wages. For an unchanged money income cannot continue to buy an unchanged quantity of goods at a higher price-level; and, unless the price-level rises, the prices of goods will not cover their marginal costs. There must therefore be a fall in employment; as employment falls, marginal costs in terms of labour will diminish and therefore real wages rise. (Since a change in money wages is always accompanied by a change in real wages in the same direction, if not in the same proportion, no harm will be done, and some advantage will perhaps be secured, if one prefers to work in terms of real wages. Naturally most 'classical economists' have taken this line.)

I think it will be agreed that we have here a quite reasonably consistent theory, and a theory which is also consistent with the pronouncements of a recognisable group of economists. Admittedly it follows from this theory that you may be able to increase employment by direct inflation; but whether or not you decide to favour that policy still depends upon your judgment about the probable reaction on wages, and also – in a national area – upon your views about the international standard.

Historically, this theory descends from Ricardo, though it is not actually Ricardian; it is probably more or less the theory that was held by Marshall. But with Marshall it was already beginning to be

qualified in important ways; his successors have qualified it still
further. What Mr Keynes has done is to lay enormous emphasis on
the qualifications, so that they almost blot out the original theory.
Let us follow out this process of development.

II

When a theory like the 'classical' theory we have just described is
applied to the analysis of industrial fluctuations, it gets into difficulties in several ways. It is evident that total money income experiences great variations in the course of a trade cycle, and the classical
theory can only explain these by variations in M or in k, or, as a third
and last alternative, by changes in distribution.

1.   Variation in M is simplest and most obvious, and has been relied
on to a large extent. But the variations in M that are traceable during
a trade cycle are variations that take place through the banks – they
are variations in bank loans; if we are to rely on them it is urgently
necessary for us to explain the connection between the supply of
bank money and the rate of interest. This can be done roughly by
thinking of banks as persons who are strongly inclined to pass on
money by lending rather than spending it. Their action therefore
tends at first to lower interest rates, and only afterwards, when the
money passes into the hands of spenders, to raise prices and incomes.
'The new currency, or the increase of currency, goes, not to private
persons, but to the banking centres; and therefore, it increases the
willingness of lenders to lend in the first instance, and lowers the rate
of discount. But it afterwards raises prices; and therefore it tends to
increase discount.'[1] This is superficially satisfactory; but if we
endeavoured to give a more precise account of this process we should
soon get into difficulties. What determines the amount of money
needed to produce a given fall in the rate of interest? What determines the length of time for which the low rate will last? These are
not easy questions to answer.

2.   In so far as we rely upon changes in k, we can also do well
enough up to a point. Changes in k can be related to changes in
confidence, and it is realistic to hold that the rising prices of a boom
occur because optimism encourages a reduction in balances; the
falling prices of a slump because pessimism and uncertainty dictate

[1] A. Marshall, *Money, Credit, and Commerce*, p. 257.

an increase. But as soon as we take this step it becomes natural to ask whether k has not abdicated its status as an independent variable, and has not become liable to be influenced by others among the variables in our fundamental equations.

3. This last consideration is powerfully supported by another, of more purely theoretical character. On grounds of pure value theory, it is evident that the direct sacrifice made by a person who holds a stock of money is a sacrifice of interest; and it is hard to believe that the marginal principle does not operate at all in this field. As Lavington put it: 'The quantity of resources which (an individual) holds in the form of money will be such that the unit of money which is just and only just worth while holding in this form yields him a return of convenience and security equal to the yield of satisfaction derived from the marginal unit spent on consumables, and equal also to the net rate of interest.'[2] The demand for money depends upon the rate of interest! The stage is set for Mr Keynes.

As against the three equations of the classical theory,

$$M = kI, \quad I_x = C(i), \quad I_x = S(i, I),$$

Mr Keynes begins with three equations,

$$M = L(i), \quad I_x = C(i), \quad I_x = S(I).$$

These differ from the classical equations in two ways. On the one hand, the demand for money is conceived as depending upon the rate of interest (Liquidity Preference). On the other hand, any possible influence of the rate of interest on the amount saved out of a given income is neglected. Although it means that the third equation becomes the multiplier equation, which performs such queer tricks, nevertheless this second amendment is a mere simplification, and ultimately insignificant.[3] It is the liquidity preference doctrine which is vital.

---

[2] F. Lavington, *English Capital Market*, 1921, p. 30. See also A. C. Pigou, 'The Exchange-Value of Legal-Tender Money', in *Essays in Applied Economics*, 1922, pp. 179–81.

[3] This can be readily seen if we consider the equations

$$M = kI, \quad I_x = C(i), \quad I_x = S(I),$$

which embody Mr Keynes's second amendment without his first. The third equation is already the multiplier equation, but the multiplier is shorn of his wings. For since I still depends only on M, I_x now depends only on M, and it is impossible to increase investment without increasing the willingness to save or the quantity of money. The system thus generated is therefore identical with that which, a few years ago, used to be called the 'Treasury View'. But Liquidity Preference transports us from the 'Treasury View' to the 'General Theory of Employment'.

For it is now the rate of interest, not income, which is determined by the quantity of money. The rate of interest set against the schedule of the marginal efficiency of capital determines the value of investment; that determines income by the multiplier. Then the volume of employment (at given wage-rates) is determined by the value of investment and of income which is not saved but spent upon consumption goods.

It is this system of equations which yields the startling conclusion, that an increase in the inducement to invest, or in the propensity to consume, will not tend to raise the rate of interest, but only to increase employment. In spite of this, however, and in spite of the fact that quite a large part of the argument runs in terms of this system, and this system alone, *it is not the General Theory*. We may call it, if we like, Mr Keynes's *special theory*. The General Theory is something appreciably more orthodox.

Like Lavington and Professor Pigou, Mr Keynes does not in the end believe that the demand for money can be determined by one variable alone – not even the rate of interest. He lays more stress on it than they did, but neither for him nor for them can it be the only variable to be considered. The dependence of the demand for money on interest does not, in the end, do more than qualify the old dependence on income. However much stress we lay upon the 'speculative motive', the 'transactions motive' must always come in as well.

Consequently we have for the General Theory

$$M = L(I, i), \quad I_x = C(i), \quad I_x = S(I).$$

With this revision, Mr Keynes takes a big step back to Marshallian orthodoxy, and his theory becomes hard to distinguish from the revised and qualified Marshallian theories, which, as we have seen, are not new. Is there really any difference between them, or is the whole thing a sham fight? Let us have recourse to a diagram (Fig. 8.1).

Against a given quantity of money, the first equation, $M = L(I, i)$ gives us a relation between Income (I) and the rate of interest (i). This can be drawn out as a curve (LL) which will slope upwards since an increase in income tends to raise the demand for money and an increase in the rate of interest tends to lower it. Further, the second two equations taken together give us another relation between Income and interest. (The marginal-efficiency-of-capital schedule determines the value of investment at any given rate of interest, and the multiplier tells us what level of income will be necessary to make savings equal to that value of investment.) The curve IS can therefore be drawn showing the relation between Income and interest which must be maintained in order to make saving equal to investment.

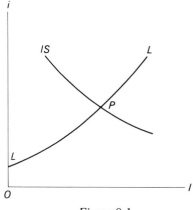

Figure 8.1

Income and the rate of interest are now determined together at P, the point of intersection of the curves LL and IS. They are determined together; just as price and output are determined together in the modern theory of demand and supply. Indeed, Mr Keynes's innovation is closely parallel, in this respect, to the innovation of the marginalists. The quantity theory tries to determine income without interest, just as the labour theory of value tried to determine price without output; each has to give place to a theory recognising a higher degree of interdependence.

III

But if this is the real 'General Theory', how does Mr Keynes come to make his remarks about an increase in the inducement to invest not raising the rate of interest? It would appear from our diagram that a rise in the marginal-efficiency-of-capital schedule must raise the curve IS; and, therefore, although it will raise Income and employment, it will also raise the rate of interest.

This brings us to what, from many points of view, is the most important thing in Mr Keynes's book. It is not only possible to show that a given supply of money determines a certain relation between Income and interest (which we have expressed by the curve LL); it is also possible to say something about the shape of the curve. It will probably tend to be nearly horizontal on the left, and nearly vertical on the right. This is because there is (1) some minimum below which the rate of interest is unlikely to go, and (though Mr Keynes does not stress this) there is (2) a maximum to the level of income which can possibly be financed with a given amount of money. If we like we can think of the curve as approaching these limits asymptotically (Fig. 8.2).

Therefore, if the curve *IS* lies well to the right (either because of a strong inducement to invest or a strong propensity to consume), *P* will lie upon that part of the curve which is decidedly upward sloping, and the classical theory will be a good approximation, needing no more than the qualification which it has in fact received at the hands of the later Marshallians. An increase in the inducement to invest will raise the rate of interest, as in the classical theory, but it will also have some subsidiary effect in raising income, and therefore employment as well. (Mr Keynes in 1936 is not the first Cambridge economist to have a temperate faith in Public Works.) But if the point *P* lies to the left of the *LL* curve, then the *special* form of Mr Keynes's theory

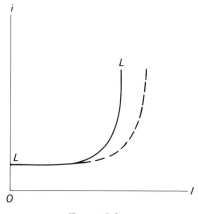

Figure 8.2

becomes valid. A rise in the schedule of the marginal efficiency of capital only increases employment, and does not raise the rate of interest at all. We are completely out of touch with the classical world.

The demonstration of this minimum is thus of central importance. It is so important that I shall venture to paraphrase the proof, setting it out in a rather different way from that adopted by Mr Keynes.[4]

---

[4] *General Theory*, pp. 201-2.

If the costs of holding money can be neglected, it will always be profitable to hold money rather than lend it out, if the rate of interest is not greater than zero. Consequently the rate of interest must always be positive. In an extreme case, the shortest short-term rate may perhaps be nearly zero. But if so, the long-term rate must lie above it, for the long rate has to allow for the risk that the short rate may rise during the currency of the loan, and it should be observed that the short rate can only rise, it cannot fall.[5] This does not only mean that the long rate must be a sort of average of the probable short rates over its duration, and that this average must lie above the current short rate. There is also the more important risk to be considered, that the lender on long term may desire to have cash before the agreed date of repayment, and then, if the short rate has risen meanwhile, he may be involved in a substantial capital loss. It is this last risk which provides Mr Keynes's 'speculative motive' and which ensures that the rate for loans of indefinite duration (which he always has in mind as *the* rate of interest) cannot fall very near zero.[6]

It should be observed that this minimum to the rate of interest applies not only to one curve *LL* (drawn to correspond to a particular quantity of money) but to any such curve. If the supply of money is increased, the curve *LL* moves to the right (as the dotted curve in Fig. 8.2), but the horizontal parts of the curve are almost the same. Therefore, again, it is this doldrum to the left of the diagram which upsets the classical theory. If *IS* lies to the right, then we can indeed increase employment by increasing the quantity of money; but if *IS* lies to the left, we cannot do so; merely monetary means will not force down the rate of interest any further.

So the General Theory of Employment is the Economics of Depression.

[5] It is just conceivable that people might become so used to the idea of very low short rates that they would not be much impressed by this risk; but it is very unlikely. For the short rate may rise, either because trade improves, and income expands; or because trade gets worse, and the desire for liquidity increases. I doubt whether a monetary system so elastic as to rule out both of these possibilities is really thinkable.

[6] Nevertheless something more than the 'speculative motive' is needed to account for the system of interest rates. The shortest of all short rates must equal the relative valuation, at the margin, of money and such a bill; and the bill stands at a discount mainly because of the 'convenience and security' of holding money – the inconvenience which may possibly be caused by not having cash immediately available. It is the chance that you may want to discount the bill which matters, not the chance that you will then have to discount it on unfavourable terms. The 'precautionary motive', not the 'speculative motive', is here dominant. But the prospective terms of rediscounting are vital, when it comes to the *difference* between short and long rates.

IV

In order to elucidate the relation between Mr Keynes and the 'Classics', we have invented a little apparatus. It does not appear that we have exhausted the uses of that apparatus, so let us conclude by giving it a little run on its own.

With that apparatus at our disposal, we are no longer obliged to make certain simplifications which Mr Keynes makes in his exposition. We can reinsert the missing i in the third equation, and allow for any possible effect of the rate of interest upon saving; and, what is much more important, we can call in question the sole dependence of investment upon the rate of interest, which looks rather suspicious in the second equation. Mathematical elegance would suggest that we ought to have I and i in all three equations, if the theory is to be really General. Why not have them there like this:

$$M = L(I, i), \quad I_x = C(I, i), \quad I_x = S(I, i)?$$

Once we raise the question of Income in the second equation, it is clear that it has a very good claim to be inserted. Mr Keynes is in fact only enabled to leave it out at all plausibly by his device for measuring everything in 'wage-units', which means that he allows for changes in the marginal-efficiency-of-capital schedule when there is a change in the level of money wages, but that other changes in Income are deemed not to affect the curve, or at least not in the same immediate manner. But why draw this distinction? Surely there is every reason to suppose that an increase in the demand for consumers' goods, arising from an increase in employment, will often directly stimulate an increase in investment, at least as soon as an expectation develops that the increased demand will continue. If this is so, we ought to include I in the second equation, though it must be confessed that the effect of I on the marginal efficiency of capital will be fitful and irregular.

The Generalised General Theory can be set out in this way. Assume first of all a given total money Income. Draw a curve CC showing the marginal efficiency of capital (in money terms) at that given Income; a curve SS showing the supply curve of saving at that *given* Income (Fig. 8.3). Their intersection will determine the rate of interest which makes savings equal to investment at that level of income. This we may call the 'investment rate'.

If Income rises, the curve SS will move to the right; probably CC will move to the right too. If SS moves more than CC, the investment rate of interest will fall; if CC more than SS, it will rise. (How much

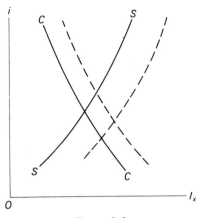

Figure 8.3

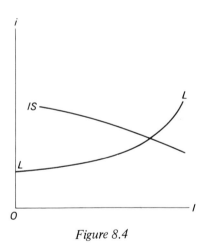

Figure 8.4

it rises and falls, however, depends upon the elasticities of the *CC* and *SS* curves.)

The *IS* curve (drawn on a separate diagram, Fig. 8.4) now shows the relation between Income and the corresponding investment rate of interest. It has to be confronted (as in our earlier constructions) with an *LL* curve showing the relation between Income and the 'money' rate of interest; only we can now generalise our *LL* curve a little. Instead of assuming, as before, that the supply of money is given, we can assume that there is a given monetary system – that up to a point, but only up to a point, monetary authorities will prefer to create new money rather than allow interest rates to rise. Such a generalised *LL* curve will then slope upwards only gradually – the elasticity of the curve depending on the elasticity of the monetary system (in the ordinary monetary sense).

As before, Income and interest are determined where the *IS* and *LL* curves intersect – where the investment rate of interest equals the money rate. Any change in the inducement to invest or the propensity to consume will shift the *IS* curve; any change in liquidity preference or monetary policy will shift the *LL* curve. If, as the result of such a change, the investment rate is raised above the money rate, Income will tend to rise; in the opposite case, Income will tend to fall; the extent to which Income rises or falls depends on the elasticities of the curves.[7]

When generalised in this way, Mr Keynes's theory begins to look very like Wicksell's; this is, of course, hardly surprising.[8] There is indeed one special case where it fits Wicksell's construction absolutely. If there is 'full employment' in the sense that any rise in Income immediately calls forth a rise in money wage rates; then it is *possible* that the *CC* and *SS* curves may be moved to the right to exactly the same extent, so that *IS* is horizontal. (I say possible, because it is not unlikely, in fact, that the rise in the wage level may create a presumption that wages will rise again later on; if so, *CC* will probably be shifted more than *SS*, so that *IS* will be upward sloping.) However that may be, if *IS* is horizontal, we do have a perfectly Wicksellian construction;[9] the investment rate bècomes Wicksell's *natural rate*, for in this case it may be thought of as determined by real causes; if there is a perfectly elastic monetary system, and the money rate

---

[7] Since $C(I, i) = S(I, i)$,

$$\frac{dI}{di} = -\frac{\partial S/\partial i - \partial C/\partial i}{\partial S/\partial I - \partial C/\partial I}$$

The savings investment market will not be stable unless $\partial S/\partial i + (-\partial C/\partial i)$ is positive. I think we may assume that this condition is fulfilled.

If $\partial S/\partial i$ is positive, $\partial C/\partial i$ negative, $\partial S/\partial I$ and $\partial C/\partial I$ positive (the most probable state of affairs), we can say that the *IS* curve will be more elastic, the greater the elasticities of the *CC* and *SS* curves, and the larger is $\partial C/\partial I$ relatively to $\partial S/\partial I$. When $\partial C/\partial I > \partial S/\partial I$, the *IS* curve is upward sloping.

[8] Cf. *General Theory*, p. 242.

[9] Cf. G. Myrdal, *Monetary Equilibrium* (see *CEET* II, p. 44).

is fixed below the natural rate, there is cumulative inflation; cumulative deflation if it is fixed above.

This, however, is now seen to be only one special case; we can use our construction to harbour much wider possibilities. If there is a great deal of unemployment, it is very likely that $\partial C/\partial I$ will be quite small; in that case IS can be relied upon to slope downwards. This is the sort of Slump Economics with which Mr Keynes is largely concerned. But one cannot escape the impression that there may be other conditions when expectations are tinder, when a slight inflationary tendency lights them up very easily. Then $\partial C/\partial I$ may be large and an increase in Income tend to *raise* the investment rate of interest. In these circumstances, the situation is unstable at *any* given money rate; it is only an imperfectly elastic monetary system – a rising LL curve – that can prevent the situation getting out of hand altogether.

These, then, are a few of the things we can get out of our skeleton apparatus. But even if it may claim to be a slight extension of Mr Keynes's similar skeleton, it remains a terribly rough and ready sort of affair. In particular, the concept of 'Income' is worked monstrously hard; most of our curves are not really determinate unless something is said about the distribution of Income as well as its magnitude. Indeed, what they express is something like a relation between the price-system and the system of interest rates; and you cannot get that into a curve. Further, all sorts of questions about depreciation have been neglected; and all sorts of questions about the timing of the processes under consideration.

The *General Theory of Employment* is a useful book; but it is neither the beginning nor the end of Dynamic Economics.

9

Methods of Dynamic Analysis

This essay was originally published in 1956 by the *Ekonomisk Tidschrift*, Stockholm, in a volume in honour of Erik Lindahl, entitled *25 Economic Essays in English, Germany and Scandinavian Languages*. The 'Addendum on Fixprice Method' at the end was added in *CEET* II (1982).

One of the greatest changes which has come over economic theory in the last thirty years (1925–55) is the transformation of economic dynamics from a pious aspiration into a respectable body of principles. It is, however, true that these principles do not quite fit together into a single coherent whole; they are still the fruits of different, though obviously related, lines of approach. What I propose to do in this paper is to make some examination of the relations which these approaches bear to one another.[1]

I

As was long ago discovered, it is impossible to make a study of method without saying something about scope. But what I have to say about scope can be kept brief and simple. For though the scope of economic dynamics has been defined in several ways, it turns out, on examination, that some of these definitions are in fact announce-

---

[1] My subject is one that has already been worked over by Erik Lindahl (see the first chapter of his *Studies in the Theory of Money and Capital*). My debt to that work (and to the corresponding parts of E. Lundberg's *Economic Expansion*) will be apparent as I proceed. But I may perhaps add at this point that since I have myself been led on different occasions (in the latter parts of *Value and Capital* on the one hand, and in my *Contribution to the Theory of the Trade Cycle* on the other) to approach dynamic theory by what look like quite different routes, one of my objects in writing has been to build a bridge between my own approaches.

ments of the *method* which the writer who advances them proposes to use; while others are restrictive definitions, which define that part of the general dynamic field on which the writer proposes to concentrate. If we look for a definition which shall define scope not method, and which shall embrace the whole of the field which practice treats as dynamic, the kind of definition to which we must come is fairly obvious. I shall take it to be the theoretical analysis of the *process of economic change*. So defined, the subject includes the study of fluctuation as well as that of growth; it includes the study of change in particular markets as well as in the whole economy; and no commitment is made in advance about the method by which the subject is to be examined. The question of method remains as a separate question; but before we pass on to that question, there is one consequence of this definition of scope which is worth a mention in passing.

One of the advantages of defining dynamics as the study of the process of change is that it does something to rehabilitate statics. For dynamics is left as much less than the whole of economics. Dynamic economists, who are (very properly) excited by what they are doing, are often tempted to make excessive claims for it. Statics (they seem to tell us) is a mere toy of the class-room, a mere introduction to dynamics, which cannot possess of its own any direct relevance to the real world. I do not believe that this is correct. There is no reason why we should be so dogmatic about the stationariness of our static models as to condemn them to hopeless unrealism. Static economics is perfectly valid economics; only it is economics arranged for the comparison of states, not for the analysis of processes. The one purpose can be as realistic as the other.

Perhaps the clearest way of showing that the distinction between statics and dynamics is not a distinction between abstraction and realism is to observe that a similar distinction persists in the wholly realistic field of economic history. One of the standard ways of writing economic history (particularly practised by political historians in their economic chapters) is to survey the *state* of the economy under consideration, as it was in various historical periods, comparing one state with another. This is the method of comparative statics. It is when the economic historian tries to throw his work into the form of a narrative that he becomes, in the theoretical sense, dynamic. Any examination of the work of economic historians will show what a difficult threshold has to be crossed at that point. It is in fact exceedingly difficult to cast economic history into a narrative form without becoming *more* abstract than one has to be on the survey method; greater realism in the matter of time-sequence has to be purchased by a higher level of abstraction in most other respects. We are, I believe, in substantially the same case in economic theory. The historian is baffled by the problem of narrating in a single sequence events that occur successively and those that occur contemporaneously; and even in theory the analysis of a number of contemporary interacting processes soon proves to be beyond our powers. It is no accident that dynamic theory tends so largely to run in terms of simple aggregative models.

II

However much we simplify the processes which are to be studied, the mere notion of an economic process has complications in itself. It is of the essence of economic behaviour that it is purposive behaviour, directed towards the future, so that it always contains within itself a time-dimension of its own. It was the main contribution of the Böhm-Bawerkian movement that it emphasised the consequential time-structure of economic activity *even in a stationary state*. For it thereby indirectly threw up the central dynamic issue – how to superimpose the pattern of change, which is one time-pattern, upon the underlying pattern of capital-using production, which is another. Though there are ways of avoiding this issue, they are bound to result in depriving the behaviour under study of its purposive character, so that the economic system is reduced to a mere mechanism. If we are not to do violence to the essential nature of the problem, a way has to be found whereby this issue can be faced.

The vital discovery which made possible the analysis of a process of change, in properly economic terms, was the introduction of accounting procedure. While economists were fumbling around to find a set of categories by which they could make a formal analysis of economic change, other people were doing the job in a professional manner. In all its main forms, modern economic dynamics is an accounting theory. It borrows its leading concepts from the work which had previously been done by accountants (with singularly little help from economists); and it is in accordance with this that social accounting should be its main practical instrument of application.

So much, I believe, is generally realised; but it is not so often observed that there are several kinds of accounting structure which are relevant to economic analysis, so that the mere decision to utilise accounting concepts does not itself produce uniform results. There are indeed two major alternatives which, in the present context, I want to distinguish; for they lead, on the one hand, to the analysis in terms of plans and realisations which is especially to be associated with the name of Lindahl, and on the other to the kind of approach of which the Keynes theory is the most famous representative. I am going to maintain that it is the second approach which arises most naturally from the application to economics of the ordinary concepts of business accounting; while the first is to be similarly associated with the concepts of a special kind of accounting – that which operates in practice in the important field of Public Finance.

III

Government accounting has several peculiar features; two of them are of particular importance for our purposes. One is the fact that governments are not obliged by any company law to present balance-sheets; it is nearly always true that their only account is a 'running' or 'income and expenditure' account. Again, unlike businesses, governments do not merely present a running account for the year which is closed at the time the account is presented; they also present a quite formal *forward* account – of the expenditure planned, and the revenue expected, for the ensuing year. Both of these peculiarities persist in the corresponding theory; the balance-sheet drops into the background, but immense stress is laid upon the distinction between backward and forward accounts – *ex post* and *ex ante.*

This latter distinction is itself sufficient to enable the Lindahl theory to clear its first hurdle. It is made abundantly clear that economic dynamics is not only concerned with what happens; it is also concerned with what is planned, or intended, or expected to happen. We do not merely have to deal with one time-scale; time reduplicates itself as in a mirror, or in a series of mirrors. Parallel to the real events, which have one course in time, are constantly changing series of planned or expected events, with similar but distinct courses. The comparison of what does happen with what is expected to happen becomes a key-point of dynamic analysis.

A second thing follows from this. Dynamic analysis is not solely concerned with the comparison between what happens in successive periods, so as to build up a story in terms of these *actual* changes;

there is also a form, or phase, of dynamic analysis which concentrates attention upon a *single period* (or *accounting period*), being concerned with the difference between what happens in that period and what is planned (at the commencement of the period) to happen in it. These differences ('windfalls') may be due to exogenous causes (acts of God or of politicians); but the more interesting windfalls are those which are traceable to inconsistencies between the plans of the various individuals (and concerns) composing the economy – assuming that there is no omniscient planning authority.

Once this approach is accepted, the general dynamic problem falls into two parts. There is, in the first place, what we may call *single-period theory*, theory which is concerned with the determination of what happens in a single period in the above sense; and secondly what we may call *continuation theory*, which is concerned with the effect of the events of a first period upon the expectations and plans which themselves determine the events of its successors. Since we do not concern ourselves with changes in the rates of flow (of output or consumption, for instance) which occur *within* the single-period, single-period theory can make a good deal of use of static method; indeed it has often been described as 'quasi-static'. I do not myself care for this description, since I am convinced that single-period theory is a part, and indeed an essential part, of dynamic analysis; but I fully admit that it needs to be completed by some form of continuation theory if it is to do its properly dynamic job of analysing a process.

IV

The properties which I have been describing must, I think, be common to all theories which work in terms of plans and realisations; but now we come to a parting of the ways. There is one form of single-period theory (a classic description of it has been given by Lindahl[2]) in which it is assumed that prices are fixed at the commencement of the period – before it is seen whether plans are consistent; a failure to fulfil plans then results in an unwanted accumulation or decumulation of stocks (or perhaps in the appearance of 'negative stocks', in the sense of unfulfilled orders). It is accordingly characteristic of this model that demands and supplies are not necessarily equal; or rather, in the accepted terminology, that

---

[2] See the chapter of his *Studies* previously cited.

ex ante demands and supplies are not necessarily equal (*ex post* demands and supplies, being adjusted for the unintended accumulations and decumulations, are equal as an accounting identity.) This is the type of single-period theory which emerges if we think along this particular track; it implies that the determination of prices is held over to be a first step in continuation theory. Prices are determined, in each successive period, largely as a consequence of the discrepancies between supplies and demands which have appeared in the period before.

Now whatever we may think about this particular framework, it was clearly one which deserved to be tried out. It is relatively realistic, and it has performed great services in the clarification of thought. Its defect, if one may put it that way, is that it is not very *efficient*. This is because so little change is allowed to occur within the single period (where it is relatively manageable) and so much has to occur at the carry-over from one period to another (where it is much harder to manage). So long as the problem is that of analysing change in a particular market only, this defect is perhaps not very serious; but it becomes much more serious when one proceeds to analysis of the economy as a whole. I believe that it is this defect which has set economists looking for an alternative theory; and which will keep them looking for alternatives, even though experience has shown that the only alternatives which are available are bound to suffer from defects in other ways.

Of the various alternatives which have been explored, that which is nearest to the above is the one worked out in my *Value and Capital* (though it was developed from a study of Myrdal and of Lindahl himself.) The essential difference between this model and that just described is that I took prices to be flexible, so that there could be no unintentional carry-over of stocks; prices could vary within the *single-period*, but the movements of prices within the period (from one part of the period to another) were neglected. It was accordingly prices, not quantities, which were likely to turn out different from what had been expected. Demands (over the period) would always equal supplies (over the period) in terms of quantity; the windfall gaps between expectation and realisation were thrown over on to the price side. Since prices are then determined, within the single-period, by an adaptation of ordinary equilibrium analysis, the results which can be achieved within the single-period part of this theory are relatively rich. Though I did not myself pursue the corresponding continuation theory very far, that was partly because there is so much less, on this approach, for the continuation theory to do. I still believe that this is a coherent approach by which an instructive dynamic theory can be built up. It gives us a functioning dynamic model, which will answer the questions we put to it.

But these advantages are purchased at a cost. The trouble with the *Value and Capital* model is that it is not sufficiently realistic. In saying this I do not merely refer to its dependence upon the assumption of perfect competition, though that is related to the defect which I have in mind. Suppose that there were only two sorts of commodities that were traded: (1) perishable goods and personal services, which *could not* be carried over from one period to another; (2) speculatively traded commodities, stocks of which were held by merchants in order to make a profit on the difference between present and future prices; an economy which contained no other goods than these could be very adequately analysed on *Value and Capital* lines. But in fact there are good reasons (connected with the heterogeneity of products and the imperfection of competition) why most non-perishable goods are not traded on speculative markets. Both the manufacturer and the retailer are, for the most part, 'price-makers' rather than 'price-takers'; they fix their prices and let the quantities they sell be determined by demand. The prevalence of this latter type of market means that a model in which quantities bear the brunt of disequilibrium fits most of the facts distinctly better. Where the *Value and Capital* analysis goes wrong is that it treats an exceptional type of market as if it were the normal case.

We have now distinguished two types of *ex ante–ex post* analysis, which may be called the '*Q*', or quantity-disequilibrium, and the '*P*', or price-disequilibrium, types respectively. There does not seem to be any reason why it should be impossible to make a synthesis of these two types. But, so far, that does not seem to have been done.

V

It is time to turn to the main alternative route, which has its accounting analogue in the field of business accounting, not in that of public finance. It is characteristic of this route that it works much less explicitly in terms of plans and expectations. This difference does not, I think, spring from any less insistence on the purposive character of the activities that are being analysed; that is common ground on both approaches. But it is felt (and it is really quite proper to feel) that *explanations* which run so largely in terms of subjective factors (*quantified* subjective factors) are unsatisfactory, because they are so largely incapable of verification. A framework which lays less stress upon such variables keeps us closer to the facts.[3]

It seems to me that a pure theorist, who had simply set himself the task of analysing a process of economic change by using a framework of business accounts, in the way that the other approach uses government accounts, would produce a scheme of analysis which would differ from that which we have been considering in the following ways. In the first place, he would drop the emphasis upon *ex ante* budgeting. Businesses have too little control over their future operations to be able to present formal forward accounts; though they do of course make estimates and plans for their own purposes, those estimates are always affected by a high degree of uncertainty. But the forward-looking aspect of a business position is in fact reflected in formal accounts in another way; it is reflected in the balance-sheet of the business – the statement of its assets and liabilities at the moment for which its accounts are drawn up.

Thus what corresponds on this route to the *ex ante–ex post* distinction on the other route is the distinction between *stock* and *flow*. There will here be a study of *flow* variables (inputs and outputs, consumption and employment), admittedly determined in large measure by expectations, but with the expectational side relatively unstressed as compared with other determinants. There will be set against this a study of *stock* variables (the valuation of the existing stock of real capital, and the network of claims and obligations that are built upon it). It is in the determination of the stock variables that the expectational side will come into its own.

Stock-flow theories, like *ex ante–ex post* theories, could be of various sorts. There could, for instance, be a Q-sort and a P-sort (utilising the distinction made above); and there could be various sorts of hybrids. The Keynes theory, as we shall see, is a very special sort of hybrid. Just for that reason, it is not convenient for our

[3] It is true that the point should not be overstressed. Expectations and plans, though often shadowy, are not wholly intangible. The forward prices that rule upon future markets are reflections, though distorted reflections, of price-expectations; while business plans are nowadays often drawn up with such definiteness that statistics of them can be collected. But in spite of these qualifications, the point seems to retain a certain amount of validity.

Once again, the analogy from historiography is helpful. While political history, and especially diplomatic history, can be superbly written in terms of *ex ante* and *ex post*, of expectations and realisations, it is hardly possible to conceive of economic history being written in such terms. This is partly a matter of the factual material with which the economic historian has to work; but is partly due to the kinds of explanation for which he is looking being different.

purpose to begin with the Keynes theory. It is better to begin with a purer case; even though in practice stock-flow theorists have not been purists, but have mixed their methods, adjusting them to the particular conditions of particular markets.

If, instead of proceeding at once to the whole economy, we begin by considering the working of particular markets, the distinction between the Q-type and the P-type of stock-flow analysis becomes readily apparent. The stock-flow P-theory of a particular market is nothing else but the regular theory of price-determination in a speculative market (of which a particularly elegant statement is to be found in the early chapters of K. Boulding's *Economic Analysis*).[4] Here, at any given moment, there are in existence given stocks of the commodity; but, over a period, these stocks are being added to by production and being drawn upon by consumption. At a moment of time, or over any sufficiently short period of time, these additions and subtractions can be taken as negligible; price is therefore determined by the Liquidity Preference of the dealers, or, in other words, by their willingness to hold stocks. (This, of course, is governed in its turn by their expectations of the future state of the market.) Thus, at each moment, price is determined by the condition that demand to hold equals the available supply; but as soon as we look at a period of appreciable length, the inflow and outflow become significant. Even if the willingness to hold stocks remained unchanged (the Liquidity Preference curve remained constant in position), an excess of supply over demand, in the *flow* sense, would cause an addition to the stocks to be held with a consequential fall in price. Thus it is true that at any given moment, price is determined by *stock* demand and supply; but it is also true that price will only remain constant, even with unchanged willingness to hold stocks, if flow demand and supply are equal.

This is the stock-flow P-theory of a particular market; it would be on these lines that we should have to proceed if we sought to construct a corresponding theory for the whole economy. In any case, we must proceed on these lines so far as we desire to make use of the P-approach, even if we only apply it to certain parts of the economy, to those markets for which it is most suitable.

Let us turn to consider the corresponding Q-type of theory, again for the case of a particular market. In a market where stocks are held by producers (or retailers) price-movements may be relatively sluggish; it is possible to follow through a process of change

---

[4] Chapters 5–7 (any edition).

in production without assuming any price-changes. (Prices may indeed be set by some mechanism which has nothing to do with supply and demand, such as the 'full-cost principle'; they may even be set in accordance with some political sliding-scale.) If prices are taken to be for the time rigid, it is not necessary (as it was in the corresponding *P*-theory) that the market should be in *stock equilibrium* at every moment; it is perfectly possible that stocks may be larger, or smaller, than their holders would desire. But it is only when stocks are at their desired level that the condition of flow demand equalling flow supply will maintain a steady level of production. For the only means which is open to (say) a manufacturer who has surplus stocks and desires to reduce them is to cut down his production below his sales; the only means which is open to him to replenish a depleted stock is to raise his rate of production above his sales. It is this chain of causation, working from sales via stocks to inputs, which is the characteristic nexus of the type of theory to which we have now come.

Suppose that we start from a position of stock equilibrium (actual stock equals desired stock), and that demand then increases beyond the point where it can be met from current output, so that it has to be met in the first place out of stocks. Then, as is well known,[5] even if the rate of production is stepped up, at the moment when demand increases, to such a point that flow supply will ultimately be sufficient to match flow demand at the new level, stock equilibrium will not be maintained. If we compare the position when the increased output is ready for sale with the initial position, we shall find that stock has diminished, while *work in progress* has increased. Flow equilibrium has been restored, but only by a disturbance of stock equilibrium. In order to restore stock equilibrium, additional investment is required – 'induced investment'.

Strictly speaking, this must always be true; but it is possible to maintain that businesses do not in practice have very precise ideas about their 'desired stock'; they will be prepared to allow their stock to move some way away from a normal figure without taking any steps to right the position. If this is so, there will be a certain range over which demand can vary without inducing any investment (or disinvestment) in stocks; the only condition which will have to be observed is that flow demands and supplies should be kept (more or less) in balance, in order that stocks should not *go on* moving in the same direction. But it is only within this range (which may of course

---

[5] Cf. Lundberg, *op. cit.* ch. 4; and *TC*, ch. 4.

be wider or narrower in different circumstances) that it can be proper to concentrate attention exclusively on flows, so as to leave induced investment out of account.

VI

With these ideas in our minds, we can on the one hand get some idea of what a *complete* stock-flow theory of economic dynamics would be like; and on the other we can begin to appreciate the true nature of the Keynes theory, which is nothing else but a drastically, and most ingeniously, *simplified* stock-flow model.

A complete stock-flow theory would presumably proceed on *P*-lines when dealing with markets for which a *P*-approach was appropriate, and on *Q*-lines when dealing with markets for which a *Q*-approach was appropriate. It would show prices in the *P*-markets being *directly* determined by stock equations, with the flow relations affecting price-expectations which would react back on current prices. It would show quantities in the *Q*-markets primarily determined by the flow equations, but with stock relations reacting back on the flow equations by the generation of induced investment (or disinvestment). Thus in both sorts of markets both stock and flow relations would come into the picture, but their role would be different in the two cases.

In contrast to this *complete* theory, we can see what it was that Keynes did. In the first place, he used a *P*-approach for one market only (that for bonds); all other markets were dealt with on *Q*-lines. (This was a superb simplification, but the procedure was by no means perfectly realistic; a complete theory would surely have used *P*-methods for quite a number of different financial markets,[6] and for some commodity markets also.[7]) Next, so far as his one *P*-market was concerned, he concentrated attention almost entirely upon the stock equation, the flow aspect of that market being pushed right into the background. (He would, I think, have justified this procedure by reference to his doctrine of the *minimum* to the rate of interest, which – so far as it is valid – ensures that there are circumstances in which excess of flow demand or supply will not

---

[6] Much of this extension has in fact been made by Professor R. F. Kahn ('Notes on Liquidity Preference', *Manchester School*, 1954).

[7] Here, of course, one suspects that Keynes was influenced by a belief that in the course of historical evolution such markets were in fact on the way out.

disturb the stock equilibrium, though this justification can only be admitted if we agree that these particular circumstances do exist in fact, as they may have seemed to do in the thirties, but hardly today.) Thirdly, so far as all remaining markets (taken to be Q-markets) were concerned, he similarly concentrated attention on one side, this time on the flow side. (That, as we have seen, is only justifiable if we take it that businesses are prepared to allow their stock – and indeed the whole make-up of their asset structure – to vary a good way away from its normal relation with output without taking steps to right the relation.) These, so it now seems to me, are the central simplifications which are the basis of the so-called 'General Theory'.

It is unnecessary to emphasise what power these simplifications give. As all experience has shown, the Keynes theory is a highly efficient theory; it is easy to use, and the range of real problems to which it can be applied is very wide. That is why it has worked a 'revolution'. But though it is needless to dilate upon this strength, one of the reasons for it has a special relevance to the present discussion, but has not yet been mentioned. It is because Keynes reduced the whole theory of the Q-markets to their flow equations that he was able, in effect, to aggregate those markets, replacing them by a single market governed by a single relation – the Consumption Function. Thus he boiled down the whole economy into the one Q-market and one P-market, linked by a single price-link – the effect of the rate of interest on (otherwise autonomous) investment.[8]

If we look at the Keynes theory in this light, we can give it full credit for its virtues – without allowing it to bamboozle us.[9] The

[8] Even with all these simplifications, all that could be boiled in this way was the stage in stock-flow theory which corresponds to the *single-period* phase in the other approach; and the Keynes theory requires *continuation* quite as much as the other theories we have considered. But Keynes himself never faced the *continuation* question; this is the origin of the difficulties about the *marginal efficiency* and *marginal productivity* of capital which he left to others to clear up. This, too, is the origin of those prophetic extrapolations to a 'Day of Judgement' which have become so unfashionable. The substitution of Growth Economics for Eschatological Economics is for the most part a phenomenon of the oscillation between optimism and pessimism to which economists are subject like other mortals; it has nevertheless been the vehicle for some slight deepening in our understanding of the process of capital accumulation.

[9] That is, for one thing, we shall not waste time in trying to find in it a formal coherence, such as is beloved by General Equilibrium theorists, but which a hybrid (and a selective hybrid at that) cannot be expected to attain. A uniform dynamic theory, of whatever type, should exhibit coherence; but the Keynes theory is not uniform, because the equilibria of its different markets do not mean the same thing. For the miseries into

real stroke of genius that went to its making was Keynes's perception that the economic system of reality was moving into a shape which made it capable of this great simplification; so that a dynamic theory of exceptional efficacy had come, at least for the time being, into reach. But the Keynes theory was not merely the child of genius, it was also the heir of luck. The world of the thirties, which was Keynesian for one reason – because the working of the price-mechanism was so largely suspended by Depression – was succeeded by the world of the forties which was Keynesian for quite another reason – because the price-mechanism was superseded by controls. In both of these worlds the Keynesian model was at home. But one has a feeling that the world of the fifties is not Keynesian in either of these ways; it may be Keynesian in its policies, but it is not Keynesian in its working. If there is any simplification which is appropriate to our present problems, it must be a simplification of a somewhat different character.

But it is not inevitable that there should be any single simplification which is appropriate. Unless we can find means of constructing a really general theory which can be put into a usable form (and that is almost too much to hope), we are bound to be thrown back, at least on occasion, upon relatively *ad hoc* methods. We shall then waste much time upon unnecessary conflicts between these methods, unless we have at the back of our minds some rough outline of a structure into which they can be fitted. To make some contribution to the formation of that outline is what I have sought to do in this paper.

ADDENDUM ON FIXPRICE METHOD

I begin with a word on the length of the single-period. One is, of course, at liberty to make it any length one likes; but if one lengthens it or shortens it, one must take the consequences. If one makes it very long, say a decade, it may not be inappropriate, at least in some economies,[10] to work in flexprice terms – with flow demands

---

which men have been led in the search for a non-existent uniformity, see the Somers-Klein controversy in *Econometrica* (1949–50) and the long hunt which has been pursued through various journals after the hare started by D. Patinkin. (A recent bibliography is given in the article by F. Hahn in *EJ*, March 1955.) [This should be somewhat qualified in the light of the analysis given below in essay 10.]

[10] I do not say that it would be appropriate, even in this long-period sense, in every economy; for it may be that there are institutional arrangements which permit of supplies being held off the market, more or less indefinitely. That applies to the labour market, as to others. One does not have to go far to find examples.

equalling flow supplies, over the period as a whole, and prices, on some sort of average over the period as a whole, being such as can assure this equality. But that will not do for the study of a process, to be regarded as a chain in which the single-periods are links; where it belongs is in static, not in dynamic analysis. For the study of a process the single-periods should surely be much shorter.

Suppose we make them months. No one would claim that over a month the flow demand for any product (current sales) and flow supply (current output) must necessarily be equal – save for the case in which the product is perishable, so that there can be no carry-over.[11] Ordinarily, inequalities will arise, reflecting themselves in accumulations and decumulations of stocks, or in unfilled orders. This is, of course, admitted, on either method. What makes the difference is that on the flexprice method it is insisted that the producer will only accumulate stocks if he thinks that the price he will be able to get, by selling them in some future period, will be better (in spite of the costs of holding) than what he could get by selling now; so in this sense the accumulation of stocks is *voluntary*. If the behaviour of all markets is interpreted in this manner, the system is regarded as being *in equilibrium* all the time. Though flow demands and flow supplies are unequal, total demands and total supplies (including what are added to stocks or taken from stocks) will be equal all the time. The flexprice method is a *temporary equilibrium* method.

The fixprice method, by contrast, is a disequilibrium method. The carry-over of stocks is not (necessarily) regarded as voluntary – though it is not at all denied that some part may be voluntary. If flow demand is less than flow supply, stock will have to be carried over; we say here that it *has to be* carried over, for the alternative policy of cutting price so as to dispose of them *within the current month* is not seriously considered. (And is not that, very often, realistic?) Thus in a fixprice model, demands and supplies do not have to be equal; there is then no equation of demand and supply to determine prices. In describing this model as a fixprice model, it is *not* assumed that prices are unchanging over time, or from one single-period to its successor; only that they do not necessarily change whenever there is demand–supply disequilibrium. It is nevertheless true that when this possibility is envisaged, one is naturally led to attach particular importance to the working of a system in which

---

[11] I have dealt with the case of perishables in *CG*, pp. 79–82. It does not need repeating here.

demands and supplies are variable, but prices do not change; for this is the case which on the other method is excluded. Once we are clear about that, the model can be elaborated to admit of price-formation on a variety of *policies* – a simple cost-plus policy being naturally the easiest to manage.

Although the fixprice method is a disequilibrium method, it cannot dispense with a concept of equilibrium – which it needs, at the least, as a standard of reference. It needs both stock equilibrium and flow equilibrium. Flexprice theory can manage with flow equilibrium alone; but fixprice theory needs both, and it is stock equilibrium which is fundamental.

To say that a firm is in stock equilibrium must mean that the goods (and claims) that are listed on its balance-sheet are the best (or appear to be the best) out of a range of alternatives. What alternatives? This is a question that in flexprice theory is hard to answer; but in fixprice theory, where we most need it, it is answerable. 'The alternative balance-sheets are alternative forms in which the capital of the unit (or its 'net worth') might *apparently* be held. A change from one to another is an exchange of equal value (at the ruling prices) for equal value. But because the system is a disequilibrium system, such exchanges cannot necessarily be made. At the best they take time. The comparison between the alternatives is nevertheless significant. For if the situation of the unit is in this sense one of stock disequilibrium, we may assume that it will endeavour to get out of that disequilibrium, when and as it can.' (*CG*, p. 88.) So stock disequilibrium is the engine, or a part of the engine, by which the process that is under analysis is carried forward.

Though it must be that in general the switching of the capital stock from one form to another takes much time, there are clearly some special, but most important, cases where it can be much quicker and much easier. Take the case of a financial firm, nearly all of whose assets are marketable securities; it can change these assets from one form to another, almost at a moment's notice. So we should say that such a firm would be, nearly always, in stock equilibrium. In the study of the markets on which such firms operate flexprice analysis should thus be rather suitable. An industrial business, by contrast, must have a large proportion of its assets in forms which make them not at all readily marketable; and even if they could be sold, they could not be replaced in new forms in a hurry. We should therefore expect that an industrial firm will always be, to some extent, in a state of stock disequilibrium. Its endeavours over time, to right that disequilibrium will be a major aspect of its policy. They will determine the time-path of the induced investment (or disinvestment) that it will undertake.

Flow equilibrium is equilibrium over a period. 'If a unit is in stock equilibrium at the beginning of the period, and is still in stock equilibrium at the end, we shall want to say that it is in flow equilibrium during the period,' (*CG*, p. 89). So flow equilibrium can just be regarded as a *maintenance* of stock equilibrium; that is quite defensible, but it is not. all that has to be said. For if stock equilibrium is to be maintained over the period, the end-stock equilibrium must be consistent with what was envisaged at the beginning; if, during the period, there had been a revision of expectations about the further future, the passage from one to the other could not be reduced to the flows that had occurred between them. This cuts both ways. 'Even though we insist on defining flow equilibrium as a maintenance of stock equilibrium, additional conditions are necessary, in addition to the stock equilibrium conditions, in order that stock equilibrium should be maintained. These conditions are quite properly defined as *conditions of flow equilibrium*. But they are necessary, not sufficient conditions. If they are satisfied, in addition to the stock conditions, then we may safely say that there is full equilibrium (or equilibrium over time). But if they are satisfied, while the stock equilibrium conditions are not satisfied, it is hard to justify describing the resulting situation as one of equilibrium at all.' (*CG*, p. 90.)

10

IS–LM – an Explanation

This paper appeared in the *Journal of Post-Keynesian Economics*, Winter (1980–81).

The *IS–LM* diagram, which is widely, though not universally, accepted as a convenient synopsis of Keynesian theory, is a thing for which I cannot deny that I have some responsibility. For it first saw the light (though there it was given different lettering) in my own paper 'Mr Keynes and the Classics' [essay 8 above]. And this is not my only connection with it; I also made use of it in some chapters (11–12) of my *Contribution to the Theory of the Trade Cycle* (1950) and again in a paper which appears as 'The Classics Again' in *Critical Essays in Monetary Theory*.[1] I have, however, not concealed that, as time has gone on, I have myself become dissatisfied with it. 'That diagram', I said in 1975, 'is now much less popular with me than I think it still is with many other people.'[2] In the reconstruction of Keynesian theory which I published at much the same time (*The Crisis in Keynesian Economics*, 1974) it is not to be found. But I have not explained the reasons for this change of opinion, or of attitude. Here I shall try to do so.

I

It will be well to begin by showing how it was that I came across this method of exposition. The clue is to be found in 'Wages and Interest: the Dynamic Problem' [*CEET* II, essay 6], the last of the relevant papers which I wrote before I saw the *General Theory*, published in 1936. It is a first sketch for what was to become the 'dynamic' model

---

[1] I still believe that the use I made of it in the latter paper is perfectly legitimate. I am much less sure about the version in *TC*.

[2] See below, p. 272.

of *Value and Capital*. It shows (I think conclusively) that that model was already in my mind before I met that of Keynes.

When I did read him, I recognised at once that my model and Keynes's had some things in common. Both of us fixed our attention on the behaviour of an economy *during a period* – a period that had a past, which nothing that was done during the period could alter, and a future, which during the period was unknown. Expectations of the future would nevertheless affect what happened during the period. Neither of us made any assumption about 'rational expectations'; expectations, in our models, were strictly exogenous. (Keynes made much more fuss over that than I did, but there is the same implication in my model also.) Subject to these *data* – the given equipment carried over from the past, the production possibilities within the period, the preference schedules, and the given expectations – the actual performance of the economy within the period was supposed to be determined, or determinable. It would be determined as an equilibrium performance, with respect to these data.

There was all this in common between my model and Keynes's; it was enough to make me recognise, as soon as I saw the *General Theory*, that his model was a relation of mine and, as such, one which I could warmly welcome. There were, however, two differences, on which (as we shall see) much depends.

The more obvious difference was that mine was a flexprice model, a perfect competition model, in which all prices were flexible, while in Keynes's the level of money wages (at least) was exogenously determined. So Keynes's was a model that was consistent with unemployment, while mine, in his terms, was a full employment model. I shall have much to say about this difference, but I may as well note, at the start, that I do not think it matters much. I did not think, even in 1936, that it mattered much. *IS-LM* was in fact a translation of Keynes's non-flexprice model into my terms. It seemed to me already that that could be done; but how it is done requires explanation.

The other difference is more fundamental; it concerns the length of the *period*. Keynes's (he said) was a 'short-period', a term with connotations derived from Marshall; we shall not go far wrong if we think of it as a year. Mine was an 'ultra-short-period'; I called it a week. Much more can happen in a year than in a week; Keynes has to allow for quite a lot of things to happen. I wanted to avoid so much happening, so that my (flexprice) markets could reflect propensities (and expectations) as they are at a moment. So it was

H

that I made my markets open only on a Monday; what actually happened during the ensuing week was not to affect them. This was a very artificial device, not (I would think now) much to be recommended. But the point of it was to exclude the things which might happen, and must disturb the markets, during a period of finite length; and this, as we shall see, is a very real trouble in Keynes.

In the rest of this article, I shall take these two issues separately, beginning with the fixprice–flexprice question, which is the easier.

II

It will readily be understood, in the light of what I have been saying, that the idea of the *IS–LM* diagram came to me as a result of the work I had been doing on three-way exchange, conceived in a Walrasian manner. I had already found a way of representing three-way exchange on a two-dimensional diagram (to appear in due course in chapter 5 of *Value and Capital*). As it appears there, it is a piece of statics, but it was essential to my approach (as already appears in 'Wages and Interest: the Dynamic Problem', 1935) that static analysis of this sort could be carried over to 'dynamics' by redefinition of terms. So it was natural for me to think that a similar device could be used for the Keynes theory.

Keynes had three elements in his theory: the marginal efficiency of capital, the consumption function, and liquidity preference. The market for goods, the market for bonds, and the market for money: could they not be regarded in my manner as a model of three-way exchange? In my three-way exchange I had two independent price parameters: the price of A in terms of C and the price of B in terms of C (for the price of A in terms of B followed from them). These two parameters were determined by the equilibrium of two markets, the market for A and the market for B. If these two markets were in equilibrium, the third must be also.

Keynes also appeared to have two parameters – his Y (income *in terms of wage units*) and r, the rate of interest. He made investment depend on r and saving on Y; so for each value of r there should be a value of Y which would keep saving equal to investment – excess demand on the market for goods then being zero. This gave a relation between r and Y which I expressed as the *IS* curve. The demand for money depended on Y (transactions balances) and on r (liquidity preference). So for any given supply of money (*in terms of wage units*) there should be a relation between r and Y

which would keep the money 'market' in equilibrium. One did not have to bother about the market for 'loanable funds', since it appeared, on the Walras analogy, that if these two 'markets' were in equilibrium, the third must be also. So I concluded that the intersection of *IS* and *LM* determined the equilibrium of the system as a whole.

Now this was really, at that stage, no more than a conjecture, for I had not properly shown that the Walras analogy would fit. In Walras, all markets are cleared; but in *IS–LM* (following Keynes) the labour market is not cleared; there is excess supply of labour. Does this, by itself, upset the Walras model? I think that by now it is generally accepted that it does not. It will nevertheless be useful, for what follows, to check the matter over in detail.

In strictness, we now need four markets, since labour and goods will have to be distinguished. But before giving them those names, let us look at the matter in terms of a general Walrasian four-goods model.

We then say that commodities A, B, C and X are being traded, with X as standard (*numéraire*). Prices p_a, p_b, p_c are reckoned in terms of the standard; $p_x = 1$. Demands and supplies on the ABC markets are functions of the three prices. The three equations $S_a = D_a$ and so on are sufficient to determine the three prices. Further, since

$$S_x = p_a D_a + p_b D_b + p_c D_c, \qquad D_x = p_a S_a + p_b S_b + p_c S_c,$$

when the supply and demand equations are satisfied for ABC, that for X follows automatically.

There is just this one identical relation between the four equations. We could use it to eliminate the X equation, as just shown, or to eliminate any one of the other equations, while retaining the X equation. Thus the system of three prices for ABC can be regarded as determined by equations for ABC, or by equations for BCX, CAX or ABX.

Thus far Walras. But now suppose that one of the commodities is sold on a fixprice market, where the price is fixed in terms of the standard, but where the equation of supply and demand does not have to hold. The actual amount sold will be equal to the demand or to the supply, whichever is the lower. So let p_a be fixed, with the equation $D_a = S_a$ removed. The remaining (variable) prices can still be determined from the equations $S_b = D_b$, $S_c = D_c$, for the p_a which appears as a parameter in these equations is now a constant. If it turns out that at these prices $S_a > D_a$, it is only D_a that can actually be traded. When calculating S_x and D_x, we must use this *actual* D_a for both D_a and S_a. With that substitution, we have $S_x = D_x$, as before.

And it is still possible, using this construction, to let the equation for the standard, $S_x = D_x$, replace one of the equations otherwise used, as could be done in the all-round flexprice case. For with D_a substituted for S_a, $p_a(S_a - D_a) = 0$ is an identity. The only terms in $S_x - D_x$ that survive, on application of this identity, are those which relate to the flexprice commodities B and C. The subsystem of BCX will then work in the regular Walrasian manner. We can determine p_b and p_c from any pair of the three equations that are left.

In this way, the Walrasian analogy gets over its first hurdle; but there is another, close behind it, which may be considered more serious. We have so far been making demands and supplies depend only on prices; and for the pure case of multiple exchange with flexible prices, that may probably be accepted. But as soon as a fixprice market is introduced, it ceases to be acceptable. It must be supposed that the demands and supplies for B and C will be affected by what happens in the market for A. That can no longer be represented by the price, so it must be represented by the quantity sold. Assuming, as before, that there is excess supply in the A market, this is D_a. So demands and supplies for B and C will be functions of p_b, p_c and D_a. The BCX subsystem would then *not* be complete in itself; but the whole system, with D_a included as a parameter, would still work in the way that has been described.

We would then have three variables to be determined, p_b, p_c and D_a – and four equations. They are the demand–supply equations for BCX (the X equation being constructed with the *actual* D_a, as before); and there is also the demand equation for D_a, which makes D_a a function of p_b and p_c. As before, any one of the BCX equations can be eliminated. The system is determined, whichever equation we choose to eliminate.

The model is still very formal; but now it is the same kind of model as the *IS–LM* model. We could represent that as a three-way (ABX) model, in which there is just on price (p_b, which becomes the rate of interest) that is determined on a flexprice market, and one quantity (Y) which plays the part of D_a. I have deliberately taken a case which in the same formal terms is slightly more complicated, since I have admitted two flexprice markets, for B and for C. It may indeed be useful to show that there is, in principle, no difficulty in introducing a second flexprice market – or, for that matter, introducing several. It could be useful, even for macro-economic purposes, to introduce a second flexprice market – for instance, a market for foreign exchange.

But that is not the reason I have introduced the extra market. The important use of a four-way model, in this connection, is that it enables us to consider the market for goods and the market for labour separately. And when we take them separately, quite interesting things happen.

One could construct a model in which only the market for labour was a fixprice market, and not only the rate of interest but also the price (or price level) of finished products was flexible. That would fit very exactly into the scheme which has just been outlined. with demand–supply equations determining D_a (employment) and the two flexible prices p_b, p_c. It is possible that Keynes himself sometimes thought in terms of that sort of model (see, for example, *General Theory*, ch. 21); but it cannot be this which *IS-LM* is supposed to represent. For Y is taken to be an index not only of employment, but also of output, so the prices of products also are supposed to be fixed in terms of the standard; and it is hard to see how that can be justified unless the prices of products are derived from the wage of labour by some markup rule. But if that is so, we have not one, but two, fixprice markets.

Say that A and B are fixprice markets, while C is flexprice. As long as we follow the Walrasian practice of working entirely in terms of price parameters, there is no trouble. p_a and p_b are then fixed, so that all demands and supplies are functions of the single variable p_c. p_c is determined on the market for C (or, equivalently, on the market for X) as before. And the actual amounts of A and B that are traded are D_a or S_a, D_b or S_b – whichever, at the equilibrium p_c, turns out to be the lower.

But now suppose that, as before, we change the parameters, making demands and supplies functions of D_a and D_b (assuming that there is excess supply in both markets), not of p_c only. One would at first say that at a (provisionally given) p_c, D_a would be a function of D_b and D_b of D_a; and there need be nothing circular about that. There are just these two 'curves' in the $(D_a D_b)$ plane (like supply and demand curves); at their intersection, the equilibrium is determined.

It must be this which, in the *IS-LM* model, is supposed to happen. We are now to take A to be the labour market, C the market for loanable funds (as before), and B the market for finished products (consumption goods and investment goods not being, so far, distinguished). p_a is the fixed money wage; p_b, the fixed price level of the finished products; p_c, the rate of interest, the only price that is left to be determined on a flexprice market.

How, then, do we identify the 'curves'? One, which makes D_b (effective demand for products) a function of D_a (employment) is easy to find in Keynes. D_b depends on D_a, since the consumption component of D_b increases when employment increases (the consumption function), while the investment component depends on the rate of interest, provisionally given. There is no trouble about that. But what of the other 'curve' – the dependence of D_a on D_b, of employment on effective demand? Keynes took it for granted that they must go together, but the matter needs looking into. For it is here that there is a danger of going seriously wrong by neglecting time.

III

It is not true, of course, that time has been wholly neglected. As I said at the beginning, all the prices and quantities that have figured in the analysis must belong to a period; the past (before the period) and the future (beyond the period) have always been playing their regular parts. What has been neglected is the flow of time within the period. It is here that the length of the period is important.

In my own version ['Wages & Interest' or *VC*], the period ('week') was kept very short, so that little could happen within it. The actual outputs of products and (probably also) the actual input of labour would be largely predetermined. What could vary, considerably, would be prices. So for the study of price formation on flexprice markets, the 'week' had something to be said for it.[3] But that was not what Keynes was interested in; so he had to have a longer period.

It is not unreasonable to suppose that the prices which are established in flexprice markets, during a 'week' (or even at a point of time) do reflect the expectations of traders, their liquidity positions, and so on. That is to say (it is equivalent to saying), we may fairly reckon that these markets, with respect to these data, are in equilibrium. And one could go on, as we have in fact been seeing, even while maintaining the 'week' interpretation, to admit that there are some markets which are fixprice markets, in which demands and supplies do not have to be equal. Then it is only to the markets which are flexprice markets that the equilibrium rule applies. Now it would be quite hard to say, in terms of such a model, that effective demand would determine employment. It is so tempting to say that there can be no output without labour input, so that an increase in demand must increase employment (as Keynes effectively did).

---

[3] No more than something. I have myself become pretty critical of the *VC* temporary equilibrium method when applied to flow markets. (I do not question its validity for the analysis of markets in stocks.) See ch. 6 of *CG*.

But the question is not one of the relation between input and output, in general; it is a question of the relation between current demand and current input, both in the current period. It is at once shown, on the 'week' interpretation, that current output is largely predetermined; while, if the price of output is fixed, current demand may be greater or less than current output (stocks being decumulated or accumulated). How, then, is current input to be determined? We can only make it determinate, as a function of current demand, if we can bring ourselves to introduce some *rule*, according to which the extent of excess demand (or supply) in the current period will affect the employment that is offered, again in the current period. If we have such a rule, we can complete the circle, and show, in the current period, effective demand and employment simultaneously determined.

It is quite a question whether we would be justified, in general, in imposing such a rule.[4] For the effect on current input of excess demand or supply in the product market is surely a matter of the way in which the excess is interpreted by decision makers. An excess which is expected to be quite temporary may have no effect on input; it is not only the current excess but the expectation of its future which determines action. It may be useful, on occasion, to suspend these doubts, and so to make models in which current input depends on excess demands (or supplies) in the product markets according to some rule. But one can hardly get a plausible rule while confining attention to what happens within a single period. So it would seem that the proper place for such a proceeding is in sequential models, composed of a succession of periods, in each of which the relevant parameters have to be determined; there is then room for linkages between the periods, and so for lags. I have myself made some attempts at the construction of such models.[5] I think they have their uses, but they are not much like *IS-LM*.

If one is to make sense of the *IS-LM* model, while paying proper attention to time, one must, I think, insist on two things: (1) that the period in question is a relatively long period, a 'year' rather than a 'week'; and (2) that, because the behaviour of the economy over that 'year'[6] is to be *determined* by propensities, and suchlike

---

[4] My mind goes back to a conversation I had, a few years ago, with a distinguished economist, who might at an earlier date have been reckoned to be a Keynesian. I was saying to him that I had come to regard J. S. Mill as the most undervalued economist of the nineteenth century. He said, 'Yes, I think I understand. *Demand for commodities is not demand for labour.* It is true, after all.'

[5] In particular, in *CG* (chs. 7-10).

[6] The *year* must clearly be long enough for the firm to be 'free to revise its decisions as to how much employment to offer' (Keynes, *General Theory*, p. 47, n. 1).

data, it must be assumed to be, in an appropriate sense, *in equilibrium*. This clearly must not imply that it is an all-round flexprice system; the exogenously fixed money wage, and (as we have seen) the exogenously fixed prices of products must still be retained. But it is not only the market for funds, but also the product market, which must be assumed to be in equilibrium.

Though the prices of products are fixed, it is not necessary to suppose that there is disequilibrium in the product market. Even at the fixed price and fixed wage, when these are maintained over the relatively long period, it will pay producers to adjust supply to demand, as far as they can. For a loss is incurred in producing output that cannot be sold, and a profit is forgone when output that could profitably be sold is not produced. There are problems of adjustment, of which sequential analysis can take account; but there may be purposes for which it is legitimate to leave them to one side. We should then assume that the product markets, during the 'year', are in equilibrium and remain in equilibrium. And since it is to be continuing equilibrium, maintained throughout the 'year', this must mean that plans (so far as they relate to the proceedings of the year) are being carried through without being disturbed.

It is not, I think, inconsistent to suppose that the product markets are in equilibrium, while the labour market is not in equilibrium. For although there are some possibilities for adjusting supply to demand in the case of unemployment on the labour market (even while prices and wages remain unchanged), as by withdrawal of elderly labour from the market, or by departure of migrants, they are surely less than the corresponding possibilities in the market for products. A model which permits excess supply in the labour market, but no product market disequilibrium, is not inconsistent.

Once we allow ourselves to assume that product markets remain in equilibrium, things become easier. For once we assume that production plans, during the period, are carried through consistently, we have the relation between current input, during the period, and current output, during the period (which has been made equal to effective demand within the period) for which we have been looking. There are some difficulties about production processes which were begun before the commencement of the period, and others which will not be completed at the end of the period, but these, perhaps, may be overlooked. We can then proceed to the two 'curves' in the $(D_a D_b)$ plane, by which employment and effective demand are simultaneously determined.

The goal is reached, but at a considerable price. For how, after all, can this equilibrium assumption be justified? I do not think it can be justified for all purposes, maybe not for the most important purposes, but I have come to think that there is one purpose for which it may sometimes be justified. I have described this purpose in chapter 6 of my book *Causality in Economics* (1979); an abstract of the argument of that chapter may be given here.

We are to confine attention to the problem of explaining the past, a less exacting application than prediction of what will happen or prescription of what should happen, but surely one that comes first. If we are unable to explain the past, what right have we to attempt to predict the future? I find that concentration on explanation of the past is quite illuminating.

We have, then, facts before us; we know or can find out what, in terms of the things in which we are interested, did actually happen in some past year (say, the year 1975). In order to explain what happened, we must confront these facts with what we think would have happened if something (some alleged cause) had been different. About that, since it did not happen, we can have no factual information; we can only deduce it with the aid of a theory, or model. And since the theory is to tell us what would have happened, the variables in the model must be determined. And that would seem to mean that the model, in some sense, must be in equilibrium.

Applying these notions to the *IS-LM* construction, it is only the point of intersection of the curves which makes any claim to representing what actually happened (in our '1975'). Other points on either of the curves – say, the *IS* curve – surely do not represent, make no claim to represent, what actually happened. They are theoretical constructions, which are supposed to indicate what *would have happened* if the rate of interest had been different. It does not seem farfetched to suppose that these positions are equilibrium positions, representing the equilibrium which corresponds to a different rate of interest. If we cannot take them to be equilibrium positions, we cannot say much about them. But, as the diagram is drawn, the *IS* curve passes through the point of intersection; so the point of intersection appears to be a point on the curve; thus it also is an equilibrium position. That, surely, is quite hard to take. We know that in 1975 the system was not in equilibrium. There were plans which failed to be carried through as intended; there were surprises. We have to suppose that, for the purpose of the analysis on which we are engaged, these things do not matter. It is sufficient to treat the economy, as it actually was in the year in question, as if it were in equilibrium. Or, what is perhaps equivalent, it is permissible to regard the departures from equilibrium, which we admit to have existed, as being random. There are plenty of instances in applied economics, not only in the application of *IS–LM* analysis, where we are accustomed to permitting ourselves this way out. But it is dangerous. Though there may well have been some periods of history, some 'years', for which it is quite acceptable, it is just at the turning points, at the most interesting 'years', where it is hardest to accept it.

What I have been saying applies, most directly, to the *IS* curve; what of the other?

In elementary presentations of the *IS–LM* model, the *LM* curve is supposed to be drawn up on the assumption of a given stock of money (the extension to a stock of money given in terms of wage units comes in only when the level of money wages is allowed to vary, so I shall leave it to one side). It is, however, unnecessary to raise those puzzling questions of the definition of money, which in these monetarist days have become so pressing. For I may allow myself to point out that it was already observed in 'Mr Keynes and the Classics' [essay 8 above] that we do not need to suppose that the curve is drawn up on the assumption of a given stock of money. It is sufficient to suppose that there is (as I said)

a given monetary system – that up to a point, but only up to a point, monetary authorities will prefer to create new money rather than allow interest rates to rise. Such a generalised (*LM*) curve will then slope upwards only gradually – the elasticity of the curve depending on the elasticity of the monetary system (in the ordinary monetary sense).[7]

That is good as far as it goes, but it does not go far enough. For here, again, there is a question of time reference; and it is a very tricky question. The relation which is expressed in the *IS* curve is a flow relation, which (as we have seen) must refer to a period, such as the year we have been discussing. But the relation expressed in the *LM* curve is, or should be, a stock relation, a balance-sheet relation (as Keynes so rightly insisted). It must therefore refer to a point of time, not to a period. How are the two to be fitted together?

It might appear, at first sight, that we must proceed by converting the stock relation into a relation which is to hold for the period – treating it, in some way, as an average of balance-sheet relations over the period. But this has to be rejected, not merely because it is clumsy, but because it does not get to the point. It has been shown that, if we adopt the equilibrium interpretation, on the *IS* side, the economy must be treated *as if* it were in equilibrium over the period

[7] P. 208 above.

that means, on the *IS* side, that the economy must remain in flow equilibrium, with demands and supplies for the flows of outputs remaining in balance. It would be logical to maintain that on the *LM* side the economy must be treated similarly. There must be a *maintenance* of stock equilibrium.

I have examined the relation between stock equilibrium and flow equilibrium in chapter 8 of my *Capital and Growth* (1965), where I have shown that the maintenance of stock equilibrium over the period implies the maintenance of flow equilibrium over the period; so it is a sufficient condition for the maintenance of equilibrium over time, in the fullest sense. A key passage is the following:

Equilibrium over time requires the maintenance of stock equilibrium; this should be interpreted as meaning that there is stock equilibrium, not only at the beginning and end of the period, but throughout its course. Thus when we regard a 'long' period as a sequence of 'short' periods, the 'long' period can only be in equilibrium over time if every 'short' period within it is in equilibrium over time. Expectations must be kept self-consistent; so there can be no revision of expectations at the junction between one 'short' period and its successor. The system is in stock equilibrium at each of these junctions; and is in stock equilibrium with respect to these consistent expectations. That can only be possible if expectations - with respect to demands that accrue within the 'long' period - are *right*. Equilibrium over time thus implies consistency between expectations and realisations within the period. It is only expectations of the further future that are arbitrary (exogenous) as they must be.[8]

That is the formal concept of full equilibrium over time; I do not see how it is to be avoided. But for the purpose of generating an *LM* surve, which is to represent liquidity preference, it will not do without amendment. For there is no sense in liquidity, unless expectations are uncertain. But how is an uncertain expectation to be realised? When the moment arrives to which the expectation refers, what replaces it is fact, fact which is not uncertain.

I have suggested, in my most recent book (*Causality in Economics*), a way of cutting the knot, but I do not have much faith in it.

We must evidently refrain from supposing that the expectations as they were before April (some data in the middle of the 'year') of what is to happen after April, were precise expectations, single-valued expectations; for in a model with single-valued expectations, there can be no question of liquidity. And we must also refrain from the conventional representation of uncertain expectations in

---

[8] Pp. 92-3. I have made a few minor alterations in wording to make it possible to extract the passage quoted from the rest of the chapter.

terms of mean and variance, since that makes them different in kind from the experiences which are to replace them. There is, however, a third alternative. Suppose we make them expectations that the values that are expected, of the variables affecting decisions, will fall within a particular range. This leaves room for liquidity, since there are no certain expectations of what is going to happen; but it also makes it possible for there to be an equilibrium, in the sense that what happens falls within the expected range. A state of equilibrium is a state in which there are no surprises. What happens (during the period) falls sufficiently within the range of what is expected for no revision of expectations to be necessary. (p. 85.)

As far as I can see, that is the only concept of equilibrium over time[9] which leaves room for liquidity.

IV

I accordingly conclude that the only way in which *IS–LM* analysis usefully survives – as anything more than a classroom gadget, to be superseded, later on, by something better – is in application to a particular kind of causal analysis, where the use of equilibrium methods, even a drastic use of equilibrium methods, is not inappropriate. I have deliberately interpreted the equilibrium concept, to be used in such analysis, in a very stringent manner (some would say a pedantic manner) not because I want to tell the applied economist, who uses such methods, that he is in fact committing himself to anything which must appear to him to be so ridiculous, but because I want to ask him to try to assure himself that the divergences between reality and the theoretical model, which he is using the explain it, are no more than divergencies which he is entitled to overlook. I am quite prepared to believe that there are cases where he is entitled to overlook them. But the issue is one which needs to be faced in each case.

When one turns to questions of policy, looking towards the future instead of the past, the use of equilibrium methods is still more suspect. For one cannot prescribe policy without considering at least the possibility that policy may be changed. There can be no change of policy if everything is to go on as expected – if the economy is to remain in what (however approximately) may be regarded as its

---

[9] I should here make an acknowledgement to G. L. S. Shackle, who in much of his work has been feeling in this direction.

existing equilibrium. It may be hoped that, after the change in policy, the economy will somehow, at some time in the future, settle into what may be regarded, in the same sense, as a new equilibrium; but there must necessarily be a stage before that equilibrium is reached. There must always be a problem of traverse. For the study of a traverse, one has to have recourse to sequential methods of one kind or another.

11

The Credit Economy

This essay first appeared as part 4 of 'The Foundations of Monetary Theory', in *Money, Interest and Wages, CEET* II (1982).

1. What I mean by a credit economy is one that contains no money that does not bear interest; so that the key instrument of monetary control must be the rate of interest, or the interest rates. Actual economies, as we have seen, are tending in that direction; so it need not surprise us to find that much may be learned about actual money by considering the pure type. It may indeed be claimed that we get from it a grasp of essentials more quickly and more easily than in any other way.

If there is no money that does not bear interest, what is money? We have to go back to the function of money as a means of payment; money is what is acceptable in the payment of debts. But what is the payment of a debt? When I pay my tradesman with a cheque that will be honoured (for otherwise there is no payment) he is exchanging my debt to him for a debt from my bank to him, while the bank has less of a debt to me (assuming that there is a surplus in my bank account). If I am working on an overdraft, I have more of a debt to the bank. The payment of a debt is an exchange of debts.

We regard it as a payment because the debts have different *quality*. It is different quality from the point of view of the creditor which is what matters. I may be quite sure that I am going to pay, but my creditor has to face the risk that I may have gone away for a holiday, just as his bill comes in. The debt to him from the bank is more reliable.

In what way is it more reliable? It is not just that he knows the hours when the bank will be open, so that the cheque can be cashed. For notes (and indeed coins) are no more than tokens; they are themselves to be regarded as debts of the banking system; all that happens when one cashes a cheque is that one exchanges one form of debt for another. Even if the bank cashiers go on strike, the debt from the bank does not lose its quality; it can still be used, though with some inconvenience.

Suppose that the creditor, to whom I pay my debt, keeps his account at a different bank from that on which my cheque is drawn. He still accepts it as a money payment, since he knows that his bank will accept it as a money payment; debts from the one bank, and from the other, have (from the points of view of all concerned) equal reliability. We normally expect that that will be the case; but if I had drawn my cheque on a bank of which he had never heard, and which (so far as he could tell) might be purely imaginary, he would not have accepted it as a payment.

2. One can construct, in the light of these reflections, two pure models of a credit economy, each of which has its uses. I call them the *monocentric* and *polycentric* respectively.

It is characteristic of a monocentric model that it has just one 'central' entity, promises to pay by which have superior quality (in that they are more widely acceptable) than promises by any other entity. The continuance of that superiority is taken for granted, so that there is just this one 'monetary authority'. The polycentric model has no such single centre. But there will still be differences in the qualities of promises by different entities; so there will be some, at any particular moment, which have highest quality. If there is just one which at the moment has the highest quality, it acts, for the moment, like a monocentre; but there is no certainty that it will retain that position. It may be, on the other hand, that there are several that have established an equal reliability, each maintaining a willingness to convert its promises, at a fixed rate, into those of the others. If there is perfect convertibility, each has some of the properties of a monocentre; but there is no single 'monetary authority'.

It will surely be noticed that a monocentric model is likely to be most relevant to the problems of a national economy, especially when the international aspects of that economy – external trade and capital movements – are being left out of account. The monocentre can then be identified with the Central Bank (or may be with Government including central bank); or, in some cases, with the whole of the banking system, when commercial banks are closely controlled by the central bank and Government). The polycentric model has most relevance to international problems.

3. I begin with the simplest type of monocentric model, a type which may fairly be described as the Wicksellian type. There is just one bank, providing credit money, the only money there is; and there are no other financial bodies. The only form in which savings can be held is as deposits in the bank, and it is only from the bank that those undertaking investment can borrow. The only means of control

that is available to the bank is the rate of interest which it pays (and charges). We call this the *money rate* of interest.

It is tempting to say that a system such as this would be *in equilibrium*, over a period, if the net increase in the volume of loans being made by the bank was equal to the net increase in the volume of deposits. For this would mean that the volume of money that was circulating outside the bank would be remaining unchanged over the period. Wicksell himself was sometimes inclined to this interpretation of equilibrium; but there is really no reason, in general, why it should be useful. The volume of money that was in circulation might be constant and yet, in other directions to which importance might reasonably be atributed, the system might fail to be in what we should want to call an equilibrium. So there is another criterion, which also makes it appearance in Wicksell's work, according to which the system is in equilibrium if the price-level is remaining constant. Then the equilibrium rate of interest is that which maintains constant prices. This is not the same thing, and it is perhaps more appealing.

But we need not stop there.[1] There are after all many indices of prices, which do not always move together; so that there should be an equilibrium rate of interest corresponding to each. One of them is a wage-index, so there should be an equilibrium rate which would keep the wage-level constant. Or, if wages are *sticky*, it could be interpreted as a rate which would give a desired level of employment (à la Keynes). And if it is not the wage-level which has become sticky, but a conventional rate of rise in the wage-level which has become sticky, there could be an equilibrium rate of interest which (in the same sense) would fit that rate of rise in the wage-level. To keep the money rate at that 'equilibrium' level would not cure inflation; all it could do would be to ensure (by being high enough) that monetary policy was not, in itself, aggravating inflation – and (by being low enough) that the activity of the economy was not being depressed by monetary policy.[2] All these things, which I need not remark have become very topical things, are already in sight of the simple Wicksellian model.

---

[1] It was the achievement of G. Myrdal's *Monetary Equilibrium* to have made this clear.

[2] If the rate of inflation, that is set by this wage-behaviour, is itself regarded as intolerable, there may be a case for keeping the money rate above the equilibrium that is set by this behaviour, to bring pressure to bear upon the 'stickiness'. That is not ruled out.

4. Still it is not good enough. For what about uncertainty, and the cost of making transactions, which I have repeatedly emphasised are at the heart of monetary problems? They have got left out. Let us try to put them back, and see what happens.

Not much needs to happen on the side of the savers. Their deposits in the bank are certain; they can deposit what they like, and will get the rate of interest which the bank is offering, to all alike. But on the side of the bank's advances it is a different story. We must no longer think of the bank just fixing a rate of interest at which it is willing to lend, and letting anyone who is prepared to pay that rate have the money. The bank will have to attend to the prospects of particular borrowers and to their character; so whether, in its judgement, they can be relied upon to repay. This is a question of the information which is available to the bank.

One can conceive of a situation when the bank would be receiving deposits but was finding it difficult to find suitable borrowers. It would thus be withdrawing money from circulation; and this could go on on such a scale that, in none of the senses that have been distinguished, could there be an equilibrium. Should one then say that the money rate is too high? That would only make sense if a way out could be found by lowering it. But to lower the rate which the bank was charging to borrowers would not necessarily help it to find new borrowers; it does not in itself provide a better way of finding them. To lower the rate that it paid on deposits might indeed do something to discourage deposits; but, when we remember that the savings may in large measure be planned as reserves (and, at the point to which we have now come, it is right to give some weight to that), even a zero rate on deposits might well fail to choke them off to the extent required.

We are thus, already, in sight of the famous crux – an excess of 'saving' over 'investment' that by interest policy cannot be righted. But it is much too soon to push on to fanciful remedies (negative rates of interest or money dropped from helicopters) which so readily suggest themselves when the issue is looked at in these simple terms. We should first consider if we have not been placing too great a responsibility upon our myopic bank.

5. To insist, as in this First Version of the model we have been doing, that all borrowing and lending must take place through the bank, is quite unnecessary. If the bank is unable to search out suitable borrowers, why should not some of the savers search them out for themselves? There is no reason why we should deny them the

possibility of making more direct contacts. In so far as they do this, they will have less to deposit with the bank; so the surplus of funds, which we have been supposing to be going into the bank, will be moderated. It should, however, be noticed that since the alternative of depositing with the bank remains open to the savers, and the liquidity of their lendings to the firms (as it will now be convenient to call them) must be less than that of their deposits with the bank, the rate of interest that is offered by the firms[3] must be greater than the deposit rate of the bank. This will still act as a minimum to the system of interest rates which in this Second Version begins to develop.

It is indeed this deposit rate which acts as the king-pin of the system, playing much the same part as was played by *the* money rate in our original Wicksellian model. For the alternative of depositing, at the fixed deposit rate of the bank, is always open to the savers, while the alternative of borrowing directly from the bank is not so regularly open to the firms. We are not excluding the possibility of the bank doing some direct lending to the firms – at a rate which (we should now say) would be somewhat higher than the rate it was paying on deposits. For the model is now to allow for transaction costs; the bank will have costs of administration, and these must be covered. The firms will get what they can at this rate (which we may fairly suppose will be lower than what they pay on direct loans from the savers); but they want more than that, and it can be got from the savers.

It will be noticed that in this Second Version the bank is less important than it was in the First; but it still retains some power of control, through its deposit rate.

6. The solution that has so far been found for the information problem is very imperfect; it has really added nothing more than an opportunity for the firms to raise some part of the funds which they require by borrowing from their friends. A modern economy does not rely much on that, though there have been times in history when it has been important. Its place has largely been taken by an alternative of much greater potency – the introduction of financial intermediaries, which make a direct attack on the information problem.

---

[3] Or its equivalent, in terms of prospect offered, if the direct lending to the firms takes the form of subscription to equities.

The financial intermediary can prosper[4] if it can make use of specialised knowledge about the prospects of particular kinds of real investment so that it can make advances to firms, or investments in the securities of firms, which the bank would not know were sound investments; and if it can acquire resources which enable it to make those financial investments at a less loss of liquidity than they would entail upon the private saver. But it cannot prosper unless it makes a profit; this implies that it must borrow at a lower rate than that in which it lends, there being a sufficient difference to cover its administrative expenses, and to compensate it for the additional risk with which it (in its turn) is involved in every extension of its operations.

Thus its 'in-rate' (as we may call it – the rate at which it borrows) and also its 'out-rate' will have to be fitted into the structure of rates, which had already appeared in our Second Version. It is not necessary that the in-rate of the financial intermediary should be higher than the rate which is paid by the firms (directly) to the bank, or by the firms (directly) to the savers; for it may be expected that the intermediary may be able to attract funds from the bank and from the savers, by offering a greater degree of security (by pooling of risks) than the firms could do directly. And it need not necessarily charge a lower out-rate than is charged by the bank, since it will be willing to do business with the firms which the bank would not do. It is however clear that its in-rate must be appreciably higher than the bank's deposit rate, and its out-rate must be higher than its in-rate, if it is to function at all.

It will surely be granted in this Third Version of it that our Wicksellian model has taken a big step towards reality. The particular institutions, which play the parts I have ascribed to the 'bank' and to the 'intermediaries', will no doubt differ from country to country, and from time to time. But that some bodies will be found which play something like the parts in question can hardly be doubted. We have made room for many sorts of lending, between our four sectors – savers and bank, intermediaries and firms – and account could be taken of flows of funds within the sectors without much difficulty. We could have gone on to introduce a Government, as a privileged borrower, offering high security (in money terms) and, if it likes, high liquidity;

[4] I here borrow a passage from *CG* (pp. 266-7), which I can fit, with very little alteration, into the present context.

thus being a strong competitor for bank funds, if it chooses to be. Alternatively, we might treat the Government as belonging, in some measure, to each of the four sectors; thus establishing a special route for flow of funds between them.

7.   This is no place for enlarging upon such applications; there yet remains a vital question about the Third Version, which I cannot avoid. How much is left (when we allow for risks, and for the growth of financial institutions to deal with those risks) of the original Wicksell construction – the money rate and the equilibrium rate, in one or other of the senses we have found ourselves giving to the latter? We can still identify the money rate with the deposit rate of the bank, which still stands as the *base* of the interest rate system. But what has happened to the equilibrium rate, which we were to set against it?

Let us simplify a little (I think it is only a little) by supposing that marginal funds – those required for a marginal increase in the value of its investment programme – will always be raised by the firms from the intermediaries, and by the intermediaries from the bank. There is then a straightforward sequence. The savers deposit in the bank at an interest rate r_0; the bank lends to the intermediaries at interest r_1; the intermediaries to the firms at r_2. r_1 must exceed r_0 to cover the administrative costs of the bank; r_2 must exceed r_1 not only because of administrative costs, but also to provide a liquidity premium. So r_2 exceeds r_0 by two margins, those of the bank and of the intermediaries.

And having gone so far, we may allow ourselves to go further. Let us suppose that there is a rate R, which will stand for the return which the firms expect to get from marginal investment; this will have to exceed r_2 by another liquidity premium. We could then say that it would be R which, from the point of view of the Wicksell construction, would need to be kept at an equilibrium level, the level which would be appropriate to the kind of equilibrium which it was sought to attain.

To get as far as that one has had to simplify, simplify drastically; still we have come into sight of an essential point. There is bound to be a gap (depending on liquidity preferences, in a broad sense, and on transaction costs) between anything that can be directly controlled by an interest rate policy *of the bank*, and the yield on investment (R) which is the key to equilibrium. If the gap is narrow, and can be relied upon to be narrow, interest policy can be quite effective; but if the gap is wide, and undependable, there is a formidable obstacle in its way.

Let us, however, remember that the problem is an information problem. In order to make wise decisions on the big issues that are here in question, many sorts of information need to be gathered; they can hardly be gathered without having many listening points. The financial intermediaries are listening points; the question is one of transmission, from those points to the centre. We have so far been supposing that the only means of communication between the bank at the centre and the intermediaries on the circumference are rates of interest charged (or offered); though these could be generalised into 'terms of lending' without much difficulty. All dealing, that is to say, is 'at arm's length'. There have undoubtedly existed financial systems which have worked in this manner; but it is by no means inevitable that a system should work in this manner. When the intermediaries are well established, the relations between them and the centre can be much closer. It seems to follow from the preceding analysis that it is desirable that they should be closer. Control must have power if it is to be effective. Whatever we think about monopoly and competition, in the rest of the economic system, there are good reasons, in this monetary sphere, for not being afraid of some concentration.

Whatever the links between the centre and the intermediaries, the collection of information, the information required, can never be perfect. The system will still be subject to shocks; things will happen which no one (who was in a position to take action) had foreseen. It is a system which is based upon arrangements for risk-taking, in the face of an uncertain future; as such it is bound to be fragile. An arm's length system is particularly fragile. A serious blow to one part can have wide repercussions. Closer association, by making it easier to find a 'lender of last resort' reduces the fragility.

8.   That is all that I shall say here about the monocentric model, which I recognise to be no more than a part of the monetary theory which on this line of thought is required. It should evidently be matched by a similar analysis of polycentric models; but I can offer no more than the beginnings of that.

One can distinguish (at least) two pure types of polycentric model. The first is that in which there are separate centres, but they are providing (or seeking to provide) what is in effect a common money. It makes no difference if the monies provided are given different names; what is essential is the fixity of the rates of exchange between them. Each of the banks, that is, declares itself ready to exchange its promise to pay for that of any other, at this fixed rate of exchange. There is perfect convertibility at the fixed rates.

It is at once apparent that it will be impossible to maintain this convertibility (except momentarily) unless the deposit rates of all the banks are the same; for if any bank held to a deposit rate which was lower than that which was being paid by the other banks, it would find itself losing its deposits. And this means that it will be impossible for any bank, acting singly, to force a reduction in the common deposit rate; but it will be possible for a single bank, acting alone, to force a rise in the common rate – for by raising its rate, it can force the others to follow its example. So such a system, as is beginning to be understood, has a natural deflationary bias. This can indeed be overcome if there is some bank which is so much stronger than the others that it can face a withdrawal of funds with equanimity; or if it has some other way than interest policy of 'giving a lead' to the others, thus bringing about some sort of agreement on common action. But in any of these cases the system is moving in the direction of monocentricity. It is even more apparent here than it was in our monocentric analysis, that a system in which all transactions are 'at arm's length' will not work.

The second type will readily be recognised as that of non-fixed exchanges. Convertibility at fixed rates is abandoned, but convertibility, on the market, is maintained. Does this restore, for the individual centres, their interest-rate autonomy? It seems often to be supposed that it does so; but the answer surely is, not very much. Suppose that there is just one bank (the bank of country X) which abandons the fixed rate of exchange. It is then possible for it to reduce its deposit rate below the common rate maintained by the others; but only if its X-currency depreciates in terms of the others, and if the depreciation is expected to be *temporary*. For if it is expected to be temporary, a depositor at the X bank, though he gets a lower rate of interest, in terms of X-currency, than he could get elsewhere, in terms of other currencies, can expect to make up the difference, in terms of other currencies, when the X-currency recovers. Thus he need not lose anything, in terms of the other currencies, by holding his deposit at the X-bank.

This is indeed what was noticed by Keynes, in the twenties, when he advocated a 'widening of the gold points', as a means of increasing the national bank's autonomy, giving it at least a little more elbow-room. And it was this which led Hawtrey to develop the argument as a general argument in favour of exchange fluctuation, *about a fixed parity*.[5] The fixed parity is essential. An exchange depreciation,

[5] See my paper on Hawtrey, in *EP*, pp. 128–9.

which is not expected to be temporary, does nothing to hold the funds that are capable of movement.

The moral, it will no doubt be said, is that convertibility, *at any rate of exchange*, should be abandoned. That some degree of impediment to convertibility, in a world of sovereign states, is necessary to make the international monetary system workable, does seem probable. But this is a slippery slope; to find impediments that do not themselves do great damage cannot be an easy matter. I myself regard it as part of a more general issue – that which I posed at the end of my first considered work on monetary theory, in 1935.[6] A monetary system – a sophisticated monetary system, with much 'fluidity' – is inherently unstable; it needs to have frictions imposed upon it to make it work. They will be frictions from the point of view of the arm's length 'price-mechanism', which I do not at all deny has a part – a great part – to play. From that point of view they are a nuisance. Still we need them.

[6] Essay 7 above.

Part IV
Methods

The papers that I have selected for this section focus primarily on the problems of integrating time into economic analysis in general, and of creating a theory of dynamics in particular. The first is a classic in the history of economic thought. ' "Revolutions" in Economics' (1976) is concerned with the development and change of economic theories, and presents a critique by example of the more grand theories of the evolution of knowledge to be found in writers such as Kuhn and Lakatos. A more gradualist approach is suggested, with theorists reflecting the changing problems of the economy which is the object and focus of their attention. In particular, classical and modern thought is distinguished according to its focus on production and distribution on the one side and exchange on the other.

The second piece, included here as essay 13, is an extract from *A Theory of Economic History* (1969). The book has been somewhat neglected by economists (but not by historians). It is included here for three reasons. It discusses the relationship between economics and history, and it suggests how economic history might be studied. But it also suggests where Hicks' own theories come from, how he constructed his theories of dynamics and growth as an attempt to provide a theory of the long run, a theory of economic change.

The third paper, 'Time in Economics' (1976) (essay 14), is an explicit treatment of time. It draws on the Austrian approach of *Capital and Time* (1972), and may be regarded as the major precursor of *Causality in Economics* (1979), to which the reader is referred. In particular the relationship between *time in economics* and *sequential causality* discussed in chapter 7 of *CE* should be noted. The paper presented here focuses on the irreversibility of time, and hence the difference in method in treating the past and the future.

Finally the selection is completed with an autobiographical note, 'The Formation of an Economist' (1970).

12

'Revolutions' in Economics

This paper arose out of a conference on methodology, in memory of Imre Lakatos, that was held at Nafplion, Greece, in September 1974. It was not itself given at that conference, but was written after it, as a personal reaction to the papers which were given at it. It was nevertheless published in the second volume of its proceedings: *Method and Appraisal in Economics* (ed. Spiro Latsis, Cambridge University Press, 1976).

The study of scientific 'revolutions', in which one system of thought (or 'research programme') has given place to another, has been shown, by Lakatos and his followers, to be a powerful tool in the methodology of natural science. Economics also has had its 'revolutions ; it is fruitful to study them in much the same manner. I think, however, that when one looks at them comparatively, one finds that their significance is very largely different.

This is a matter of importance, for economics itself. Economics is more like art or philosophy than science, in the use that it can make of its own history. The history of science is a fascinating subject; it is important (as has been shown) for the philosophy of science; but it is not important to the working scientist in the way that the history of economics is important to the working economist. When the natural scientist has come to the frontier of knowledge, and is ready for new exploration, he is unlikely to have much to gain from a contemplation of the path by which his predecessors have come to the place where he now stands. Old ideas are worked out; old controversies are dead and buried. The Ptolemaic system may live on in literature, or it may form the framework of a mathematical exercise; it has no direct interest to the modern astronomer.

Our position in economics is different; we cannot escape in the same way from our own past. We may pretend to escape; but the past crowds in on us all the same. Keynes and his contemporaries echo Ricardo and Malthus; Marx and Marshall are still alive. Some of us are inclined to be ashamed of this traditionalism, but when it is properly understood it is no cause for embarrassment; it is a consequence of what we are doing, or trying to do.

The facts which we study are not permanent, or repeatable, like the facts of the natural sciences; they change incessantly, and change without repetition. Considered as individual events, they are often events of great interest. Every business has a history of its own, every consumer a history of his own; any of these histories may have its own drama when we come close to it. But, as a general rule, it is not our business as economists to come close. We are trying to detect general patterns amid the mass of absorbing detail; shapes that repeat among the details that do not repeat. We can only do this if we select something less than the detail which is presented to us. In order to analyse, we must simplify and cut down.

Further, in practice, we must simplify quickly. Our special concern is with the facts of the present world; but before we can study the present, it is already past. In order that we should be able to say useful things about what is happening, before it is too late, we must select, even select quite violently. We must concentrate our attention, and hope that we have concentrated it in the right place. We must work, if we are to work effectively, in some sort of blinkers.

Our theories, regarded as tools of analysis, are blinkers in this sense. Or it may be politer to say that they are rays of light, which illuminate a part of the target, leaving the rest in the dark. As we use them, we avert our eyes from things that may be relevant, in order that we should see more clearly what we do see. It is entirely proper that we should do this, since otherwise we should see very little. But it is obvious that a theory which is to perform this function satisfactorily must be well chosen; otherwise it will illumine the wrong things. Further, since it is a changing world that we are studying, a theory which illumines the right things now may illumine the wrong things another time.[1] This may happen because of changes in the world (the things neglected may have grown relatively to the things considered) or because of changes in our sources of information (the sorts of facts that are readily accessible to us may have changed) or because of changes in ourselves (the things in which we are interested may have changed). There is, there can be, no economic theory which will do for us everything we want all the time.

Accordingly, while we are right to allow ourselves to become wrapped up in those theories which are useful now, we are unwise if

---

[1] As an example of this, see the discussion of the evolution of market theory in ch. 5, of my *CG* (1965).

we allow ourselves to forget that the time may come when we shall need something different. We may then be right to reject our present theories, not because they are wrong, but because they have become inappropriate. Things which we formerly left unnoticed (more or less deliberately unnoticed) may rise up and become essential; we shall have to bring them in, even if that means averting our attention from things we thought important before. That is the *special* reason why economics is prone to revolutions – revolutions which appear, while they are occurring, to be steps in advance, though from a different point of view they may take on quite another character.

The revolutions may be large or small. Big revolutions are (fortunately) rare. The Keynesian revolution is the obvious example of a big revolution; there are not more than two or three others which might conceivably be compared to it. It is possible that big revolutions are more likely to take their origins outside the ranks of academic economists in the narrow sense (Keynes was only a part-time academic economist). For big revolutions can only occur when something rather far away from the previous concentration of attention comes to the forefront, so that its recognition compels a major readjustment. Small revolutions, that are revolutions in my sense nonetheless, can more easily be made by academics. Working in 'blinkers' is uncongenial to the academic mind; it is difficult to teach the concentration without keeping an eye on what is around it. So it comes naturally to us to be on the watch for ways of bringing into attention things which have been only just left out; we have a bias in favour of inclusiveness and generality, even at the cost of ineffectiveness. We do keep that sort of watch fairly well.

There are, however, two ways in which we may keep our watch One is by generalisation, by constructing 'more general' theories theories which put more things into their places, even if we can do less with them when we have put them there.[2] This is a perfectly respectable activity; but what I am here concerned to point out i that it is not the only way in which we can do that particular business. The same function can be performed by the history of economics ii another way. If we seek to discover how it was, and why it was, tha concentrations of attention have changed, and theories (effective theories) have changed with them, we find ourselves 'standing back just as we do when we pursue the generalisation method; we ge something of the same gain, and it may be that we run less risk o losing our appreciation of 'effectiveness' as we get it. But I have ne

---

[2] Keynes's theory is of course not a general theory in this sense; it is a superbly effectiv theory, which gains power by what it leaves out.

need to champion one of these ways of broadening our minds against the other. There is plenty of room for both.[3]

The first of the 'revolutions' which I shall be considering is that which led to the establishment of 'classical' economics – the system of thought which was taken over by Adam Smith from the Physiocrats in France. If one asks what it is that distinguishes those great (and highly 'effective') economists from their relatively ineffective predecessors, the answer is surely to be found in the vision of the economic process which they possessed, a vision which made it possible for them to think economic problems through, not in separate bits, but together. This vision was not a vague sense of everything being inter-related; it had content that is capable of being identified and described.

There is an exact indication of that content in the full title of Adam Smith's book – *An Inquiry into the Nature and Causes of the Wealth of Nations*. If we take that title, not as a mere label in the modern manner, but as a description which means what it says, its meaning is apparent: wealth is production; the wealth of a nation is what we now call the national product.[4] Adam Smith is to tell us what the social product of a nation is, what is meant by its being large or small; what is meant by its growing. That is 'nature'. Then he is to tell us why the social product is large or small, and why it grows. That is 'causes'.

Much of what we say, and much of what Smith said, on these matters seems uncontroversial. The social product is large when the quantities of the factors of production that are used to make it are large, and when those large quantities are used with high efficiency. The social product grows by growth in the factors of production, by increase in the numbers and in the efficiency of labour, and by the accumulation of capital. And it grows by improvements in the efficiency with which capital is applied to labour; that is, by improvements in the efficiency with which the factors of production are

---

[3] I have emphasised another set of reasons why we should study the history of economics – its function as a means of communication – in my paper on 'Capital Controversies' (*EP*, 1977). See also *CEET* II, p. 238, and *CEET* III, pp. 372-3.

[4] We are nowadays so accustomed to thinking of wealth as capital wealth that it may not be easy to realise that in Smith wealth is normally taken in a 'flow' sense. Even in the first sentence of his book there is a snag which worries the modern reader. 'The annual labour of every nation is the fund which originally supplies it with all the necessities and conveniences of life which it annually consumes.' The repeated *annual* emphasises *flow*; but what about *fund*? I suggest that we get nearest to Smith's meaning if we interpret *fund* to mean *revolving fund*. This would square with what he says later (in book 2) about capital. The *flow* interpretation of the sentence, which is meant to set course for the whole work, and must therefore be coherent with the title, would then become clear.

combined. These statements sound obvious but when we take them to be obvious, we are not taking them literally, as (I believe) Smith did, or was at the least beginning to do.

There is, of course, no question that the flow of wealth is production; things are produced, and it is in these products that the flow of wealth consists. But the things that are produced are heterogeneous; it is not obvious that we can take them together and reduce them to a common 'stuff'. What is implied in the classical approach is that for essential purposes we can take them together. We can represent them by a flow of wealth, which is so far homogeneous that it can be greater or less. It was the study of this flow of wealth which the classics called *political economy*.[5]

How did Smith and his successors come to think in this way? By analogy, surely, with the experience of business. The products of a business may be heterogeneous, but they are reduced to a common measure by being valued in terms of money. It is in money terms that we can tell whether the turnover of one business is greater than that of another; cannot we do the same for nations? Adam Smith always found it easy, indeed too easy, to jump from the firm to the whole economy; it is not surprising that he found the analogy compelling. That, at the least, is the way he must have begun.

He soon found, however, that the money measure could not be used without precaution. It was necessary to distinguish between market values (which might not be significant as a means of valuation) and 'natural' or normal values which should be; and it was necessary to find a 'standard of value' so as to be able to correct for changes in the value of money. Thus, already in Smith, *political economy* is based upon a theory of value. It is of the first importance to emphasise that the primary purpose of that theory of value is not to explain prices, that is to say, to explain the working of markets; its primary purpose is to identify the values which are needed for the *weighting* of the social product, the reduction of the heterogeneous commodities which compose it to a common measure.

This, admittedly, is not very clear in Smith; it is much clearer in Ricardo. It was as a means of reducing heterogeneous commodities to a common measure that Ricardo used his labour theory of value. But it is not simply that device which marks the originality of Ricardo. The transition from Smith to Ricardo was itself a minor 'revolution'; but it did not come about, in the scientific manner,

[5] *Political economy* is identified by Smith with 'the nature and causes of the wealth of nations' (Smith, 1976, vol. 2, pp. 678–9). For the subject as defined by Smith's title, it was, I would maintain, a most appropriate name. It is not appropriate for a great part of what we now call economics, so one can understand why it was abandoned.

because of the need to take account of new facts, revealed by experiment or observation, facts which, however, had been *there* all the time. It did come about as a result of the need to accommodate new facts, but they were genuinely new facts, facts which had come into existence in the course of history – new *events*. Ricardo's rent theory, and the growth theory which followed from it, were reactions to the problems of his own time – the problems of feeding a growing population, forced upon attention, first by the Napoleonic blockade, and then in terms of reconstruction after the War. Ricardian economics is a remarkable intellectual achievement; but it could not have taken the form it did, except under the pressure of particular events.

As time went on, the land problem became less acute; thus though Ricardo's theory remained, for it had no intellectual rival, it became less and less *relevant*. So the time came when economics was ready for another 'revolution'. In fact there were two revolutions, at about the same time; one made by Marx, the other by Jevons, Walras and Menger. As a result of these two revolutions, economics was divided; economists proceeded, for many years, on quite separate tracks. How do we describe these revolutions, and how do we explain them?

In relation to the classical political economy, the distinguishing feature of the work of Marx is its distributism. Classical economics had been a theory of production and distribution, but production came first. *The Wealth of Nations*, as indicated, is a book about production ('nature' and 'causes'); though Adam Smith says much, incidentally, about distribution, what he says is unsystematic. It is true that if one judges Ricardo by that famous passage in the preface to his *Principles*, he is stressing distribution, against what he held to be its neglect by Adam Smith. 'To determine the laws which regulate this distribution is the principal problem of Political Economy.' (That, of course, is the way Marx took Ricardo; it explains why Marx, and Marxists, have always had some affection for Ricardo.) Nevertheless, in spite of this passage, the general tendency of Ricardo's work is to treat distribution as secondary. He was interested in distribution because of the importance which he attached to the effects of distribution on production, not because he had much interest in distribution *per se*. It is only in the third of the major classics, in John Stuart Mill's *Principles*, that there is much attention to distribution for its own sake. By that change of emphasis Mill opened the way to Marx.

The half-way house which we find in Mill explains a good deal. At the date when Mill was writing, the fact of the Industrial Revolution was unmistakable; a great increase in productive power had already

J

occurred. But it had not brought with it the social gains which 'friends of humanity' (Ricardo's phrase) had expected from it. Thus already, to Mill, increase in production had come to seem to be of less importance than improvement in distribution. Further increase in production did not much matter; so the achievement of a distributive or 'socialist' society seemed near at hand. That was where the classical vision, in Mill, appeared to have led; and from that point Marx could fairly easily take over.

The other revolution is not so easy to describe, or to explain. The economists who led it are commonly called 'marginalists'; but that is a bad term, for it misses the essence of what was involved. The 'margin' is no more than an expression of the mathematical rule for a maximum (or minimum); any sort of economics is marginalist when it is concerned with maximising.[6] (Ricardo himself could be quite marginalist at times.) The essential novelty in the work of these economists was that instead of basing their economics on production and distribution, they based it on exchange. I therefore propose to make use of a term which was sometimes used, at the time in question, to mean the theory of exchange; it was called catallactics.[7] So I shall re-name the so-called marginalists as catallactists.

There is, of course, no doubt that exchange is a basic feature of economic life, at least in a 'free', or what Marx would have called a 'capitalist' economy. By none of the classical economists would that have been denied. But while the classics looked at the economic system primarily from the production angle, the catallactists looked at it primarily from the side of exchange. It was possible, they found, to construct a 'vision' of economic life out of the theory of exchange, as the classics had done out of the social product. It was quite a different vision.

How do we explain the rise of catallactics? It can, I think, be explained in more than one way. Some will want to explain it as a reaction against socialism – hardly, at first, against Marx who must have been practically unknown to the first catallactists, but against the more general socialist tendencies which were already 'in the air'. One can make a case for that. It can be claimed that political economy is always in some sense socialist, catallactics individualist; though one cannot make that fit the history unless one distinguishes between means and ends. The Old Political Economists were socialists (or at

---

[6] I am, of course, aware that there are problems of maximising which cannot be developed in terms of marginal *equations*.

[7] See for instance Edgeworth, *Mathematical Psychics* (1881), p. 30. The term has been used more recently by von Mises in *Human Action* (1949).

least 'social') in the ends they set up; but they were individualist in practice, because they held that individualism was the way to the achievement of their social ends. As long as that was tenable, the conflict between ends was not acute. Whether one's objective was the 'welfare' of society or the freedom of the individual, the path to be followed was the same. Those to whom the one mattered more and those to whom the other mattered more could march under the same banner; they did not need to emphasise their differences. But as faith in the 'hidden-hand' declined, as the 'socialists' became socialist, the die-hard individualist was bound to cut adrift. He perceived, as he had not had to perceive before, that his objectives differed from those of his former allies. He was bound to insist upon his rejection of purely social ends, and to make a fuss about his rejection of them.

I admit that this is one strand which can be recognised in the work of the more politically minded catallactists. It appears in Pareto, at some stages of his work, and in an extreme form in some members of the Austrian school, especially Ludwig von Mises.[8] It is certainly one way in which the catallactic approach can be used; there are living writers, in America and elsewhere, who continue to use it in this manner. The exchange economy is a free economy; so to those who put freedom at the head of their values, it is bound to have a particular attraction. For it seems to show that a world is workable in which we are all allowed to go our own ways, our different ways, with a minimum of interference from other people.[9]

There is this individualist strand, especially in later work, but it will hardly do as an explanation of the 'revolution'. One can find it in Pareto, and perhaps even in Wicksell,[10] but in the work of the first generation (Jevons, say, or Menger) where is it? The most that could be argued in their case is that they were responding to a challenge. The socialists had made it impossible for the exchange economy to be taken for granted; whether one was for it, or against it, the time had come when it needed to be better understood. There may be something in that; but even that does not have to be the main answer.

I have insisted that the Old Political Economy, like other 'powerful' economic theories, was a concentration of attention. It gained

[8] See in particular von Mises's book *Die Gemeinwirtschaft* (1922) which was translated into English under the title *Socialism* (1959).
[9] *'Ce n'est pas qu'elle gouverne bien, mais elle gouverne peu'* as someone in Anatole France says of the Third Republic. The British classical economists would never have said that of *their* state.
[10] It is in his book on public finance (*Finanztheoretische Untersuchungen*, 1896) that Wicksell carries his individualism to the most extreme lengths.

strength by its omissions, by the things it put on one side. Some of the things it put on one side were rather obvious. Thus throughout the century in which it was dominant, there had been numerous writers who had refused to put on the Smithian 'blinkers'; they had been unwilling to think in the way in which that system of thought required them to think. But they had been unable to develop any system of thought with comparable potency. That is just what it was that Walras and Menger did.[11]

I would therefore maintain that the principal reason for the triumph of catallactics – in its day it was quite a triumph – was nothing to do with socialism or individualism; nor did it even have much to do with the changes that were then occurring in the 'real world'. The construction of a powerful economic theory, based on exchange, instead of production and distribution, had always been a possibility. The novelty in the work of the great catallactists is just that they achieved it.

The appeal of catallactics lay in its intellectual quality, much more than in its individualism. The first catallactists were poor mathematicians, but they were thinking mathematically; and the mathematics that is implied in their theories has proved to be capable of enormous development. Already, before that happened, there was enough of intellectual interest to set its mark on the minds of many economists (who were now, it should be noticed, to a large extent academic economists). Though 'marginal utility' had its difficulties (difficulties of which we in our time have become increasingly aware) it was becoming easier to think of 'individuals' having given wants, or given utility functions, than to swallow the homogeneous 'wealth' of the Old Political Economy. It was easier to think of the economic system as a system of inter-related markets (Walras) or as an adjustment of means to ends (Menger) than to keep up the fiction of the social product any longer.

I have devoted this much space to the 'marginal revolution' (or 'catallactist revolution') because it seems to me to be the best example in economics of something which fits the Lakatos scheme. It provided a new way of taking up the economic problem; not just a new theory, but a new approach which was capable of much development. It was not (I have tried to show) in the main a reaction to contemporary

---

[11] The Lausanne and the Austrian versions of catallactics are by no means identical, and it is possible that Jevons's version, if he had completed it, would have constituted a third variety. But it is noticeable that as time has gone on, these versions, at first distinct, have grown together. Later catallactists, such as Wicksell and Schumpeter and many more modern writers, have drawn upon Menger and upon Walras in equal measure. So the distinction between them is not one which we shall need to emphasise for our present purpose.

events. The possibility of a utility theory had been there all the time; what the catallactists showed was that something could be done with it.

I pass on to what happened afterwards, in this century. That, from the point of view I am here adopting, was not just the Keynesian revolution; there was another thing too. You may be thinking that what I have called catallactics should be given a more familiar name – micro-economics; it is true that what I have called the catallactist revolution can be regarded as the rise of micro-economics. But if I used that term I might find myself saying that Keynesianism was macro-economics; and that is not right. There are two kinds of modern macro-economics. One is Keynesian; the other is quite different.

If we must have a founder for this other kind of macro-economics, it must be Pigou. Pigou of the *Economics of Welfare*,[12] or perhaps of *Wealth and Welfare*.[13] Long before the (relevant) work of Keynes! But what I mean by the other kind of macro-economics is not welfare economics in the modern sense; for what happened in the new welfare economics (in which I myself played my part) was that welfare economics was captured by the catallactists and it has never got quite free. If one looks at the whole of Pigou's book, not just at its (now) misleading title, one sees that it is a revival of the classical political economy. It is a book on production and distribution, in the classical manner. The definition of the real social product; how it can be increased; and how it is divided up. There is a line of descent, from Pigou, through my own *Theory of Wages*[14] to a great deal of modern growth theory (which, if one looks at it critically, is quite un-Keynesian). I think, for instance, of much of the work of Professor Solow. It is surely in Lakatos's sense a 'research programme'; it has been capable of much development, and it is by no means extinct.

If we are to think clearly about it, we must give it a name. I tried, at one time, to keep the classical name, and to call it political economy. But that does not do. I am now inclined to match catallactics, and to call what I am now talking about as plutology. (I know that the only writer who has previously used that term was a catallactist! But he was not of great importance; his ghost will doubtless forgive us.) Plutology is good Greek for theory of wealth.

Classical political economy, then, is the old plutology; that which descends from Pigou is the new. Why has it come up, and why has it

---

[12] First edition 1920.
[13] (1912).
[14] *TW* (1932).

flourished? Surely the reason for its success is the availability of the statistical material on which it can feed. We now have vast quantities of statistical material, on the macro-level; much more abundant (at least apparently) than the empirical material for micro-economics. The old plutologists did not have this material; that is why their work appears so abstract. They did not have the statistics to give it flesh and blood.

Why do we have these statistics, which they did not? It is not the case, as might be supposed from natural science analogies, that the lack of statistics, of this kind, was shown up by the classical theories; and that gave an incentive to collect them. There was something of this, but it was not the main thing. The statistics are a by-product of a great historical change, the great extension of the powers of the State which has occurred in this century. That, in its turn, is partly to be ascribed to political changes; but it is also, very importantly, a consequence of the cheapening of the costs of administration, which has made it possible for modern governments to collect information on a vastly greater scale than was previously practicable. One must always remember, when reading the older economists, that they were desperately short of facts. Nowadays we are swamped by floods of facts, or what appear to be facts, welling, all the time, out of the machines.[15]

I turn, finally, to Keynes. Keynesianism also, as it has developed, has had to accommodate the flood of facts; but it is clear that it did not start in that way. The 'social accounting Keynesianism' which is now in all the textbooks (and in the articles of journalists) was quite a late development; it is not really present even in the *General Theory*. If one looks at that book in terms of what led up to it (not in terms of what happened afterwards), one sees where it comes out. Where it belongs, when it is so considered, is not in the field of general (or 'real') economics – to which nearly all I have hitherto been saying refers. Where it belongs is in monetary economics; and since monetary statistics have long been abundant (much more abundant than most other statistics until the present century) monetary economics has always been topical; it has always had a close relation to the circumstances of the time in which it has been written; it has had to change as they have changed.

As I have stated elsewhere (at more length)[16] it is my own view that if the Keynes story is to be told properly (in its historical context) it should begin before Keynes. It begins with Hawtrey: *Currency and*

---

[15] Cf. what I say on the 'Administration Revolution' in *TEH* (1969), pp. 99, 162-6.
[16] In my paper on Hawtrey (*EP*, 1977).

Credit (1919). It must begin there, for there is a large part of Keynes's *Treatise* (1930) which is a reply to Hawtrey. A reply, on the matters where Keynes and Hawtrey differed; these are important, but they can only be seen in proper proportion once we have realised that on the most basic matter they were on the same side. Neither of them held that the economic system is automatically self-righting. The 'instability of capitalism' is nowadays commonly held to be a characteristically Keynesian doctrine; but it is already there – in Hawtrey. It has never been better stated than in the first chapter of Hawtrey's book, the chapter that is called 'Credit without Money'. In Hawtrey as in Keynes, the system has to be stabilised, by policy and by some instrument of policy. It was over the instrument of policy that they differed.

As the difference began, it looked rather small. Both agreed that the instrument was a rate of interest; but Hawtrey looked to the short rate, Keynes to the long. At this point I would accept that Keynes was more up to date. It was a change in the structure of the industrial system which Keynes perceived, and one on which Hawtrey was much less clear, making fixed capital investment of greater importance than it had been in the past, which impelled Keynes to make his first departure from the Hawtrey system. Another example, you will notice, of a theoretical development echoing a historical process.

But then Keynes discovered that his long rate was not only less directly susceptible to banking control than Hawtrey's short, but that it was very likely to be found that just when it was wanted it could not move enough. So he moved away from monetary methods to the 'fiscal' methods which have later been so largely associated with his name. That is a process that is taking place *inside* the *General Theory*. The structure of the book dates from the time when the long rate was pre-eminent; but as the work develops he cuts the ground under his own feet. Thus it was, that what began as monetary theory became 'fiscalism'.

It was nevertheless the particular circumstances of the 1930s which had this effect; it was because of his desire (his very proper desire) to apply his theory to the particular conditions of the time in which he was living that he moved in this way. At other times he might have reacted differently; one can even be fairly sure, from a general knowledge of his work, that he would have reacted differently. So it does no honour to Keynes to go on applying his theory, without drastic amendment, to the very different circumstances of the time in which we are now living. The Keynes theory has 'dated', just as the Hawtrey theory 'dated'. That does not mean that we must go back to the Hawtrey theory, or to still older theories, as many contemporaries would like to do. We must still push on. One can yet recognise that there may be something dramatically appropriate – nice for the historian, though not for those who have to live through it – if it should turn up, as now seems to be likely, that it is on the field of primary commodities (which Hawtrey emphasised, but Keynes, at least in the *General Theory*, so much under-emphasised) that the Age of Keynes will have met its nemesis.

I have covered a wide field – I had to! Let me sum up by returning to what I said at the beginning. What we want, in economics, are theories which will be useful, practically useful. That means that they must be selective. But all selection is dangerous. So there is plenty of room for criticism, and for the filling in of gaps, building some sort of bridge between one selective theory and another. There is plenty of room for academic work, doing that sort of a job. Much of it, I am well aware, works in its own 'blinkers', seeing the mote that is in one's brother's eye but not the beam that is in one's own. That, I am afraid, is the nature of the case. Still, one could learn a little humility.

There is also, one must not forget, the application to history – not to the history of thought, with which I have here been concerned, but to economic history in the other sense. It is not only for application to the present that we need economics; we need it also for the interpretation of the past. If what I have said is true, this is a most delicate matter. We should not analyse (say) nineteenth-century history in terms of nineteenth-century theories; for our knowledge of the facts of that time is different from that of contemporaries, and the questions we ask are different from those that contemporaries asked. Yet we have to be careful in the application of modern theories, which arise out of modern experience. Neither is necessarily right.

13

Theory and History

This is an extract from chapter 1 of *A Theory of Economic History* (1969).

Economic history is a large subject – an enormously large subject. It extends, in one of its dimensions, over the whole world; in another, over the whole span of human history, from the 'dark backward and abysm of time', the earliest ages of which anthropologists and archaeologists have given us some fragmentary knowledge, right up to that edge of the unknown future, the present day. I call it economic history; but I am not interpreting economic history in a narrow sense. I am certainly not claiming that it envelops the whole of history, or that one should always be looking for economic motives behind apparently non-economic behaviour; but I do not want to contract its boundaries, as is so often done in these days with the boundaries of economics itself. In spite of the vogue of 'Quantitative Economic History', economic historians are under less temptation than economists to see their subject as purely quantitative. This is not only for the reason that as we go back in time the figures become so patchy; there is a deeper reason, too. We are bound to find, as we go back into the past, that the economic aspects of life are less differentiated from other aspects they they are today. Economic history is often presented, and rightly presented, as a process of specialisation; but the specialisation is not only a specialisation among economic activities, it is also a specialisation of economic activities (what are becoming economic activities) from activities of other sorts. This is a specialisation which is not yet complete and can never be complete; but it has gone far enough for us to imitate it in our studies. We contract the boundaries of our subjects, and of our sub-subjects, to make them more manageable; and we are enabled to do this because our academic specialisation corresponds to something which is in fact happening in the 'real world'. But it is not all that is happening in the world; we suffer, and we know that we suffer, by getting so far apart. A major function of economic history, as I see it, is to be a forum where economists and political scientists, lawyers, sociologists, and historians – historians of events and of ideas and of technologies – can meet and talk to one another. In what sense can one attempt a 'theory of history'? Theory and history, many would say, are opposites; at best, alternatives; it is not the business of a historian to think in theoretical terms. Or perhaps it would be conceded that he may make use of some disconnected bits of theory to serve as hypotheses for the elucidation of some particular historical processes; no more than that. I think I understand this scepticism, and I have some sympathy with it. I have more sympathy with it than with the grand designs of a Toynbee or a Spengler, the makers of historical patterns which have more aesthetic than scientific appeal. My 'theory of history' will quite definitely not be a theory of history in their sense. It will be a good deal nearer to the kind of thing that was attempted by Marx, who did take from his economics some general ideas which he applied to history, so that the pattern which he saw in history had some extra-historical support. That is much more the kind of thing I want to try to do.

It does not seem unreasonable to suppose that we can draw from social science, not only (in view of what has just been said) from economics, some general ideas which can be used by historians as a means of ordering their material. I suppose that most historians are coming to grant that this is so. What remains an open question is whether it can only be done in a larger way, so that the general course of history, at least in some important aspects, can be fitted into place. Most of those who take the latter view would use the Marxian categories, or some modified version of them; since there is so little in the way of an alternative version that is available, it is not surprising that they should. It does, nevertheless, remain extraordinary that one hundred years after *Das Kapital*, after a century during which there have been enormous developments in social science, so little else would have emerged. Surely it is possible that Marx was right in his vision of logical processes at work in history, but that we, with much knowledge of fact and social logic which he did not possess, and with another century of experience at our disposal, should conceive of the nature of those processes in a distinctly different way.

One of the things which we have learned – a general point which must be emphasised at the outset – is to distinguish between those historical questions which can usefully be discussed in terms of the notion of statistical uniformity, and those which cannot. Every historical event has some aspect in which it is unique; but nearly always there are other aspects in which it is a member of a group, often of quite a large group. If it is one of the latter aspects in which we are interested, it will be the group, not the individual, on which we shall fix our attention; it will be the average, or norm, of the group which is what we shall be trying to explain. We shall be able to allow that the individual may diverge from the normal without being deterred from the recognition of a statistical uniformity. This is what we do, almost all the time, in economics.[1] We do not claim, in our demand theory for instance, to be able to say anything useful about the behaviour of a particular consumer, which may be dominated by motives quite peculiar to himself; but we do claim to be able to say something about the behaviour of the whole market – of the whole group, that is, of the consumers of a particular product. We can do this, it must be emphasised, without implying any 'determinism'; we make no question that each of the consumers, as an individual, is perfectly free to choose. Economics is rather specially concerned with such 'statistical' behaviour.

The historical phenomena to which a theory of history might apply are those which, in the light of our interest in them, can be regarded as having this statistical character. Most of the phenomena of economic history (however widely considered) do have it; the questions we want to ask about economic history deal mainly with groupings that can be made to possess it. But the distinction is not, in principle, a distinction between economic and other kinds of history. In any department of history we may find ourselves looking for statistical uniformities. The distinction is between an interest in general phenomena and an interest in particular stories. Whenever our interest is in general phenomena, theory (economic or other social theory) may be relevant; otherwise usually not.

To take some examples. Suppose we take the view (which on some versions is quite a tempting view) that there would have been no French Revolution if Louis XVI had not been so lazy and inattentive[2] – that it could have been avoided if he had just had the virtues of a conscientious civil servant, like his ancestors Louis XIV or Philip II of Spain – then the French Revolution, regarded from that angle, would be a particular story, not one of the phenomena to which historical theory could be applied. Even so, it might be regarded from other angles from which it would look different. If we

---

[1] When we stop doing so, as sometimes happens in the 'theory of the firm', we get into trouble.

[2] 'He was bored with his job (son métier l'ennuyait)', so Madelin puts it (*La Révolution*, Paris, 1933, p. 29).

regarded it as an expression of social changes, which would have occurred in France even under a better ruler, and which did occur in other countries in less spectacular ways, it would become a particular instance of a more general phenomenon, which could be theoretically discussed. Or if our interest were in the reasons for this concentration of power, which made it possible for the defects of one man to have such disastrous consequences, that again could be made into a theoretical question, though it would be even less of an economic question than the former. But these are relatively sophisticated questions which go much below the surface of the fact of the French Revolution.

As an obvious contrast, consider the 'Industrial Revolution' in England, the change in the organization of industry in England which was going on at much the same time. Some of the story of that Revolution can be told, and has been told, in particular biographies; but there is no biography that is central. No one would dream of claiming that there was any one particular man, any single inventor or entrepreneur, without whose activity the English Industrial Revolution could not have occurred.[3] Though there is a sense in which the Industrial Revolution is an event, it is itself a statistical phenomenon; it is a general tendency to which theory is unmistakably relevant.

A theory of history will have to be concerned with such general phenomena; it is to history conceived in that way that it will have to apply. Such is by no means the whole of history; I have tried to make it quite clear that I do not think it is. There is another kind, which is not concerned with such general issues; which makes it a virtue to run in terms of individuals, their deeds, their characters, their relations with one another. It has to be concerned (too much for some modern tastes) with famous people; for it is only such people who have left enough record behind them for it to be possible for us to bring ourselves into personal contact with them. Sometimes we can get it directly, through their own writings; sometimes only indirectly, when enough is left for them to be brought back to life by the dramatic skill of historian or biographer. I am sure that kind of history should not be undervalued. It is relevant, even here; for it is unsafe to exercise one's imagination on the past – even to the extent

---

[3] There is an enjoyable attempt by an economic historian to tell a good part of the story of the American Industrial Revolution biographically (J. R. T. Hughes, *The Vital Few*, Boston, 1966). But I do not think (and I do not suppose that Professor Hughes would think) that it invalidates my point.

that it is needed for 'theoretical' purposes – unless it has been warmed by that 'old-fashioned' history.[4]

After all, the way in which the economist develops his hypotheses is by asking himself the question, 'What should I do if I were in that position? It is a question that must always be qualified by adding: if I were that kind of person'. If I were a mediaeval merchant, or a Greek slave-owner! It is only by getting a feel of what people were like that one can begin to guess.

The task which lies before us can now be described. It is a theoretical enquiry, which must proceed in general terms – the more general the better. We are to classify states of society, economic states of society; we are to look for intelligible reasons for which one such state should give way to another. It will be a sequence not altogether unlike the 'Feudalism, Capitalism, Socialism' or Marx, or the stages of economic developments of the German Historical School.[5] But our presuppositions are less deterministic, less evolutionary than theirs, and that will make a difference. It is only a *normal* development for which we are looking, so it does not have to cover all the facts; we must be ready to admit exceptions, exceptions which nevertheless we should try to explain. We are not to think of our normal process as one which, on being begun, is bound to be completed; it may be cut short from external causes, or it may encounter internal difficulties from which only sometimes there is a way of escape. All these possibilities will be admitted. Though we distinguish an underlying trend to which we may be willing to give the name of 'progress' or 'growth' or 'development', it is progress that is often interrupted, and which only too often takes disagreeable, even terrible forms. After all, why not? We are accustomed to thinking of our last two centuries as a period of economic development, but it is

---

[4] Though the passage from the old style of history-writing (such as Macaulay's) to the new (of which the new *Cambridge Modern History* is an outstanding example) may seem to bring the historian nearer to the economist, it is not an unmixed advantage even from the latter's point of view. It is so easy for the economist to forget that the 'actors' in his models (if the models are to be practically useful) should have at least one characteristic of real people, that they do not know what is going to happen; so they must take their decisions in the light of possibilities that look as if they might be realised, but which (as we now know from hindsight) are not going to be realised. Diplomatic history may seem at first sight to be the department of history which is furthest removed from economics; but since it is in the documents of diplomatic history that contingency planning is at its most explicit, it has lessons for the economist.

[5] For a classical criticism of the views of the Germany Historical School (so influential around 1900), see W. Eucken, *Grundlagen der Nationalökonomie* Godesberg, 1947) ch. 4.

a development that has been irregular ('cyclical') and has many dark places to it. Why should the same not hold further back?

Every statistical time-series can be analysed, by purely mechanical methods, into trend and cycle; it is a natural human way of thinking, applicable, in a rough way, to non-numerical data also. Why should we not treat the Economic History of the World as a single process – a process that (at least so far) has a recognizable trend? Even the rises and declines of civilizations can find a place among the cycles that are imposed upon it.

Where shall we start? There is a transformation which is antecedent to Marx's Rise of Capitalism, and which, in terms of more recent economics, looks like being even more fundamental. This is the Rise of the Market, the Rise of the Exchange Economy. It takes us back to a much earlier stage of history, at least for its beginnings; so far back indeed that on those beginnings (or first beginnings) we have little direct information. But there are several ways in which we can deduce, fairly reliably, what must have occurred.

It is evident, in the first place that the transformation was a gradual transformation; some of its later stages come much more clearly into the light of day. Secondly, it was not a transformation that occurred once for all; there are societies which have slipped back from being exchange economies, after which the same tale has been gone through again. Thirdly, there are 'underdeveloped' countries which have only undergone the transformation in quite recent times; some, even now, have not completed it. From these various sources we have a good deal of indirect evidence; so that we can fairly safely deduce what must have happened, for the first time, many centuries B.C.

14

Time in Economics

This paper was published in a Festschrift in honour of Nicholas Georgescu-Roegen, entitled *Evolution, Welfare and Time in Economics* edited by A. M. Tang *et al.* (1976).

Two years ago I published a book called *Capital and Time*. You might reasonably expect that in the present lecture I should just be going on with what I did in that book. This is in fact one of the things to which I shall be coming; but such continuation is only one of the things which I have in mind. My subject here is much broader. It concerns a principle which has come up, in several ways, in the work of Professor Georgescu; so it should be a suitable topic for a paper that is being written for him. It has also come up, sometimes in similar ways, more often in different ways, in much of my own work. I have not always been faithful to it, but when I have departed from it I have found myself coming back to it. It is clearly his principle; but I think I can claim that on the whole it has been mine as well.

It is a very simple principle: the irreversibility of time. In space we can move either way, or any way; but time just goes on, never goes back. We represent time on our diagrams by a spatial coordinate; but that representation is never a complete representation; it always leaves something out. And it is not only in simple diagrams that we represent time by space; there are highly sophisticated models which, in effect, do the same thing. It is quite hard to get away, in any part of our thinking, from the spatial representation. We represent time by a 'trend variable'; but that is again the same thing; it does not fully show time going on.

One of the principal consequences of the irreversibility of time is that past and future are different. Not just different as front and back are different; you cannot turn past into future, or future into past, as by turning round you can turn back into front. The past is past, over and done with; it is there and cannot be changed. 'Not heaven itself upon the past hath power' – the line of Dryden which I was already quoting, on nearly the first occasion when I came to grips with the issue, in *Value and Capital* (1939).[1] The past, however, has this virtue that we can have knowledge of it, knowledge of fact. The knowledge that we have, or can have, of the past is different in kind from what we can know of the future; for the latter, at best, is no more than a knowledge of probabilities. This may happen, or that may happen. But it is something quite definite which *has* happened.

It is true that our knowledge of the past is incomplete. All we know is what has been remembered, or recorded; or perhaps it has left some mark upon the present world from which we can deduce what happened, probably what happened. Thus even our knowledge of the past is largely a matter of probabilities. But these probabilities are different from probabilities about the future. Past populations, for instance, are recorded at census dates; if we want a figure for population between census dates we have to estimate it. Yet the estimation of population in 1885, when populations in 1880 and in 1890 alone are recorded, is a matter of getting as near as we can to a *right* figure. The country did have a population in 1885; by using more and more of relevant information available to us now we can in this (no doubt favourable) case be fairly sure that we cannot be far wrong. With estimates of the future, the situation is quite different. There is no *right* figure for population in 2000, no right figure *now*. There will be a right figure when 2000 comes, but only when that date is passing into the past.

It is already apparent from this simple example how complicated these time-relations can be; how easy it is to slip into ways of thinking which treat past and future alike. How easy it is to forget, when we contemplate the past, that much of what is now past was then future. Action is always directed towards the future; but past actions, when we contemplate them in their places in the stream of past events, lose that orientation toward the future which they undoubtedly possessed at the time when they were taken. We arrange past data in time-series, but our time-series are not fully in time. The relation of year 9 to year 10 looks like its relation to year 8; but in year 9 year 10 was future while year 8 was past. The actions of year 9 were based, or could be based, upon knowledge of year 8; but not on knowledge of year 10, only on guesses about year 10. For in year 9 the knowledge that we have about year 10 did not yet exist.

---

[1] *VC*, p. 130. The poem from which I took the quotation purports to be a translation from Horace, but the correspondence with its 'original' is far from close.

What I have been saying, so far, must sound very obvious. But its consequences for economics are quite far reaching.

One application, which I shall do no more than mention, is to Social Accounting. We are tempted to say that the net investment of a year is the difference between opening and closing stock – the difference between the value of the capital stock at the end of the year and at the beginning. We know that we must correct, for inflation or deflation, changes in the value of money which may have occurred within the year. But this does not get to the root of the matter. The value that is set upon the opening stock depends in part upon the value which is expected, at the beginning of the year, for the closing stock; but that was then future, while at the end of the year it is already present (or past). There may be things which were included in the opening stock because, in the light of information then available, they seem to be valuable; but at the end of the year it is clear that they are not valuable, so they have to be excluded. Such revisions, due to new information, may occur at any time. Suppose that information comes in during year 2 which makes it clear that the capital stock at the end of year 1 was over-valued. This may well mean that the net investment of year 1, calculated at the end of year 1, was over-valued – at least it seems to be over-valued from the standpoint of the end of year 2. It needs to be written down for its mistakes – mistakes which only in. the course of time have become revealed.[2]

I leave that on one side, and pass to other applications, of which the first is a simple application to consumer theory. The point is very simple; yet it is one which in most presentations (including some for which I have been personally responsible) gets most blatantly left out. It is immensely convenient, in economics, to suppose that 'the consumer' (as we call him) has a fully formed scale of preferences, by which all the choices that are available to him on the market can be ordered. I am still of the opinion that there are many purposes (including, very probably, the most important purposes) for which that assumption can be justified. But it is itself a very odd assumption; to take it, as many economists do, as being justifiable for all purposes, must, I now believe, be wrong.

The picture which is called to mind by this conventional assumption is that of the consumer (or his wife) paying a weekly visit to the super-market, having been given just so much to spend out of the

[2] See *CT*, pp. 164-6. Also a paper entitled 'The Concept of Income in relation to taxation and to business management' which was given at a meeting of the International Institution of Public Finance in 1979 and is reprinted in *CEET* III.

family income. She picks up goods from the shelves; then, as she adds up the cost in her mind, she finds that it comes to more than her allowance. So she has to give up some of the things she wanted to buy, or has to substitute something cheaper. She juggles things about until she finds the collection which is within her budget and which suits her best.

Such a consumer I would agree, 'reveals her preferences'. But consider the case of another consumer decision, a decision of what car to buy, or whether to buy a new car. If it is asked how that decision is made it is surely a matter of deciding *what one can afford*. I can afford this; I cannot afford that. But what is meant by not being able to afford it? The conventional answer, by the economist, is to say that if the car is acquired, something else will have to be given up; and that 'something else' is more desired than the car. That is to say, the consumer is supposed to re-think his whole budget, identifying the collection of goods which would have to be given up if the car was purchased. Now it may sometimes happen that a consumer proceeds in that way, but it seems unlikely that it will often happen. It seems much more likely that he proceeds with some idea, based upon previous experience, of what he can afford. He judges whether or not to buy a car, not by re-thinking his whole budget, but by a single test.

From this point of view the replacement of the old consumer theory – the marginal utility theory – by the modern theory of ordinal preferences (a replacement in which I myself have played a part) was not so clear an advance as is usually supposed. Marshall's consumer, who decides on his purchases by comparing the marginal utility of what is to be bought with the marginal utility of the money he will have to pay for it, is more like an actual consumer, at least so far as some important purchases are concerned, than Samuelson's consumer, who 'reveals his preferences'. The marginal utility of money, on which Marshall relies, is much more than the mere Lagrange multiplier, the role to which it has been degraded. It is the means by which the consumer is enabled to make his separate decisions, and to make them fairly rationally, without being obliged to take the trouble to weigh all conceivable alternatives. It is the means by which he decides *what he can afford.*

But his estimate of the marginal utility of money, to him, is based upon his past experience. It is by experience that he learns the standard by which his desires for the things he would like to buy are to be judged. In static conditions, when income is steady (or fairly steady) and prices are steady (or fairly steady), it is a reliable standard; and it was of course in terms of such conditions that Marshall's theory was originally set out. But when income is changing (or when many prices are changing) it becomes less reliable. It is based on the past; when the present is seriously unlike the past it becomes a less reliable guide. The *lags* with which consumption responds to a change in real income, though they are partly a matter of constraints set by commitments (including as commitments the possession of durable goods), must also be a matter of the time which is taken for the marginal utility of money, as it appears to the consumer, to respond to the change. To make fully rational decisions in fundamentally new conditions is by no means easy.

The matter is probably of greater importance in times of inflation than it is in more settled conditions. I believe that we miss the point about inflation when we look at it, as we so usually do, in terms of index-numbers. In terms of index-numbers there has always been some inflation (or deflation); an index-number of prices hardly ever stays quite constant from year to year. Yet there have been conditions in which there has been no inflation, in a highly significant sense. This is when there are many prices which are not changing, or changing very little. So long as that condition holds, the standard which the consumer makes for himself, out of his past experience, is a reliable standard; so he can make his decisions, deciding what he can afford fairly rationally. This is to be contrasted with the condition that is now being experienced in so many countries, when all prices, or nearly all prices, have broken loose from their moorings. That is true inflation; apart from its other costs (which are more familiar) there is this other cost – that rational decisions, even within the field of consumption, become so much harder to make.

That is all I have to say on this particular matter. I turn to wider questions. The parts of economics where the distinction with which I began is of greatest importance are the theory of capital and (as we shall see) the theory of markets.

As far as capital theory is concerned, the story goes back a long way. It appears, very strikingly, in the history of the Austrian school, a group of economists who (as everyone knows) were particularly concerned about the relations of capital and time. The two progenitors of the Austrian school were Menger and Böhm-Bawerk (Wieser, at this time of day, seems very secondary; while Schumpeter and Hayek belong to later generations). At a casual reading, Menger and Böhm appear to be saying much the same thing; so it is something of a shock when one discovers that in the view of Menger (as recorded by Schumpeter)[3] Böhm-Bawerk's theory was 'one of the greatest errors ever committed'. What was it in Böhm that so annoyed Menger? I believe it is simply that in Menger time is unidirectional. Menger's theory is an economics *in* time but Böhm's is an economics *of* time, in which time is no more than a mathematical parameter – a parameter of what we should now call capital-intensity. (Of course, there are passages in which Böhm gets closer to Menger than he does in the structure of his theory; but to say that in Böhm time is just a parameter of capital-intensity is not so far wrong.) In Menger time is much more than that.

I do not suppose that Menger ever read Wicksell; but if he had read Wicksell's version of Böhm's theory (the version which has become more familiar to most economists) he would have found that his judgment was amply confirmed. For he would have found that in the hands of Wicksell the theory became no more than a theory of a stationary state, no more than that. In a stationary state one moment of time is just like another. The stationary state is out of time; time has stood still. In Menger, time never stood still.

I do not claim that Menger had more than the beginnings of a theory of an economy *in* time. But he did have that; a clear indication is his theory of liquidity.[4] What Menger had to say on liquidity is deeper than what was said by anyone else before Keynes; indeed I think it is deeper than what is in Keynes. I know that I had to go on thinking about liquidity for many years after Keynes before I realised that I had got to a point which Menger had reached, in effect, nearly a hundred years before. For Menger had grasped, already, that the holding of liquid reserves, in money or near-money, is only one aspect (though no doubt the most important aspect) of a much more general kind of behaviour. It is a matter of provision against an uncertain future – not passive provision (like insurance) but active provision, providing oneself with the ability to take action to meet emergencies which may arise in the future, and which are such that their particular shape cannot be accurately foreseen. Obviously, then, there can be no question of liquidity, in either the wide or the narrow sense, in a stationary state. Liquidity is a problem of the economy *in* time.

---

[3] *History of Economic Analysis* (1954), p. 847.

[4] *Grundsätze der Volkswirtschaftslehre* (translated by Dingwall and Hoselitz as *Principles of Economics*), chapters 7 and 8. There can be no doubt that Menger would have been on the side of Marshall, rather than on that of Pareto, with respect to the point about consumer theory discussed above, and essentially for the reason given. I owe the beginnings of my understanding of this to conversations with Professor Rosenstein-Rodan.

I have begun with this old story because it presents the issue so sharply. In later work, it has been thoroughly muddled. The man who began the muddling was Keynes.

Keynes's theory has one leg which is *in* time, but another which is not. It is a hybrid. I am not blaming him for this; he was looking for a theory which would be effective, and he found it. I am quite prepared to believe that effective theories always will be hybrids – they cannot afford to bother about difficulties which are not important for the problem in hand. Complications (and for a simple theory the flow of time is a complication) must be allowed for when they have to be allowed for; but if there is any place where we can avoid them, avoid them we will. In facing the world that may well be good policy; but when a hybrid theory is subjected to classroom criticism, places are bound to be exposed which are not easy to defend.

There are many passages – many famous passages – in which Keynes proclaims his theory to be *in* time; he makes quite a fuss about it. 'The dark forces of time and ignorance which envelop our future'[5] – everyone knows them. Take these passages at their face value, as they are so often taken, and one would suppose that Keynes was actually producing a full theory of economics *in* time – the theory which Menger had adumbrated but had certainly not carried through. Yet that is not so; there is only a part of the Keynes theory which is *in* time. He has (very skilfully) divided his theory into two parts. There is one, that concerned with the Marginal Efficiency of Capital and with Liquidity Preference, which is unquestionably *in* time; it is basically forward-looking; time and uncertainty are written all over it. But there is another, the multiplier theory (and indeed the whole theory of production and prices which is – somehow – wrapped up in the multiplier theory) which is out of time. It runs in terms of demand curves, and supply curves and cost curves – just the old tools of equilibrium economics. A state of equilibrium, by definition, is a state in which something, something relevant, is *not* changing, so the use of an equilibrium concept is a signal that time, in some respect at least, has been put to one side.

For Keynes's own purpose, I have insisted, this was justifiable; but what a muddle he made for his successors! The 'Keynesian revolution' went off at half-cock; so the line, which I believe to be a vital line, was smudged over. The equilibrists, therefore, did not know that they were beaten; or rather (for I am not claiming that they had been

[5] *The General Theory of Employment, Interest and Money*, p. 155.

altogether beaten) they did not know that they had been challenged. They thought that what Keynes had said could be absorbed into their equilibrium systems; all that was needed was that the scope of their equilibrium systems should be extended. As we know, there has been a lot of extension, a vast amount of extension; what I am saying is that it has never quite got to the point.[6]

I shall make no attempt in what follows to work through the whole of what has happened; that would be a vast job, and I much doubt if I am capable of doing it. What I can do, and am perhaps well fitted to do, is to look over my own work, since 1935, and to show how some aspects of the struggle, and the muddle, are reflected in it. I can at least explain how it has been that, in one way after another, I have found myself facing the issue, and (very often) being baffled by it.

I begin (as I am sure you will want me to begin) with the old *IS–LM* (or *SI–LL*) diagram, which appeared in a paper I gave to the Econometric Society within a few months of the publication of the *General Theory*.[7] The letter which Keynes wrote me about that paper has now been published.[8] I think I am justified in concluding from that letter that Keynes did not wholly disapprove of what I had made of him. All the same, I must say that that diagram is now much less popular with me than I think it still is with many other people. It reduces the *General Theory* to equilibrium economics; it is not really *in* time. That, of course, is why it has done so well.

Much more to the point is *Value and Capital* (1939). A good deal of that book was written before I saw the *General Theory*; though Keynes came in at the end, even the so-called 'dynamic' part was begun under the influence of Lindahl. Lindahl, it is surely fair to say, was most decidedly *not* an equilibrist; the distinction between past and future (*ex ante* and *ex post*) was at the centre of his work. Thus, even before I read Keynes, I was finding myself confronted with a parallel problem: how to build a bridge between equilibrium economics and an economics which should be securely *in* time. (Since the first part of my book was very thoroughgoing, quite static, equilibrium economics, the problem came up in my work even more sharply than it did in Keynes's.) I built a kind of a bridge, but, as I now see very well, it was a very imperfect bridge, not so very

---

[6] I make no claim that I am the first to say this; it seems to me to be in substance the main point which emerges from the influential book by Axel Leijonhufvud, *On Keynesian Economics and the Economics of Keynes* (1968).

[7] Essay 8 above. See also essay 10.

[8] In Keynes, *Collected Writings*, vol. 14, p. 79; also in my *EP*, p. 144.

unlike the imperfect bridge that had been built by Keynes. My theory also was divided; there was a part that was *in* time and a part that was not. But we did not divide in the same place. While Keynes had relegated the whole theory of production and prices to equilibrium economics, I tried to keep production *in* time, just leaving *prices* to be determined in an equilibrium manner. I wanted, that is, to go further than Keynes, keeping closer to Lindahl. But I could only do so by an artificial device, my 'week', which was such that all prices could be fixed up in what would now be called a 'neo-Walrasian' or 'neo-classical' manner, on the 'Monday'; then, on the basis of these predetermined prices, production *in* time could proceed. It was quite an interesting exercise; it did bring out some points – even some practically important points – fairly well; but I have become abundantly conscious how artificial it was. Much too much had to happen on that 'Monday'! And, even if that was overlooked (as it should not have been overlooked) I was really at a loss how to deal with the further problem of how to string my 'weeks' and my 'Mondays' together.

In *Value and Capital* terms, there were these two problems left over; they correspond fairly well, though not precisely, with what could be expressed in Keynesian (or Marshallian) language. Keynes (he would no doubt have admitted) had been mainly concerned with constructing a general theory of Marshall's *short period*. All he had said about the things included in Marshall's long period had been pretty sketchy; and, except in relation to financial markets, the things with which Marshall had been concerned in his theory of exchange (or barter) had got quite left out. Whether one prefers that statement, or my statement (as just given), does not much matter. What does matter is that the Keynes theory and the *Value and Capital* theory were weak in corresponding ways. They both lacked, at one end, a satisfactory theory of *markets*; and at the other end, they lacked a satisfactory theory of *growth.*

Since these deficiencies were so different, it is scarcely surprising that what has come out of them has been very different. I shall have to take them quite separately.

Growth theory, say since Harrod and Domar (or perhaps since von Neumann), has been the scene of a tremendous come-back of equilibrism. Trying to push on beyond Keynes it has slipped back behind him. What made this possible was the discovery of the Regularly Progressive Economy, or 'steady state'. A stationary state, as found in the Classics or in Wicksell, was a very poor instrument for the study of saving and investment, even in the long-run; for in a

Stationary State both net saving and net investment must by definition equal zero. The Steady State, with its constant growth rate, admitted positive saving, so it looked much better. It could be tidied up, on equilibrium lines, just as well as the Stationary State; for though the quantities of inputs and outputs did not remain unchanged over time, their ratios did. In ratio terms, the Steady State was still quite stationary. Thus, so long as attention was fixed on ratios (and the growth rate itself is a ratio), the Steady State could be absorbed into full-brown equilibrium economics, in which one point of time is just like another. It was just as much 'out of time' as the Stationary State itself.

I shall not say much about Steady State economics; for in spite of all that it has meant for the economics of the fifties and sixties, it is my own opinion that it has been rather a curse. I do not merely mean that the impression that has been given to non-economists (through the mediation of statisticians) that there is something natural about a constant growth rate has been a curse. That is obvious; maybe it will be one of the (few) advantages of the present economic crisis that it will teach us to get over it. I also mean that it has encouraged economists to waste their time upon constructions that are often of great intellectual complexity but which are so much out of time, and out of history, as to be practically futile and indeed misleading. It has many bad marks to be set against it.

I must, however, admit that I have myself spent much time on steady state economics – the Harrod type, the Joan Robinson type, the Kaldor type, the von Neumann type, the Solow type – one after another. I felt that I had to learn them, and the best way to learn them is to write out one's own version. But in the successive versions which I have produced, I have always been making some effort to get away.

Thus in my *Trade Cycle* book (1950) I began with my version of Harrod. I am not particularly proud of that book, but it does have the virtue that it makes some attempts to get back *into* time. One is by introducing lags, though that is a device which is more appropriate in econometrics than in economic theory. By making *present* behaviour depend upon *past* experience, one does something to re-introduce the flow of time; but, I fully admit, not very much. Another route of escape was my concept of Autonomous Investment – a concept which equilibrists, very naturally, have found hard to swallow. As first introduced, it looks like a piece of steady state economics; and there, admittedly, it is out of place. But I did go on, in the later parts of the book (which have received much less

attention) to allow Autonomous Investment to change autono-
mously. I believe that at that point my model did become less
deterministic, and so less equilibrist.

The next stage in the story, so far as I personally am concerned,
was my *Capital and Growth* (1965), written fifteen years later. It is a
long gap, and, of course, it is true that during these years much that is
relevant had been done by others. A large part of *Capital and Growth*
is just a survey of what they had been doing. They had taken the
capital stock of the Harrodian steady state – much too 'macro' in
its original form – and had broken it down into its components:
capital goods of different specifications, different durabilities, and
different 'vintages'. They had been able to do this by a massive
injection of matrix algebra. I had to learn the matrix algebra, which
had come into fashion since the days of my mathematical education
– and it took me quite a time! They had also developed a new kind
of 'dynamic equilibrium' in which not even ratios are kept constant;
a plan, a consistent plan, is nevertheless developed between time 1
and time 2. (This goes back to von Neumann and to Ramsey and
includes much work descended from them: turnpike theorems,
optimum saving theorems and the like.) Though these are not steady
state theories, they are nevertheless equilibrium theories. One point
of time is not like another, even in the ratio sense; yet the whole of
the plan is looked at together. The plan is mutually determined;
there is no movement from past to future, except in the sense that
there is also a movement from future to past. There is no room for
the unexpected.

I had to learn these things; and a great part of *Capital and
Growth* is occupied with setting out my version of them. But there
are some signs, even in *Capital and Growth*, that I was trying to get
away. There are many of them in the opening chapters (which are
chiefly of a critical character); and there are some, even in the latter
part of the book, though that is mainly concerned with the steady
state, or with the other kind of 'dynamic equilibrium'. There is the
monetary chapter (23); but that really belongs to the theory of
markets, to which I shall be coming later. There is a funny chapter
on 'Interest and Growth' (22), which tries to break away; but it is an
unsuccessful break-out since it is still using the tools of steady state
economics, which are obviously unsuitable. Most important is the
chapter called 'Traverse' (16). This was a first attempt at a formal
theory of an economy which is not in a steady state, not in 'Growth
Equilibrium' – an economy which has a history, so that things
actually happen. Since it is a system in which the actors do not know

what is going to happen next, it at once appears that flexibility (which disappears from sight in the steady state) is a matter of major importance. The method that is used in that chapter is not, as I have since become convinced, very suitable; but I do not regret having made the attempt. Some quite interesting things did come out. I was able, in particular, to throw some new light (or what to me was new light) upon the *role* of prices – to show how different it is in an uncertain world from what it appears to be in equilibrium economics.[9]

So we come to *Capital and Time* (1973), as I promised. People, I can see from reviews, have not known quite what to make of it; it probably needed a preface (such as I have been giving, in fact, in this essay) so that it could be explained. The whole of the second part of *Capital and Time* is called 'Traverse'; it corresponds to that single chapter in *Capital and Growth*. It is in fact the case that the chief (almost the whole) purpose of the latter book is to seek a better way of doing what I was trying to do in the former 'Traverse' chapter. In that former chapter I was trying to build a theory which should at least be rather more *in time*, while using a fairly conventional steady state model as a basis. It did not do. So I tried, in the later book, to build my 'Traverse' on a different steady state model, which I hoped, and I think I showed, could get one just a little further. But this new steady state model (descended from Böhm-Bawerk through one of the less read chapters of *Value and Capital*)[10] would, I knew, be unfamiliar to most of my readers. So the whole (or nearly the whole) of the first part of *Capital and Time* is taken up with explaining it.

But this first part is *not* the important part. Taken by itself, its conclusions are quite negative. It just shows that you get the same steady state results in my model as in other models, a thing which was to be expected *a priori* but needed to be demonstrated in detail. The results come out rather neatly, so it may be that it will be found (even by equilibrists) to be quite useful, if only for teaching purposes. But that is all.

Even in Part II, I had to start very slowly. If I had started with a fine set of plausible assumptions, drawn from the real world, I am sure I should have got nowhere. I had to build up my model bit by bit. I began from a steady state (but that was simply because I had to have something firm, which I thought I understood, from which to start), but the point of the steady state (in Part II) is that it is to be *disturbed*. I made a lot of use – perhaps too much use – of what I

[9] *CG*, esp. pp. 194–7.
[10] *VC*, ch. 17.

called a Simple Profile, a production plan which admitted the construction of a plant and then its utilisation, but not much else. It is not surprising that some of the results which I got with the Simple Profile were much the same as those which others have got by more conventional methods. I am again not ashamed of my 'fixwage' hypothesis, with which I still think it was proper to begin; I did indeed push on quite a long way beyond it. Nor am I ashamed of the 'static expectation' assumption, which made firms choose their plans on the basis of today's prices, or rather price ratios; that again I think was the right way to begin. Though I did not do much to modify this assumption, I don't think it would be hard to modify it. But this is no place to discuss these matters in detail. What I want to emphasise is that in Part II I was trying to build something up. It ends with a chapter called 'Ways Ahead'; that was meant as a signal that I was sure I had not finished the job.

Most of my critics have been (and no doubt will be) equilibrists; but there is one, for whom I have great respect, who has opened fire from the other flank. Professor Ludwig Lachmann, of the University of Johannesburg, South Africa, is (like Professor Hayek) a chief survivor of what I distinguished as the Mengerian sect of the Austrian school. It is clear that his view of me is like Menger's view of Böhm-Bawerk. He cannot, of course, abide the steady state.[11] Even the modest uses of it which I have made (and perhaps, until now, I have not sufficiently emphasised that they are meant to be very modest uses), even these fill him with dismay. Even the explanations which I have now been giving (and which are meant, incidentally, to assure him that I am more on his side than on the other) will, I fear, fail to placate him. His ideal economics is not so far away from my own ideal economics, but I regard it as a target set up in heaven. We cannot hope to reach it; we must just get as near to it as we can.

There is one further thing I want to say about *Capital and Time*. I was trying in Part II to analyse a growth process *sequentially*; there were things which emerged almost as soon as one tried to do that, even if one was not succeeding in doing it very well or very completely. I began, for instance, to understand why there had been so much trouble with that old distinction between autonomous and induced inventions, a distinction for which I must admit I had myself some responsibility in days gone by.[12] It is a static distinction, quite out of time, though it concerns a matter where some time-reference is essential. When one puts it back *into time*, it looks quite different.

---

[11] See his review of *CT* in the *South African Journal of Economics* (September 1973).
[12] See *TW*, ch. 6.

As I said in the book:

the technology, and the technological frontier, now become suspect.... The notion of a technology, as a collection of techniques, laid up in a library to be taken down from their shelves as required, is a caricature of the inventive process....Why should we not say that every change in technique is an invention, which may be large or small? It certainly partakes, to some degree, of the character of an invention; for it requires, for its application, some new knowledge, or some new expertise. There is no firm line, on the score of novelty, between shifts that change the technology and shifts that do not.[13]

One can say that, and still admit a distinction between autonomous and induced invention, but the distinction must now be of a more dynamic character. An induced invention is a change in technique that is made as a consequence of a change in prices (or, in general, scarcities); if the change in prices had not occurred, the change in technique would not have been made. I now like to think of a major technical change (one that we may agree to regard as autonomous, since, for anything that we are concerned with, it comes in from outside) as setting up what I now call an Impulse. If the autonomous change is an invention which widens the range of technical possibilities, it must begin by raising profitability and inducing expansion; but the expansion encounters scarcities, which act as a brake. Some of the scarcities may be just temporary bottle-necks which in time can be removed; some, however, may be irremovable. Yet it is possible to adjust to either kind of scarcity by further changes in technical methods; it is these that are the true *induced inventions*. The whole story, when it is looked at in this way, is *in time*, and can be in history; it can be worked out much further, and can, I believe, be applied.[14]

That is rather a mouthful; it deserves a lecture to itself; but there I must leave it. For I have still to say something (it cannot, at this stage, be very much) about the other 'deficiency' which, as I explained, was left unfilled in the thirties. I must turn, that is, to the theory of *markets*.

How – just how – are prices determined? In *Value and Capital* (even in the 'dynamic' part of *Value and Capital*) I had been content to be what is now called neo-Walrasian; prices were just determined by an equilibrium of demand and supply. And I am afraid that for many years I got no further, or very little further. When I was asked

---

[13] *CT*, p. 120.

[14] I have tried to draw some more practical consequences in a paper entitled 'Industrialism' (*EP*, pp. 20–44).

to review Patinkin's book, which really raised the issue, I quite failed to see the point.[15] It was only by slow degrees that it began to sink in.

Walras himself, it is true, had been much less obtuse. He had seen that for a market to work in his way (the way in which so many others have followed him) some market *structure* was necessary. But the market structure which he posited was very special. One would be tempted to think that it was invented by Walras just to give the right result if there were not some evidence that there did exist examples of markets which did work in much this way, and could well have been familiar to him.[16] One, in fact, may have been the Paris Bourse itself!

These, however, would be very sophisticated markets, requiring a lot of organisation; for who is to pay the official who is to 'cry' the prices, or (as Clower would call him) the 'auctioneer'?[17] There must be a prior agreement among the parties to play the game according to these rules; but how is such an agreement to come about? A proper theory of markets must clearly include the Walras-type market as a particular case; but I think it needs to start much further back.

The simplest form of exchange is barter; and (since Edgeworth) we know how that works. One might begin with a market (or pre-market) – a sort of village fair – in which all transactions were barter transactions between a pair of individuals, each giving up something

[15] 'A Rehabilitation of "Classical" Economics' (*EJ*, June 1957).

[16] So I was told by Keynes himself. I had sent him the article on Walras which I had published, entitled 'Leon Walras' (*Econometrica*, 1934). I have a letter from him about it dated 9 December of that year. The substantial part of the letter is as follows: 'There is one small point which perhaps I may be able to clear up. . . . You enquire whether or not Walras was supposing that exchanges actually take place at the prices originally proposed when these prices are not equilibrium prices. The footnote which you quote [p. 345 of my paper, p. 44 of the 4th French edition of the *Elements* which I was using] convinces me that he assuredly supposed that they did not take place except at the equilibrium prices. For that is the actual method by which the opening price is fixed on the Paris Bourse even today. His footnote suggests that he was aware that the Agents de Change used this method and he regarded that as the ideal system or exchange to which others were approximations. As a matter of fact, this is also the method by which opening prices are fixed on Wall Street. It is unfamiliar to us because the only London example which I can think of is the daily 'fixing' of silver by the bullion brokers. In all these cases there is an application of Edgeworth's principle of re-contract, all those present disclosing their dispositions to trade and the price which will equate offers and demands is arrived at by an independent person, known in New York as the specialist.'

It is much to be desired that the methods of trading on organised markets, in different countries and at different times, should be studied systematically.

[17] Robert Clower and Axel Leijonhufvud, 'The Coordination of Economic Activities: A Keynesian Perspective' (*The American Economic Review* May 1975).

which he wants relatively less in exchange for something which he wants relatively more. But such simple barter, as the textbooks have long been telling us, is bound to leave some opportunities for advantageous trading unexploited; so one must go on from that to introduce some form of triangular trade. At that point, two things happen. One is the evolution of some form of money; in a more complete account than I can offer here, that would have to be fitted in.[18] The other is that there arises an opportunity for the development of specialised merchanting – a merchant being defined as one who buys not for his own use but in order to sell again. It is easy to see that once the market has passed a certain size, so that problems of communication become important, there will have to be specialised merchants (or, perhaps, some substitute for them).

I am very convinced that for the purpose in hand, the specialised merchant is the key figure. When Gerschenkron reviewed my *Theory of Economic History*, he entitled his review 'Mercator Gloriosus'[19] – indicating that from his point of view, the point of view of the historian, I had made too much of the merchant. I dare say that he is right. But I am sure that from the point of view of economic understanding I was right. The role of the merchant in the development of market organisation is crucial.

Once merchants exist there are three kinds of dealings to be distinguished: (1) dealings between merchants, (2) dealings between merchants and non-merchants, and (3) direct dealings between non-merchants, which in some particular cases may still survive. The most obvious example of direct dealings between non-merchants, surviving into otherwise sophisticated economies, is the market in private dwelling-houses. We rarely find house-merchants holding stocks of dwelling-houses (for rather obvious reasons); but there remains a problem of communication, which is dealt with in another way. This is by the appearance of house agents, a particular kind of commission agent, who has the function of bringing buyer and seller together, and consequently of advising them of the price at which they should trade. He charges a commission to cover the cost of his services (which may formally be paid by the buyer or by the seller, but the price is in fact so adjusted that it falls to some extent on both). In a complete theory of markets, the commission agent would have to find a place.

The market for dwelling-houses is a notoriously 'imperfect' market; the most perfectly organised markets are at the other end –

[18] I started the job in the first lecture of 'The Two Triads' (*CEMT*). See also *TEH*, ch. 3.
[19] *EHR* (November 1971).

the markets on which specialised traders trade with one another. It is here that we should look for the Walras-type market and for other sophisticated types. For when merchants habitually trade together, they develop needs for assurance about the carrying-through of their dealings – needs for legal assurances about property and contract, and other related matters – and it is worth their while to pay something in order to get these rules policed and enforced. All this is very important, but it is just one end of the spectrum of market structures.

At the centre, however, is what remains: dealings between merchants and non-merchants. It is here that we meet the shop-keeper and the wholesaler. They buy to sell again, so must buy before they sell, so they must hold stocks. The holding of unsold stocks is expensive, so their appearance is again an indication that information is imperfect. They are giving those who buy from them the service that they can buy the things they want when they want them. The provision of that service is expensive; for the costs that they incur in providing it they properly charge.

In this sort of market, with sharply specialised merchants, there is no question who fixes prices; it is the merchant himself. When he finds his stock running down, so that he is in danger of failing to meet the demands that they be made upon him, he will first try to get more from other merchants; if they have ample stocks, all is well; but if their stocks also are running down, he will have to offer higher prices, to the other merchants or to outside producers, in order to get more stock. Then he will charge a higher price to consumers in order to cover the rise in his costs. Such a market may well be quite similar, in many ways, to the textbook competitive market; but until we take uncertainty and costs of information into account we cannot show how it works.[20]

I believe that there was a stage in the development of capitalism when a market such as I have been describing was the typical market – for consumers' goods, and for many sorts of producers' goods also. But I greatly doubt if it can still be regarded as the typical market. What has upset it is the taking over of the mercantile function by the producers themselves. The manufacturers do it directly, the primary producers indirectly, through the formation of their own associations or by selling organisations equipped with political power. This is, of course, the point at which the question of monopoly becomes so important. But that, again cannot in general be understood unless we look at it *in time*, as an aspect of the evolutionary process we have

[20] See my chapter on 'The Method of Marshall' (*CG*, ch. 5).

been considering. Why is it that the theory of monopolistic competition, or imperfect competition, to which so much attention was paid in the thirties, now looks so faded? Because it is quite shockingly *out of time*.[21]

There is a practical conclusion from what I have just been saying to which I should like to draw attention. You have a long tradition in in the United States of anti-monopoly action; and in my own country, in recent years, it has been ineffectively imitated. I do not think it has been much of a success, even with you. On the line of thought I have been sketching out, one can see why. It is an attempt to go back from the late stage of capitalism – the producer-dominated stage – to the earlier stage, before the producers took over. But this earlier stage depended for its functioning upon a merchant class, an independent merchant class; and that cannot be raised from the dead by a stroke of the pen, or by an Act of Congress. It would have to grow up; to bring it back would be quite a job.

One final salute – to Georgescu. He has chosen a cosmic way of demonstrating the irreversibility of time.[22] Since he was addressing himself to a science-based culture, that (I am sure) was a good way of going about it. For my part, I am very ignorant of science; though I have dabbled in mathematics my spiritual home is in the Humanities. It is because I want to make economics more human that I want to make it more time-conscious; and since I am approaching the task from that end I am content with a more earthy way of going about it. We are nevertheless, I believe, on the same side. We are both of us evolutionists, but not straight-line, or 'exponential', evolutionists. It is the *new* things that humanity has discovered which makes its history exciting; and the new things that may be found in the future, before humanity blows itself up, or settles down to some ghastly 'equilibrium', make a future worth praying for, and worth working for.

---

[21] I made an attempt to start the business of bringing it back into time in 'The Process of Imperfect Competition' (*OEP*, February 1954); but I do not pretend that I got very far.

[22] Georgescu-Roegen, *The Entropy Law and the Economic Process* (1971).

15

The Formation of an Economist

This was written as one of a series of recollections by internationally known economists. It appeared in the *Banca Nazionale del Lavoro Quarterly Review*, September, 1979.

If I am asked how it was that I became an economist, I can give nothing better than the regular economic answer: in order to earn my living. At the moment when the decision had to be made, I had just taken my first degree at Oxford. I had had a very good general education, but a very unspecialised education, which did not clearly point in one direction rather than another. It had been paid for by 'scholarships', awarded on competitive examination (at the ages of 13 and 17); at that stage my main subject was mathematics. But I had turned away from mathematics; I took my degree in 'philosophy, politics and economics', a new course just established at Oxford, a course which was perhaps better devised for the training of politicians than of academics. (Hugh Gaitskell, Harold Wilson, Edward Heath and Reginald Maudling all had that background.) But I wanted to be academic; and though I had done very little economics, I was advised that economics was an expanding industry, so I would have a better chance of employment if I went that way. So I did.

Economics, at Oxford, was very 'social'; so they started me working on labour problems. I did my thesis on skill differentials in the building and engineering trades. But I had been well advised that there was a market for economists; so when I came to seek employment for myself, I was able to get what I wanted. From 1926–35 I taught at the London School of Economics; and I learned at the London School of Economics. Within those nine years I passed from the state of appalling ignorance, from which I started, to my first theoretical achievements: the invention of the elasticity of substitution (*Theory of Wages*, 1932), the distinction of income and substitution effects ('Reconsideration of the Theory of Value', in collaboration with Roy Allen, *Economica*, 1934)[1] and the liquidity spectrum ('A Suggestion for Simplifying the Theory of Money', *Economica*, 1935).[2] Already, before I left LSE, I had done what I still feel to be some of my best work.

How had this happened? Those nine years at LSE fall very sharply, from my point of view, into two parts. They are separated, in 1929, by the arrival of Lionel Robbins as head of department. In the three years before that time I had been working mainly by myself. I had access to that already splendid library, and I got advice from my colleagues on what I should read, but I was not a member of a group. After 1929 I was a member of a group, the group which Robbins built up around him. We were all of us quite young people and most of us are still surviving. Apart from Robbins himself, there were Hayek and Roy Allen, Richard Sayers, Nicholas Kaldor and Abba Lerner, together with Marian Bowley and Ursula Webb (Ursula Hicks after 1935). So the work which I did in these latter years was in large measure a collective work.

I go back to the years of preparation which preceded. There were two things which happened during those years which need to be recorded.

One of them, in the first of those years, was that Hugh Dalton[3] (then temporary head of the economics department) said to me 'you read Italian, you ought to read Pareto'. So it was reading the *Manuale* which started me off on economic theory.[4] I was deep in Pareto, before I got much out of Marshall.

---

[1] Essay 1 above.

[2] Essay 7 above.

[3] Dalton had learned his economics at Cambridge, where he was a pupil of Pigou; but by the time I knew him his interest in economics was waining. He had started upon his political career, and was aiming at being Foreign Secretary in a future Labour government. It is well known that when the time came, he was disappointed in that ambition, and had to go back to economics as Chancellor of the Exchequer. But by 1945 his economics was seriously out of date.

His lectures, which I attended in 1926, were a bit like political speeches. 'I always begin with population – good spicy subject, gets 'em interested' he said to me himself.

He had learned Italian when serving with the British army in Italy in 1918. He had a great affection for Italy, but felt himself unable to visit Italy during fascism. My Italian had begun by stumbling through Dante, while I was still at school; I had gone on to read fairly widely in Italian literature. But it was not until 1933, after I had published *Theory of Wages*, that I made my first contact with Italian economists, visiting, in Turin, Einaudi and Cabiati, del Vecchio at Bologna and Marco Fanno at Padua.

[4] I was naturally led from Pareto to Walras and Edgeworth. My time at Oxford was too late for me to have been able to go to Edgeworth's lectures; and I doubt if by my teachers at Oxford he was even mentioned. So it was not until I got to LSE that I found *Mathematical Psychics*.

The other was a long interlude in the second year, when I went to South Africa. The professor at the University at Johannesburg (their sole teacher of economics!) had died very suddenly. The authorities sent to London for a temporary replacement, while they made up their minds on the appointment of a successor. No one senior to me would take it, but I was tempted – on the whole very fortunately. I had to lecture on a wide variety of subjects, from statistics to economic history; but somehow I managed.

My own interest, at that time, was still in labour problems; and from that angle South Africa was a revelation. I came from a country where Trade Unions could still be thought of, by their well-wishers, of whom I had been one, as agents for the advancement of labour in general. But in South Africa they stood for no more than the interests of a minority, for White labour only. So much has been heard, in later years, of the colour problem in South Africa that it will hardly be credited that Dalton had given me an introduction to his 'fellow-socialist', the leader of the South African Labour Party, then in coalition with the Nationalists, the begetters of *apartheid*, with whom I could soon see that they belonged. Thus I got a new view of Trade Unions, I began to think of them as monopolists, so that it was by the application of monopoly theory that their effects were to be understood. The reservation of skilled jobs to White labour, and the confinement of the best land in the country to White ownership, were the economic obstacles in the way of progress for the Black majority. In a free market system these would wither away, so I became a free market man, even before I left South Africa.

Thus, when the Robbins circle began to form, I fitted in. I readily accepted his rejection of inter-personal comparability of utilities (then considered as a rationale for progressive taxation), for the rejection was in line with the ordinalism I had got from Pareto. And I was readily seduced by the great 'neo-classical synthesis' (as it effectively was, though that name has been mainly applied to later varieties), according to which a competitive system, free of monopoly elements, which would only grow if they were buttressed by state 'interference', would easily find an 'equilibrium'. I was willing to apply this doctrine, even to the labour market; though there I had some reservations, which survive in some chapters of *Wages*. My *Wages* book, however, is in its main lines thoroughly 'neo-classical'.

It was surprising, to outside observers, that these very Right-ish doctrines could have had such a vogue at the London School, which was popularly considered to be a hotbed of socialists. We did indeed have our eminent socialists, such as Laski and Tawney (Dalton, by now, had gone off into politics); but it was significant of the tolerant atmosphere of the School that personal relations with them were friendly. There was indeed a substratum of 'liberal' political principles which our socialists and our free market men had in common.

LSE was not only tolerant, it was also, to a high degree, international. (It has become even more international since that time!) What we economists thought we were doing was not only to bring to life the inheritance of the British Classical Economists, but also to widen the horizons of the British economists of our own time by bringing in a refreshment from what was being done, and had been done, in other countries. I got mine, as has been seen, from Walras and Pareto; Robbins, on the other hand, was looking to the Americans (Chicago was already another home of free market economics) and even more to the Austrians. Books written in other languages had not then been translated into English; but I managed enough German to read the Austrians, and also Wicksell and Myrdal (at that time only available to me in German). I have never learned Swedish, but, as will be seen, I have been deeply influenced by Swedish economics.

It was not only through books that one made these contacts. Eminent economists, from many countries, would pass through London, and when they came to London they would come to the School. Thus it was that I made the acquaintance of Taussig and Viner, of Mises and Schumpeter, of Ohlin and Lindahl; as well as of a younger generation of Austrians, often on their way to exile, for Austria was already falling under Hitler's shadow.[5] Hayek himself came to London before the Hitler revolution; he came to tell us about Austrian economics; and he did.

My reaction to Hayek's teaching, at that time, I have described elsewhere;[6] and I have also set out, in another place,[7] the change in

---

[5] Ursula spent a semester at the University of Vienna in 1931, so she had first-hand experience of the incipient Nazification. But it was not difficult for the rest of us, associating with German and Austrian exiles, to have a feeling of what was coming. When I went to Cambridge in 1935 (of which more below) I found an atmosphere that was very different. I remember how shocked I was to hear Pigou, a very great economist but curiously insular, remarking at that time that he supposed that Hitler was going to 'bomb the frogs' (i.e. the French). None of our business! And it was even later that Claude Guillebaud (Marshall's nephew and later editor) wrote a book on the *Economic Recovery of Germany*, praising the economic policy of Hitler as an application of Keynesian economics. (I would not like to leave that reference without saying that Guillebaud was a good friend of mine in Cambridge; he was the only other British economist I have known who knew the last canto of the *Paradiso* by heart.) The vogue of appeasement at Oxford during those years is notorious; but the sleep at Cambridge was still more profound.

[6] 'The Hayek Story', in *Critical Essays in Monetary Theory* (1967).

[7] 'Recollections and Documents', *Economic Perspectives* (1977). [See also the paper on 'LSE and the Robbins Circle', *CEET* II.]

my own ideas which was intertwined with it. Here I will merely say that I began, once again, from Pareto, making an attempt, first of all a very crude attempt, to make the Paretian system less static, so as to be able to incorporate planning over time, planning for a future which was not known in advance. Hayek was making us think of the productive process as a process in time, inputs coming before outputs; but his completest, and most logical, account of intertemporal relations was confined to a model in which everything worked out as intended – a model of 'perfect foresight'.[8] In his *Prices and Production* (1932), the lectures through which we first got to know him, things were allowed to go wrong, but only for monetary reasons; it was only because of monetary disturbances that an exception was allowed to the rule that market forces must tend to establish an equilibrium. If money could only be kept 'neutral', all would be well. (An anticipation of latter-day monetarism!) In the models I tried to construct, in which people did not know what was going to happen, and knew that they did not know what was going to happen, there was no place for 'neutral money'.

I was aware, before I left LSE in 1935, and before the appearance of Keynes's *General Theory* at the beginning of 1936, that the direction in which my mind was moving was not dissimilar to his. (He told me so himself, in some correspondence I had with him.[9]) But I did not begin from Keynes; I began from Pareto, and Hayek.[10] But I had gone on by 1935 to draw consequences from my new approach; and I had realised that I had separated myself from the faith in the free market which had been dominant among my colleagues. After I had read them my *Simplification* paper (at the end of 1934) they must have been aware of what was happening; but, as I have said, the atmosphere at LSE was tolerant, and I have been able to keep them among my friends.[11]

It was not because I was becoming Keynesian (as in a sense I was) that in the summer of 1935 I removed to Cambridge. I went there in consequence of an invitation from Pigou, and it was because of the friendship I had already formed with Robertson[12] that I was attracted.

---

[8] ('Das intertemporale Gleichgewichtsystem', in *Weltwirtschaftliches Archiv*, 1928).

[9] Reprinted in 'Recollections and Documents', cited.

[10] There is evidence for this, in the paper on 'Equilibrium and the Cycle', which is reprinted in *CEET* II.

[11] I think that Hayek, and perhaps Vera Lutz, have been the only ones of us who in later years have been fully constant in the old faith. Even Robbins has departed from it, to a considerable extent.

[12] I have described my early relations with Robertson in 'Recollections and Documents'. See also the memoir of him which I wrote for the British Academy, and which is reprinted as a preface to the selection of his *Essays on Money and Interest* (1966).

Cambridge, however, was already riven by disputes between Keynesians and anti-Keynesians; and since I was associated with Pigou and Robertson, I found myself regarded, at least by some Keynesians, as being in the 'anti' camp. The ISLM version of Keynes's theory,[13] which I myself produced, but which has never been highly regarded by orthodox Keynesians, did not help me.

My chief occupation during those years at Cambridge (1935–8) was the writing of *Value and Capital*. This is not at all a Cambridge book; it is a systematisation of the work I had done at LSE. It is represented as a work of bridge-building, not so much between micro- and macro-economics (as others have often regarded it) as between the static neo-classical system, which has been regarded as the foundation of free market economics, and the 'dynamic' models where past and future are properly distinguished, in which I had by that time become more interested. My own dynamic model is presented in terms that have some relation with Keynes's work; but it is not very Keynesian. It owes much more to what I had got from the Swedes, from Myrdal and Lindahl. It was from Myrdal that I got the idea of 'temporary equilibrium', a momentary market equilibrium in which price-expectations are taken as data; it was Lindahl, with his pioneering work on the social accounting framework, who taught me how (formally at least) to string my temporary equilibria together.[14]

I do not now think that the monetary chapters in *Value and Capital* are at all good; it is not from them, but from the *Simplification* paper of 1935, that my later work on money has proceeded. There is little about liquidity in *Value and Capital.*

By the time *Value and Capital* was published, I had removed to Manchester, where I remained during the war years. The British universities were only partly closed down, so there still was work to be done, though most of the teaching I had to do was rather elementary. I took advantage of this to write my *Social Framework*, which seems to have had the widest circulation of any of my books. It should have been called *The Social Accounts*, for its novelty consisted in the systematic use of social accounting material for elementary teaching; but the idea of social accounting was then unfamiliar, so I was persuaded to fall back on that unsatisfactory title.

---

[13] 'Mr Keynes and the Classics', *Econometrica* (1937); essay 8 above.

[14] I read Myrdal's *Monetary Equilibrium*, in German, at the beginning of 1934; it was through Myrdal's references to him that I first heard of Lindahl. I found these references very exciting; but I could not follow them up, since I could not read Swedish. So it was a great moment when I actually met him at LSE. He had come to London to get help in the translation of his essays into English; I was able to find a helper for him. A year later, on another visit to see that helper, she had to tell him that we had decided to get married. 'Ah!' he said in his imperfect English 'I had my doubts'.

Value and Capital had been published at the beginning of 1939; so it got distributed throughout the world before the War broke out. But I was thereafter cut off from the reactions that were forming to it; it was only after the War that I found out what had been happening.[15]

In the second half of 1946, I made my first visit to the United States. I there met again some old friends, such as Schumpeter and Viner; but I also made my first contacts with the younger generation, who were soon to become famous. At Cambridge (Mass.) I met Samuelson; in New York I met Arrow; and at Chicago Milton Friedman and Don Patinkin. I did not know them, but they knew me; for I was the author of *Value and Capital*, which (as has since become obvious) was deeply influencing their work. They regarded it as the beginning of *their* 'neo-classical synthesis' – no more than the beginning, for they and their contemporaries, with far more skill in mathematics than mine, were sharpening the analysis I had merely roughed out. But I am afraid I disappointed them; and have continued to disappoint them. Their achievements have been great; but they are not in my line. I have felt little sympathy with the theory for theory's sake, which has been characteristic of one strand in American economics; nor with the idealisation of the free market, which has been characteristic of another; and I have little faith in the econometrics, on which they have so largely relied to make their contact with reality. But I make no pretence that in 1946 I was even beginning to get clear about all this. It took me many years before I could even begin to define my new position.

I can see, looking back, that there is quite a gap between my early contributions, substantially completed by 1950, and the work on which I have been engaged from 1960 onwards. It is not that in the gap I was idle. There was work to be done in Oxford, where from 1946–52 I took part in the formation of Nuffield College; and where from 1952–65 I held the Drummond Professorship, with some general responsibilities for the organisation of post-graduate studies. And I was also much engaged in other activities, which sprang initially from Ursula's work in Public Finance, and from other work in that field in which I joined her. I have always held (as I said in the preface to *Value and Capital*) that theory should be 'the servant of applied economics'; but I have also been aware that theory gives one

---

[15] Years later, when visiting Japan, I was assured that my book had been a set book at Kyoto University since 1943. I was astonished, and asked them how it could have been possible for them to get copies. They reminded me that until December 1941 they could import through America; and then, they said, we captured some in Singapore!

no right to pronounce on practical problems unless one has been through the labour, so often the formidable labour, of mastering the relevant facts. Those which have to be mastered before one can pronounce on the macro-economic problems of developed countries are so extensive that the task of mastering them has usually to be left to specialists; but there have been simpler cases where it has appeared more manageable. During the years when the British Empire was breaking up, there were many such opportunities for British economists; they were often called on for advice in easing the transition to self-government and then independence. We have done a bit in that field, in Nigeria and in the Carribbean, in India and in Ceylon; during the fifties it was a major interest.

I pass on, as here is appropriate, to the years about 1960, which I reckon as the time of my *Risorgimento*. The first thing I had to do, on resuming my former work, was to bring myself up-to-date with what others had been doing; and I knew that I could not understand what others had been doing unless I could re-state it in my own terms. I did two exercises of that kind,[16] which took a good deal of time. But I do not feel that these things are fully my own work; they are just 'translations'.

Nevertheless, with these behind me, I could go on. I could start to build on the work I had done in the thirties, but I could do so in my own way. I could take those parts of Keynes's system which I wanted, and could reject those which I did not want. I then found myself led, only incidentally to formal models, but chiefly to new analytical concepts, which may have some power to improve understanding of what has happened in the world, and what is happening.

There are three of these which I now feel to be important enough to be distinguished.

The first is the contrast between what I have called flexprice and fixprice markets: the former being those in which prices are made by the market (by demand and supply, as in the textbooks), the latter being those in which prices are made by producers, a change in price being an act of policy. This already appears in *Capital and Growth*,[17] but its fruits have been gathered throughout my later work. I contend that flexprice markets, as they have existed in practice, depend upon the existence of intermediaries, neither producers nor final consumers

---

[16] The first was published as 'A Survey of Linear Theory' (essay 19, *CEET* III); the second is embedded in the middle chapters of *CG* (1965). The writing of the latter owed much to the tuition which I received from Michio Morishima, while he was a Visiting Fellow of All Souls College in 1963–4.

[17] Especially in ch. 5.

of the products in which they trade. My *Theory of Economic History* is largely an attempt to see the main lines of economic development as a matter of the evolution of the merchant-intermediary, and its consequences. But I have fully recognised that in the most modern times it is the fixprice market which is taking over. Thus, when I am concerned with contemporary problems, I have tried to think in terms of a *mixed* fixprice-flexprice economy.

The second is a deepening of the concept of liquidity, which, though it is Keynes's concept, was (I now feel) imperfectly explored by Keynes. He did not (at least in the *General Theory*) sufficiently stress the relation between liquidity and time. 'Liquidity is not a matter of a single choice; it is a matter of a sequence of choices, a related sequence. It is concerned with the passage from the unknown to the known – with the knowledge that if we wait we can have more knowledge'.[18]

The third is the concept of the Impulse, which grew out of *Capital and Time*, but which did not finally emerge until the essay on 'Industrialism' in *Economic Perspectives*. I think of a major invention, or other major change in circumstances, like the opening up of a new market, as generating a chain of consequences, some of which by theory can be followed out. I did not have this idea when I wrote my *Theory of Economic History*; it is needed to complete the analysis which I gave in that earlier book.

During the years since 1965, while I have been writing my later books, I have been a retired professor; but I have been allowed to continue to work at Oxford, at All Souls College. Though I have useful discussions with colleagues at Oxford, I have not been a member of a group, as I was in early days at LSE. Those who have worked closest with me have been visitors to Oxford, and post-graduate students, who themselves come and go. For though in Oxford our first degree students are mainly British, most of our post-graduate students come from abroad. When they have done their two or three years, they go back to places, often very distant places, from which they have come. Such contact as one can then maintain with them must be largely by correspondence – unless one can go and see them at their homes or places of work. I have indeed done a good deal of that.

It has so happened that a considerable number of economics post-graduates, and of other economists who have visited Oxford, have come from Italy. And it is not so far from England to Italy as it is to

---

[18] *CKE* (1974), pp. 38–9. See also my *EP* (1977), essay 3, and *CE* (1979), chs. 6 and 7.

places further afield! I have explained the importance of my knowledge of Italian (which is still, I fear, little more than a reading knowledge) in the beginnings of my economics. It has been a great thing for me that I have again been able to use it in the contacts with Italian economists which I have been able to develop during the last twenty years. We now feel that a year which does not contain a visit to Italy is a year in which there is something missing. And now, when we come to Italy, we come to see our friends.

The Published Works of John Hicks

The following abbreviations are used:

Books by the author

CE	*Causality in Economics* (1979)
CEET I	*Collected Essays on Economic Theory*, vol. I: *Wealth and Welfare* (1981)
CEET II	*Collected Essays on Economic Theory*, vol. II: *Money, Interest and Wages* (1982)
CEET III	*Collected Essays on Economic Theory*, vol. III: *Classics and Moderns* (1983)
CEMT	*Critical Essays in Monetary Theory* (1967)
CG	*Capital and Growth* (1965)
CKE	*The Crisis in Keynesian Economics* (1974)
CT	*Capital and Time* (1973)
EP	*Economic Perspectives* (1977)
EWE	*Essays in World Economics* (1959)
TEH	*A Theory of Economic History* (1969)
TW	*The Theory of Wages* (1932; second edition, 1963)
VC	*Value and Capital* (1939)

Journals and publishers

AER	*American Economic Review*
BNDLQR	*Banca Nazionale del Lavoro Quarterly Review*
BOUIS	*Bulletin of the Oxford University Institute of Statistics*
CJE	*Canadian Journal of Economics*
CUP	Cambridge University Press
Ec	*Economica*
Eca	*Econometrica*
EHR	*Economic History Review*
EI	*Economic Inquiry*
EJ	*Economic Journal*
ER	*Economic Record*
GER	*Greek Economic Review*
IA	*International Affairs*

IBR	*Irish Bank Review*
IEA	Institute of Economic Affairs
JEL	*Journal of Economic Literature*
JMCB	*Journal of Money, Credit and Banking*
JPKE	*Journal of Post-Keynesian Economics*
LBR	*Lloyds Bank Review*
MS	*Manchester School*
MSS	Manchester Statistical Society
NIESR	National Institute for Economic and Social Research
OUP	Oxford University Press
OEP	*Oxford Economic Papers*
QJE	*Quarterly Journal of Economics*
REP	*Revue d'économie politique*
RES	*Review of Economic Studies*
TBR	*Three Banks Review*
SAJE	*South African Journal of Economics*
SJE	*Swedish Journal of Economics*
ZFN	*Zeitschrift für Nationalökonomie*

Square brackets denote reprints, translations and foreign editions.

1928 'Wage-fixing in the building industry', *Ec*

1930 'Early history of industrial conciliation in England', *Ec*
'Edgeworth, Marshall and the "indeterminateness" of wages', *EJ* [*CEET* III]

1931 'Theory of uncertainty and profit', *Ec* [*CEET* II]
'A reply' (to Dobb, 'A note on "The indetermination of wages" '), *EJ*
'Quotas and import boards', in Beveridge *et al.*, *Tariffs: The Case Examined*, Longmans, Green
'The possibility of imperial preference' (with W. Beveridge), in Beveridge *et al.*, *Tariffs*
Review: Amulree, *Industrial Arbitration*, in *Ec*

1932 *The Theory of Wages*, Macmillan [Italian, 1934] (see 1963 below)
'Marginal productivity and the principle of variation', *Ec*
'Reply to Schultz: Marginal productivity and the Lausanne. School', *Ec*

Reviews: Goodfellow, *Economic History of South Africa*, in *EJ*

Simiand, *Le Salaire*, in *EJ*

Mises and Spiethof (eds), *Probleme der Wertlehre*, in *EJ*

Bresciani and Turroni, *Le vicende del Marco Tedesco*, in *Ec*

1933 'A note on Mr Kahn's paper' ('Elasticity of substitution'), *RES*
'Gleichgewicht und Konjunktur', *ZFN* [*EI*, 1980; *CEET* II]
Reviews: Taussig, *Wages and Capital* (reprint), in *Ec*

Monroe, *Value and Income*, in *ZFN*

Reichenau, *Die Kapitalfunktion der Kredits*, in *ZFN*

1934 'A reconsideration of the theory of value' (with R. G. D. Allen), *Ec* [*CEET* I]
'A note on the elasticity of supply', *RES* [*CEET* III]
'Léon Walras', *Eca* [*CEET* III]
Reviews: Isles, *Wages Policy and the Price Level*, in *EJ*

Myrdal, 'Monetary equilibrium', in Hayek (ed.), *Beiträge zur Geldtheorie*, in *Ec* [*CEET* II]

Wicksteed, *Common Sense of Political Economy* (reprint), in *Ec*

1935 'The theory of monopoly', *Eca* [*CEET* III]
'A suggestion for simplifying the theory of money', *Ec* [*CEMT*; *CEET* II]
'Wages and interest: the dynamic problem', *EJ* [*TW* (2nd edn); *CEET* II]
Reviews: Dupuit, *De l'utilité et de sa mesure* (Turin reprint), in *Ec* (*CEET* III]

von Stackelberg, *Marktform und Gleichgewicht*, in *EJ*

Roos, *Dynamic Economics*, in *EJ*

1936 'Mr Keynes's theory of employment', *EJ* [*CEET* II]
'Distribution and economic progress: a revised version', *RES* [*TW* (2nd edn)]
'Economic theory and the social sciences', contribution to a symposium on the Social Sciences, Institute of Sociology
Review: Pigou, *Economics of Stationary States*, in *EJ*

1937 'Mr Keynes and the "Classics" ', *Eca* [*CEMT*; *CEET* II]
   La Théorie mathématique de la valeur, tr. by Lutfalla, Hermann, Paris

1939 *Value and Capital*, Clarendon Press [Spanish (Mexico), 1945; Japanese, 1950; French, 1956; Polish, 1975; Hindi, 1971; Urdu, 1975; Hungarian, 1978]
   'Public finance in the national income' (with Ursula Hicks), *RES*
   'Mr Hawtrey on bank rate and the long term rate of interest', *MS* [*CEET* II]
   'Reply to Hawtrey', *MS*
   'Foundations of welfare economics', *EJ* [*CEET* I]
   Reviews: Allen, *Mathematical Analysis for Economists*, in *Ec*
         Pool, *Wage Policy and Industrial Fluctuation*, in *Ec*

1940 'Valuation of social income', *Ec* [*CEET* I]
   'A comment' (on Lange, 'Complementarity and interrelations of shifts in demand'), *RES*

1941 *Taxation of War Wealth* (with Ursula Hicks and L. Rostas), Clarendon Press
   'Rehabilitation of consumer's surplus', *RES* [*CEET* I]
   'Saving and the rate of interest in war-time', *MS*
   Education in Economics, MSS

1942 *The Social Framework: An Introduction to Economics*, Clarendon Press [Swedish, 1945; Spanish (Mexico), 1950; Greek (pirated), 1955; Portuguese, 1956; German, 1962; Sinhalese/Tamil, 1964. Also special editions: American, 1945 and Japanese, 1974 listed separately below]
   Taxation of War Wealth (with Ursula Hicks and L. Rostas), 2nd edn, Clarendon Press
   'The monetary theory of D. H. Robertson', *Ec* [*CEET* II]
   'Maintaining capital intact', *Ec*
   'The budget white paper of 1942', *Journal of the Institute of Bankers*
   'Consumer's surplus and index-numbers', *RES* [*CEET* I]
   Review: Davis, *Theory of Econometrics*, in *EJ*

1943 *Standards of Local Expenditure* (with Ursula Hicks), CUP for NIESR

The Beveridge plan and local government finance (with Ursula Hicks), MSS
Review article: Rist, *History of Monetary and Credit Theory*, in *EHR* [*CEET* II]

1944 *Valuation for Rating* (with Ursula Hicks and C. E. V. Leser), CUP for NIESR
'Four consumer's surpluses', *RES* [*CEET* I]
'Inter-relations of shifts in demand: comment' (on Robertson), *RES*

1945 *The Incidence of Local Rates in Great Britain* (with Ursula Hicks), CUP for NIESR
The Social Framework of the American Economy, adapted by Hart, OUP, New York
'Recent contributions to general equilibrium economics', *Ec*
'Théorie de Keynes après neuf ans', *REP*
Review: Pigou, *Lapses from Full Employment*, in *EJ* [*CEET* II]

1946 *Value and Capital*, 2nd edn, Clarendon Press
'Generalised theory of consumer's surplus', *RES* [*CEET* I]

1947 'World recovery after war', *EJ* [*EWE*; *CEET* II]
'"Full employment" in a period of reconstruction', *National-økonomisk Tidsskrift* [*CEET* II]
'The empty economy', *LBR*

1948 'Valuation of social income: comment on Kuznets' *Reflections*', *Ec* [*CEET* I]
Articles on consumer surplus, *Economie appliquée*
Review: Sewell Bray, *Precision and Design in Accounting*, in *EJ*

1949 *The Problem of Budgetary Reform*, Clarendon Press [Spanish, 1957]
'Devaluation and world trade', *TBR* [*EWE*]
'Les courbes d'indifférence collective', *REP*
'Mr Harrod's dynamic economics', *Ec* [*CEET* II]

1950 *A Contribution to the Theory of the Trade Cycle*, Clarendon
      Press [Italian, 1950–1; Spanish, 1954; Japanese, 1954]
      Articles on 'Value', 'Demand', 'Interest', 'Wages' and 'Rent' in
      Chambers' Encyclopaedia

1951 *Report of Revenue Allocation Commission, Nigeria*, part 2
      [*EWE*]
      Free Trade and Modern Economics, MSS [*EWE*]
      'Comment on Mr Ichimura's definition' (of related goods),
      RES
      Review: Menger, *Principles of Economics* (Dingwall and '
               Hoselitz translation), in *EJ* [*CEET* III]

1952 *The Social Framework*, 2nd edn, Clarendon Press
      'Contribution to a symposium on Monetary Policy and the
      Crisis', *BOUIS*
      Review article: Scitovsky, *Welfare and Competition*, in *AER*
               [*CEET* II]

1953 'Long-term dollar problem', *OEP* [*EWE, CEET* III]

1954 'The process of imperfect competition', *OEP* [*CEET* III]
      'Robbins on Robertson on utility', *Ec*
      'A reply' (to Morishima, 'A note on a point in *Value and
      Capital*'), *RES*
      Review: Myrdal: *The Political Element in the Development
               of Economic Theory* (Streeten translation), in
               EJ [*CEET* III]

1955 *Finance and Taxation in Jamaica* (with Ursula Hicks), Jamaican
      Government
      The Social Framework of the American Economy, 2nd edn,
      adapted by Hart and Ford, OUP, New York

1956 *A Revision of Demand Theory*, Clarendon Press [Spanish
      (Mexico), 1958; Japanese, 1958]
      'Instability of wages', *TBR* [*EWE*]
      'Methods of dynamic analysis', in *25 Economic Essays*
      (Festschrift for Erik Lindahl), Ekonomisk Tidskrift, Stock-
      holm [*CEET* II]

1957 *National Economic Development in the International Setting*, Central Bank, Ceylon [*EWE*]
Review article: 'Patinkin: a rehabilitation of "Classical" economics?' in *EJ* [*CEMT* as 'The classics again']

1958 'Measurement of real income', *OEP* [*CEET* I]
Development under Population Pressure (Ceylon), Central Bank, Ceylon [*EWE*]
'A "value and capital" growth model', *RES*
Future of the Rate of Interest, MSS [*CEMT*]
'World inflation', *IBR* [*EWE*]

1959 *Essays in World Economics*, Clarendon Press (including previously unpublished articles: 'National economic development in the international setting'; 'Manifesto on welfarism' [*CEET* I]; 'Unimproved value rating (East Africa)'; 'A further note on import bias' [*CEET* III]; 'The factor-price equalisation theorem' [*CEET* III]) [Japanese, 1965; Spanish, 1967]
Review: Leibenstein, *Economic Backwardness and Economic Growth*, in *EJ*

1960 *The Social Framework*, 3rd edition, Clarendon Press
'Linear theory', *EJ* [*Surveys of Economic Theory*; *CEET* III]
'Thoughts on the theory of capital: the Corfu conference', *OEP*

1961 'Prices and the turnpike: the story of a mare's nest', *RES* [*CEET* III]
'The measurement of capital in relation to the measurement of other economic aggregates', in Lutz and Hague (eds), *The Theory of Capital*, IEA [*CEET* I]
'Pareto revealed', *Ec* [*CEET* III]
'Marshall's third rule: a further comment', *OEP* [*TW* (2nd edn)]

1962 'Liquidity', *EJ* [*CEMT*; *CEET* II]
'Evaluation of consumers' wants', *Journal of Business*
Reviews: Meade, *A Neo-Classical Growth Model*, in *EJ*
         Sen, *Choice of Techniques*, in *EJ*

1963 *The Theory of Wages*, 2nd edn, Macmillan [Spanish, 1973]
International Trade: The Long View, Central Bank of Egypt

'The reform of budget accounts' (with Ursula Hicks), *BOUIS Review*:   Friedman, *Capitalism and Freedom*, in *Ec*

1965 *Capital and Growth*, Clarendon Press [Spanish, 1967; Italian, 1971; Polish, 1982]
      Robertson, A Memoir, British Academy [reprinted as intro-
      duction to Robertson, *Essays in Money and Interest*,
      1966]
      Review: Lipsey, *An Introduction to Positive Economics*, in
               Ec [*CEET* III]
               Scitovsky, *Papers on Welfare and Growth*, in *AER*

1966 After the Boom, IEA
      'Growth and anti-growth', *OEP*
      'Essay on balanced economic growth', *The Oriental Economist*
      (Tokyo)

1967 *Critical Essays in Monetary Theory*, Clarendon Press (includ-
      ing previously unpublished articles: 'The two triads';
      'Monetary theory and history'; 'Thornton's "Paper Credit"';
      'A note on the *Treatise*'; 'The Hayek story') [Spanish,
      1971; Italian, 1971; Japanese, 1972)]

1968 'Saving, investment and taxation', *TBR*

1969 *A Theory of Economic History*, Clarendon Press [Swedish,
      1970; Japanese, 1971; Portuguese (Rio), 1971; French,
      1973; Norwegian, 1974; Spanish, 1974]
      'The measurement of capital – in practice', *Bulletin of the
      International Statistical Institute* [*CEET* I]
      'Autonomists, Hawtreyans, and Keynesians', *JMCB* [*EP* as
      'Hawtrey']
      'Direct and indirect additivity', *Eca* [*CEET* III]
      'Value and volume of capital', *Indian Economic Journal*
      Review: Pesek and Saving, *Money, Wealth and Economic
               Theory*, in *EJ*

1970 'A neo-Austrian growth theory', *EJ*
      'Elasticity of substitution again: substitutes and complements',
      OEP [revised version in *CEET* III as 'Elasticity of substitu-
      tion reconsidered']
      'Capitalism and industrialism', *Quarterly Journal of Economic
      Research* (Tehran)

'Expected inflation', *TBR* [*EP*]
Review: Friedman, *The Optimal Quantity of Money*, in *EJ*
[*CEET* II as 'The costs of inflation']

1971 *The Social Framework*, 4th edn (much enlarged), Clarendon
Press [Japanese, 1972; Portuguese (Rio), 1972]
'A reply to Prof. Beach' ('Hicks on Ricardo on machinery'),
EJ

1972 'The Austrian theory of capital and its rebirth in modern
economics', *ZFN* [in Hicks and Weber (eds), *Carl Menger
and the Austrian School of Economics*, Clarendon Press,
1973; *CEET* III]
'Ricardo's theory of distribution', in Preston and Corry
(eds), *Essays in Honour of Lord Robbins*, Weidenfeld and
Nicolson [*CEET* III]

1973 *Carl Menger and the Austrian School of Economics* (edited
with W. Weber), Clarendon Press
Capital and Time, Clarendon Press [Italian, 1973; Spanish
(Mexico), 1976; Japanese, 1973; French, 1975]
'Recollections and documents', *Ec* [*EP*]
'The mainspring of economic growth', *SJE* [*EP*; *AER*, 1981]
'British fiscal policy' (with Ursula Hicks), in Giersch (ed.),
Fiscal Policy and Demand Management, Mohr, Tübingen
'On the measurement of capital', *The Economic Science*
(Nagoya University, Japan)

1974 *The Crisis in Keynesian Economics*, Basil Blackwell [Italian,
1974; Spanish, 1976; Japanese, 1977; Hungarian, 1978]
The Social Framework of the Japanese Economy (with
Nobuko Nosse), OUP
'Preference and welfare', in *Economic Theory and Planning:
Essays in Honour of A. K. Das Gupta*, OUP, Calcutta
'Real and monetary factors in economic fluctuations',
Scottish Journal of Political Economy [*EP*; in Manti
(ed.), *The 'New Inflation' and Monetary Policy*, Macmillan,
1976].
'Industrialism', *IA* [*EP*]
'Capital controversies: ancient and modern', *AER* [*EP*]

1975 'The scope and status of welfare economics', *OEP* [*CEET* I]
'What is wrong with monetarism', *LBR*

'Revival of political economy: the old and the new' (reply to Harcourt), *ER*

'The quest for monetary stability', *SAJE*

'The permissive economy', in Hicks *et al.*, *Crisis '75?*, IEA

1976 'Some questions of time in economics, in Tang *et al.* (eds), *Evolution, Welfare and Time in Economics* (festschrift for Georgescu-Roegen), Lexington Books [*CEET* II]

'Must stimulating demand stimulate inflation?' *ER* [*CEET* II]

'"Revolutions" in economics', in Latsis (ed.), *Method and Appraisal in Economics*, CUP [*CEET* III]

'The little that is right with monetarism', *LBR*

Review: Whittaker (ed.), *The Early Economic Writings of Alfred Marshall*, in *EJ* [*CEET* III]

1977 *Economic Perspectives*, Clarendon Press (including previously unpublished articles: 'Monetary experience and the theory of money'; 'Hawtrey'; 'The disaster point in risk theory'; 'Explanations and revisions') [Portuguese (Rio), 1978; Italian, 1980]

'Mr Ricardo and the moderns' (with S. Hollander), *QJE* [*CEET* III]

1978 *Le Funzioni della moneta internazionale*, Bancaria

Reviews: Lachmann, *Capital Expectations and the Market Process*, in *SAJE*

Collison Black (ed.), *Papers and Correspondence of William Stanley Jevons*, vols 3–5, in *EJ* [*CEET* III]

1979 *Causality in Economics*, Basil Blackwell [Italian, 1981; Spanish (Buenos Aires), 1982]

'The concept of income in relation to taxation and to business management', *GER* [*CEET* III]

'The formation of an economist', *BNDLQR* [*CEET* III]

'Is interest the price of a factor of production?' in Rizzo (ed.), *Time, Uncertainty and Disequilibrium*, Lexington Books [*CEET* III]

'On Coddington's interpretation: a reply', *JEL*

'The Ricardian system: a comment', *OEP*

Review: Weintraub, *Microfoundations: The Compatibility of Microeconomics and Macroeconomics*, in *JEL* [*CEET* III]

1980 'IS–LM: an explanation', *JPKE* [*CEET* III]
'Equilibrium and the trade cycle' (re-translation by Schechter of German 1933 article), *EI* [*CEET* II]
Review: Presley, *Robertsonian Economics*, in *CJE* [*CEET* II]

1981 *Wealth and Welfare*, vol. I of *Collected Essays on Economic Theory*, Basil Blackwell (including previously unpublished articles: 'The rationale of majority rule; 'Valuation of social income – the cost approach'; 'Optimisation and specialisation')

1982 *Money, Interest and Wages*, vol. II of *Collected Essays on Economic Theory*, Basil Blackwell (including previously unpublished articles: 'LSE and the Robbins circle'; 'Foundations of monetary theory'; 'Are there economic cycles?')
'Limited liability: the pros and cons', in Orhnial (ed.), *Limited Liability and the Corporation*, Croom Helm [*CEET* III]
Foreword to Andrew Shonfield, *The Use of Public Power*, OUP
'Planning in the world depression', *Man and Development* (India)

1983 *Classics and Moderns*, vol. III of *Collected Essays on Economic Theory*, Basil Blackwell (including previously unpublished articles: 'The social accounting of classical models'; 'From classical to post-classical: the work of J. S. Mill'; 'Elasticity of substitution reconsidered'; 'A Discipline not a Science')
Culture as Capital, Supply and Demand, Lincei, Rome
'Edgeworth', in Murphy (ed.), *Studies of Irish Economists*
The Social Framework of the Indian Economy, with Ghosh and Mukherjee, OUP, India

Papers in process of publication

Is Economics a Science? *Interdisciplinary Science Review*
Sraffa and Ricardo – a critical view

Index